SOLDIERS BACK HOME

SOLDIERS BACK HOME

THE AMERICAN LEGION IN ILLINOIS, 1919–1939

THOMAS B. LITTLEWOOD

SOUTHERN ILLINOIS UNIVERSITY PRESS • CARBONDALE

Library of Congress Cataloging-in-Publication Data
Littlewood, Thomas B.
Soldiers back home : the American Legion in Illinois, 1919–1939 / Thomas B.
Littlewood.
   p. cm.
Includes bibliographical references and index.
1. American Legion. Dept. of Illinois—History—20th century. 2. Illinois—
History—20th century. I. Title.
D570.A12I35 2004
369'.1861'09041—dc22   2004003329
ISBN 0-8093-2587-X (cloth : alk. paper)

Printed on recycled paper.♲

The paper used in this publication meets the minimum requirements of American National Standard for Information Sciences—Permanence of Paper for
Printed Library Materials, ANSI Z39.48-1992. ⊚

For Megan Ratchford
Bryce, Chris, and Beth Hamrick
Lizzie, Caroline, and Courtney Littlewood

CONTENTS

ILLUSTRATIONS

Preface

Some of my most vivid schoolboy memories of growing up in the 1930s in a small town in the Midwest are of November 11. Every year on that date, all the schoolchildren would march to the municipal auditorium for a ceremony commemorating Armistice Day. Several portly gentlemen would be waiting on the stage. They were attorneys, judges, store owners, insurance salesmen, many of the most prominent town fathers, all wearing on this day identical blue overseas caps with gold piping. The color guard would bring the Stars and Stripes forward. One of the men, a local politician whose name was familiar to our parents, would tell us at some length what we already knew about the importance of patriotism. At precisely 11 a.m., a bugler would sound taps and then the firing squad would deliver a rifle volley, the sound echoing inside the building while the children held their hands to their ears, because most had been there before and knew what was coming.

The self-appointed overseers of our continuing education in Americanism were members of the biggest and most politically committed of the several organizations of veterans of the First World War—the American Legion. The Legion appeared in different public roles. It was, first and foremost, a fraternal association of men whose military service set them apart. One veteran who later studied the readjustment problems of his former comrades as an academic considered the Legion to have been an invaluable "social machine" that contained and redirected their anger and alienation. "The ex-soldier has lost his years, his youth, and he brings back the memory of nameless horrors," said Willard Waller. "There is no place for him in civilian society. The veterans' organization gives him a place of honor. His fellow soldiers understand him. They value his achievements. They do not tire of listening to him so long as he is willing to listen to them. . . . Through the organization, the veteran gains a stake in society."[1] The Legion developed almost immediately, to no one's surprise, into a vigorous pressure group that worked to influence public policy on behalf of veterans and their families. Concentrating at first on the welfare of children who had lost their fathers in the war, it became involved later in a variety of community service activities. The Legion also functioned as a political training ground. The political skills that "the go-getters and smooth talkers" nurtured inside the organization were put to effective use subsequently in the quest for public office.[2]

Group psychology affected active members of the Legion in different ways. The bonding that had occurred through their military service had a sometimes perverse psychological effect on their behavior in the company of comrades. Soldiers in a distant land, removed for the first time from the controls of family, church, and community, experienced a wartime sense of solidarity that carried over into their often difficult reentry into civilian society.[3] For them, being part of such an identifiable band of men who had been trained to bear arms lessened their inhibitions. Conventions and other reunions were merrymaking occasions—"moral holidays," as some have described them. Group pressures enforced a harsh ideological conformity, too, and in some places and at some times, a profoundly uncivil view of democracy's give-and-take. Many of their fellow citizens were appalled, in the most extreme cases, by the mobilization of American Legion units as auxiliary police to resist the organizational activities of labor unions and advocates of social and economic change.

What follows is a political and social history of the American Legion in one important state—Illinois—during that formative period between the two world wars. It is difficult even now to gauge the singular influence of an organization like the Legion in the wildly unsettling events of the 1920s and 1930s. Contemporary interpretations tended to be polemic. Highly sanitized "official" histories were offset, more or less, by the critical outcries of liberal journalists and commentators. Here we shall be looking anew at what happened in the beginning in that one state between the end of the Great War and the onset of World War II in 1939.

The Great War was America's first to be fought by a largely conscripted army. Draftees were selected initially not by the military and not by some central bureaucracy but by boards of local citizens. When America entered the conflict in 1917, no one could have anticipated, as the historian Jennifer D. Keene has reminded us, "how influential this generation of citizen-soldiers would become."[4] The doughboys of the American Expeditionary Force came home from France to a fretful nation facing an uncertain future. In the wake of the Bolshevist revolution in Russia, radical political movements dedicated to the overthrow of capitalism spread around the world. In the United States, labor unions were pressing hard to organize American workers in rapidly growing concentrations of industry. At the dawn of a new era of conspicuous consumption, business enjoyed generally high esteem. The ensuing social and economic turbulence led, however, to a total shattering of the civil order in some parts of Illinois. Rival unions took up arms not just against the company and its strikebreakers in the coalfields of central and southern Illinois but also against one another. In a few counties, the virulently anti–African American and anti-Catholic Ku Klux Klan filled the leadership void by actually assuming de facto law enforcement functions of local government. Flaming crosses burned on wooded hilltops all across the region. Race riots erupted in Chicago and in other American cities.

The postwar years brought a severe counterreaction by the American voters. It was, Samuel Eliot Morison observed, "the most popular war in our history while it lasted and the most hated after it was over." Servicemen returned home, Frederick Lewis Allen added, "their torn nerves crav[ing] the anodynes of speed, excitement, and passion." The nation indulged itself in a "revolution in manners and morals." The Chicago writer Ben Hecht said, "We were in the twenties a disaster-haunted society. . . . People sang louder, drank deeper, danced longer and squandered themselves in every direction. . . . They built love nests like beavers and tripled their divorce rate. High, and many of the low, gave themselves hedonistically to the pleasures of the hour."[5] Women bobbed their hair, shortened their skirts, made love in the back seats of fast cars.

The Constitution was changed to give women the right to vote in all the United States. And, after many years of agitation by temperance groups, another constitutional amendment outlawed the sale of alcoholic beverages—which led to the growth of organized crime as gangs of hoodlums took over the illicit commerce in beer and liquor. Bootleggers, speakeasies, rumrunners, the hip flask, and backwoods alky cookers were introduced into American life.

The nation turned inward. Problems near and far were ascribed to foreign influences. A society composed almost entirely of immigrants and their descendants thought it necessary to admit mostly only northern Europeans—people like most of themselves—and considerably fewer of them at that. The door closed on most Poles, Italians, Greeks, Russian Jews. Prices soared, the economy faltered, then swerved upward, then crumbled in a waste heap, bringing on the cataclysmic Depression of the 1930s.

While this upheaval was going on in Illinois, rural representatives dug in to deny the rebalancing of political power required by the massive internal migration of people from farm to city. There were more and better-organized trade unionists, radical leftists, and social activists in Illinois than in most other states. The International Workers of the World, a radical labor movement referred to as "the Wobblies," were founded in Rockford, Illinois. The American Communist Party is said to have been formed in Illinois by a coalition of foreign language federations.[6] Chicago was home to Jane Addams, founder of the settlement house movement and a well-known and widely respected pacifist. Yet with the passing years, the Legion was able to leave its contrary mark on both major political parties. Men like Scott Lucas, Everett Dirksen, C. Wayland Brooks, John Stelle, Leslie Arends, and William Dawson advanced into influential public offices. They and others worked together to forge a bipartisan coalition behind the Legion's understanding of "one hundred percent Americanism."

One cannot begin to think about public affairs in Illinois without examining the effects of sectionalism. An important theme throughout this book is the sectional tensions that existed within the Legion. During its creation, army officers from the southern states who were among the Legion's founders insisted that the state organizations would be sovereign. States would retain the authority to charter local American Legion posts. The reason for this delegation of power to the states required no explanation. Black veterans would thereby be excluded from Legion membership in the South. That proviso proved to be significant in states outside the South for reasons other than racial discrimination. In Illinois, state supremacy meant that big-city posts from Chicago would be engaged in a running struggle to operate independently of the statewide administration.

Large and diverse, Illinois was already a major industrial, agricultural, and mining state. Of pivotal importance in the national electoral system, it would prove to be equally so in the governance of the American Legion. Throughout this period just before, during, and after the Great War, the state's geopolitical climate was defined by the swirling action of sectional differences between

- the urban and rural populations;
- the bustling metropolis Chicago and the rest of the state;
- the big central city and the collar of "country towns" on its outer fringes;
- the rambunctious, hot-blooded coal mining counties in deep southern Illinois, a troubled region known as "Egypt," and the more prosperous, highly moralistic settlements in the rural northern part of the state.

By then Chicago had become arguably the country's leading labor union stronghold, a city of large, staunchly nationalistic immigrant blocs. It sometimes seemed as though everyone in Illinois was looking at everyone else with hostility and distrust. Downstaters hated and feared the big city. Chicagoans tended generally to think or care little about the rest of the state.

I first became interested in the political influence of the Legion at the state and local level while working as a journalist in Springfield after World War II. My research for a biography of the Depression governor of Illinois Henry Horner raised many interesting questions about the Legion. I began this project by scratching around for original material about the men who founded the Legion in Illinois, how they organized themselves into posts, and how their sectional differences played out at the state level. The library at the Legion's national headquarters in Indianapolis is a treasure chest of what historians call "primary sources"— recorded proceedings of state conventions, transcripts of executive committee meetings, biographical questionnaires, and post histories of varying forthrightness. While it should be understood that this book is in no sense one of those official histories, Lynda Lydick and the others on the library staff were unfailingly cooperative in making materials available. The library lives on, a priceless repository of records and memories of the Legion's past. If wars fought to an unconditional conclusion by mass armies of citizen soldiers are indeed obsolete, as we can all hope, the future of this organization and the majestic building on the memorial plaza at Indianapolis are highly uncertain. The character of the Legion is likely to change if it is to consist of retired professional soldiers and specialized technicians instead of citizens hastily mobilized for extended service.

The next steps in my research were to fit the activities of Legionnaires and their posts into the byzantine sectional politics of Illinois; to place the Illinois experience in the overall national policies of the organization; and finally to analyze whether and how the conflicts within the Legion mirrored those in the larger society. A brief bibliographic essay at the end describes works from which additional information can be obtained.

Almost every community in Illinois, no matter how large or small, is home to at least one devoted local historian. I owe a special debt of gratitude to several who helped me understand something I needed to know: Elaine Sokolowski at the Peoria library, Harley Griffin in Warsaw, George May in Metropolis, Shirley Crawford and Ruth Giffin in Aledo, E. L. Bosemworth in Olney, John Turner in Danville, William Alfeld in Carrollton, Thomas Woodstrup in Sycamore, and Major James B. McCabe, historian for the Illinois Department of Military Affairs in Springfield. Roberta Wildenradt of Sycamore rescued the dusty old minutes of auxiliary meetings from her basement. Thanks also to the staff of the Vermilion County Museum and to Louis Liebovich, Gene Callahan, Herb and Nancy Gresens, and as always, my ever tolerant mate, adviser, and mental health therapist, Barbara Littlewood.

What follows is not, and cannot be, the exhaustive story of all the seven-hundred-some posts that existed in the 102 counties of Illinois in the 1920s and 1930s. I have reconstructed one version of the events of those years, developing themes that are interrelated and, I believe, significant. But it is not the only word on these matters and certainly not the last word. Much is left unsaid.

Aspects of the study appeared in preliminary form in an article entitled "The American Legion in Illinois and the Sectional Divide, 1919–1936," *Journal of Illinois History* 3 (Winter 2000): 267–84.

SOLDIERS BACK HOME

Know'st thou not there is but one theme for ever-enduring bards?
And that is the theme of War, the fortune of battles,
The making of perfect soldiers.

—Walt Whitman, *Leaves of Grass*

The War as Prologue

The United States did not enter the Great War of 1914–18 until almost three years after the fighting started. The trouble began in the Balkans. Austria-Hungary blamed Serbian nationalism for the assassination in Sarajevo of the heir apparent to the Habsburg throne. This was a provocation the jittery, militarily weak remnants of a once powerful empire did not believe could go unanswered. Within its borders lived, besides Austrians and Hungarians, sizable communities of Germans, Czechs, Slovaks, Croatians, Poles, Bosnian Muslims, Italians, and Serbs. At this stage, the tensions between the "ill-glued" Austro-Hungarian empire and the tiny Slavic kingdom of Serbia did not appear to threaten the vital interests of Germany or Russia, much less France or Great Britain, nor in any conceivable way those of the far-off United States of America.[1] Nevertheless, their inherited burden of ethnic hatreds, imperial pretensions, and shifting borders had prompted the nation-states of Europe to enter into a series of mutual assistance agreements. So the Austrians went ahead and declared war on Serbia, confident that their much stronger friends in Germany would be standing at their side. Russia then mobilized its forces, a gesture of support for its Slavic "little brothers," the Serbs. This alarmed Kaiser Wilhelm II, who did not completely trust his cousin, the Russian czar. France, which had a cooperative treaty with Russia, feared a German attack, which is what happened. Britain was bound by yet another treaty to defend the neutrality of Belgium. Germany unwisely demanded that the Belgians step aside and allow its invading army to pass through into France. This ultimatum brought the British into the conflict. In no time, "the Allies"—France, Britain, Belgium, and Russia—were at war against "the Central powers"—Germany, Austria-Hungary, and later Turkey. "The Serbs, the cause of the trouble in the first place, had been forgotten. War was not to come to their little kingdom for another 14 months."[2] Driven back to the outskirts of Paris, the Allies repelled the invaders at the first battle of the Marne. The two sides suffered horrendous casualties in the months to follow (three hundred thousand French dead in the first four months) as they jockeyed indecisively for position along the western front.

Especially in the interior of the United States, the sentiments of the American people were divided in large measure, and often with extreme emotional conviction, by their nation of origin. Among the combatants were several countries that had sent streams of immigrants to make new lives for themselves in, among other states, Illinois. Fully 70 percent of the residents of Chicago in 1914 were immigrants or the sons and daughters of immigrants.[3] They came from Germany, the Balkans, various Slavic lands, the Russian Jewish ghettos, and countless other places. These were people who took personally the religious prejudices and border demands of their former homelands. The Polish people, from a nation now split between the German and Russian empires, constituted the largest single first-generation old-world nationality group living in Chicago. Included in the city's "Polonia" community were many recent arrivals, not yet naturalized citizens and relegated to unskilled jobs in the stockyards and steel mills. German-born Chicagoans, on the other hand, accounted for almost one-fourth of the city's workforce. They, along with the almost one hundred thousand Austrian-born residents, had been in America longer. Many of them had advanced into better-paying jobs and were dependable voters. Not directly involved in the overseas conflict, but exceedingly important in Chicago and Illinois politics, were the Irish. Their influence derived largely from their positions of power in the Democratic party organization, the Roman Catholic archdiocese (though the archbishop at the time was of German ancestry), the police department, and the Chicago Federation of Labor. Embittered by Ireland's centuries-old struggle to break loose from the British Empire, the Irish were predisposed therefore to cheer for anyone making trouble for the English. Chicago's large Jewish population included not only the more affluent German-speaking Jews from Bavaria, Prussia, Bohemia, and Austria—

many of whom had become prominent businessmen—but also other more recent Yiddish-speaking newcomers who had fled the pogroms and their tragic memories of czarist Russia. Many of them were struggling to survive as peddlers and garment makers.

Accustomed to doing business in London and Paris, eastern U.S. companies and banks continued to sell war goods and to lend money to the Allied powers. President Woodrow Wilson and members of Congress knew, though, that midwestern sensibilities were a lot different from those in the East. Spread beyond the big city into many parts of Illinois, the "German element" could and sometimes did determine the outcome of elections. In the mid-nineteenth century, groups of Germans had organized "colonization parties" in Europe to select their local destination before coming to America. "The prospect was held out that it might even be possible to form a German state," recalled one German American leader in Illinois.[4] Now their support for the German cause made the conflict abroad politically untouchable across the Midwest and the Great Plains. At a rally in Sieben Hall, one of the busiest saloons and beer gardens on Chicago's "Nord Seid," two thousand men hastened to enlist in a volunteer regiment to help the kaiser. Money was raised for the German and Austro-Hungarian Relief Society, an organization chartered by the state of Illinois. Four-inch replicas of the Iron Cross were sold as paperweight souvenirs of the war effort. Members of the Sinai Temple reprimanded Rabbi Emil G. Hirsch for his pro-German comments, which were no doubt inspired by the fact that the rabbi had nine relatives in the German army.[5] The Republican mayor of Chicago—William Hale Thompson—attracted German (and Irish) votes by famously promising, given the opportunity, to punch the king of England "in the royal snoot." Downstate, Antje Conrady Dirksen, a native of Ostfiesland, Germany, lived in the Beantown section of Pekin, not far from Peoria, with her invalid husband, Johann, and their twin sons. A picture of the kaiser hung proudly on her kitchen wall.

As the war went on and tempers grew short, the sheriff of DeKalb County found it necessary to issue an official proclamation urgently requesting that "all people refrain from public discussion of questions involved in the present crisis and maintain a calm and considerate attitude toward all without regard to their nationalities."[6] In other words, kindly keep your thoughts to yourself.

With the passing months, however, mainstream American opinion drifted increasingly against the Germans. They were accused of having burned libraries and committed atrocities against women and children in Belgium, news reports of which were denounced as "slanderous lies" by the Germania Club in Chicago. The Germans also used chlorine gas against French forces for the first time at Ypres in May of 1915. (Both sides subsequently unleashed much more deadly phosgene and mustard gas assaults later in the war.) But the major perception problem for the Germans, as they sought to keep the United States out of the war, involved submarine attacks against shipping bound for England. From the beginning, both sides tried to prevent the shipment of supplies to enemy ports. In this task, the Germans were handicapped in two important respects. Because their seacoast was much more confined, it was easier for the British to shut off access to their ports. And secondly, because they lacked the powerful surface fleet of the British, the Germans had to rely primarily on the stealth of their U-boats. In May of 1915, the British passenger liner *Lusitania* was torpedoed, resulting in a heavy loss of life, including 128 Americans. It was revealed later that the ship had also been carrying forty-two hundred crates of ammunition to the British. Then, after another passenger ship was sent to the bottom of the sea, the Germans responded to American protests by agreeing to discontinue attacks first on passenger ships and then on merchant vessels without prior warning. German Americans argued that a nation being deprived of resupply by the British blockade could not be expected to wage war without doing whatever it could to deny the enemy's sources of supply from abroad. Senators filibustered in Washington against a proposal by the administration that American merchant ships be armed. Unable to advance on the western front, the opposing armies dug into a long line of trenches separated by a no-man's-land of barbed wire. Massed cannon and machine guns fired from concrete pillboxes, making frontal assaults futile.

In 1916, meanwhile, units of the Illinois National Guard were federalized and sent to the Mexican border to help with a problem that had nothing to do with the war in Europe. They were dispatched to secure the border while regular army troops pursued the revolutionary guerrilla leader Pancho Villa back into Mexico. The states all maintained militia forces, part-time soldiers who could be used to handle emergencies within the state and who could be activated into the national military service on short notice. Officers' commissions in the Illinois National Guard were dispensed routinely as patronage rewards to politicians who enjoyed reviewing troops and being saluted. As a rule, the officer corps in the regular army had little regard for their counterparts in the guard.

Wilson's military preparedness plans, slowly and reluctantly arrived at, were blamed for his failure to carry Illinois in the 1916 presidential election. He ran poorly in many of the usually Democratic Irish Catholic precincts. But the president won enough electoral votes in other states to be reelected to a second term. Samuel Gompers, president of the American Federation of Labor, approved of the preparations for U.S. intervention in the war. Except for those in Chicago, craft unions in Illinois generally agreed with Gompers and Wilson. A militant minority in the labor movement, headed by the leaders of the central body in Chicago, were strenuously opposed, however. The president of the Chicago Federation of Labor, the Irish-born John Fitzpatrick, ignored Gompers's leadership. Fitzpatrick was a social radical who had his own foreign policy agenda. He believed in the international solidarity of all working people. In his view, the war had been brought on not by German aggressors but by profiteering munitions makers and other greedy military contractors. If there had to be a standing army at all, which he doubted, Fitzpatrick thought it ought to be "democratically officered."[7] His labor federation, the Germanic societies, and Jane Addams's pacifists all demonstrated in Chicago against U.S. intervention.

At the beginning of 1917, the Germans resumed submarine attacks against the shipping of neutral nations bound for Britain and France. It was believed in Berlin that a final desperate offensive thrust could win the war before the Yanks could arrive in force. At last, the president's patience exhausted, the United States broke off diplomatic relations with Germany and entered the war in April on the side of the Allied powers. The war in Europe became the World War. Still, five of the fifty votes against the war resolution in the House of Representatives were cast by Illinois members. Most of the two hundred thousand troops in the regular army at that time were preoccupied with the Mexican problem.

Once the waiting was over, however, the mobilization was swift and efficient. On October 23, 1917, men of the First Division of the regular army fired the first shots by American troops on the western front in France. Eventually, two million members of the American Expeditionary Force crossed the Atlantic in ships. About half of them saw combat action. By official count at war's end, 4,734,991 Americans served in the armed forces, including those who remained in the United States.[8]

There were three separate categories of military service:

1. The regular army, strengthened by wartime enlistments, plus the other regular branches: the navy and the Marine Corps.

2. National Guard regiments activated in the federal service. Guard units operated in effect as an army reserve. As the war progressed, vacancies in their ranks were filled by draftees.

3. Draftees—men who were conscripted into the "National Army." The first of three selective service registrations consisted of unmarried males twenty-one through thirty-one who were without dependents; the last inductions, two months before the end of the war, included men between eighteen and forty-five. Eleven of the twenty-nine divisions that saw action in France were draftee divisions, which were usually organized separately from the regular army.

Both of the latter two categories consisted originally of men who were from the same communities and served together in the same units, either in one of the eleven National Guard divisions or as draftees. Often they knew one another before entering the service and would return to the same towns after the war. As units were weakened by casualties and forces were reshuffled, the geographic autonomy diminished.

Mass conscription had never happened before in the United States. Previous U.S. wars had been fought mainly by state militia units and mercenaries (only 8 percent of the Union army in the Civil War consisted of draftees). This time many of the 24.2 million who registered were found to be unfit for service. As many as a quarter million of those who were called fled after receiving their induction notices.

In all, Illinois contributed 351,000 men to the military service, in these categories[9]:

National Guard—By August 1917, all the Illinois regiments, approximately twenty-five thousand strong, had been federalized. Most were assigned to the Thirty-third Infantry Division, which became known as the Prairie Division. The Thirty-third Division lost 1,171 men in the war. One infantry regiment—the Eighth—consisted of 2,008 men who served in sixteen all-black infantry companies. Four of the black companies were from Springfield, Peoria, Danville, and Metropolis. The other twelve units were from Chicago.

Regular army enlistments—numbering about 110,000 men

Navy enlistments—24,663

Marine enlistments—3,678

Army draftees—188,010 (including 8,748 African Americans who served in segregated units. Most of the black draftees were assigned to grave digging and other support duties.)

Voluntary enlistment experience varied in different parts of Illinois. In Chicago, according to one account, once war (and conscription) became imminent, "there was a rush not for the recruiting stations but for the marriage license bureau," married men being exempt from the draft.[10] Recruiters posted outside Wrigley Field one afternoon found no takers at all among Chicago Cubs fans. In other counties, "there was a disposition on the part of some, and of many of their parents, to exaggerate their importance as indispensable men in industry and agriculture," these being grounds for draft exemption. Generally, however, recruiting was more successful downstate. Groups of young men enlisted together in many downstate communities. In Vermilion County, for example, enlistments exceeded the first draft quota. Mothers and sisters raised money for a boot fund to provide hip boots for the men bound for the muddy trenches in France. In Decatur, mothers knitted woolen sweaters and gloves that slipped over the hand and wrist, leaving the trigger fingers free.[11]

In tiny Mercer County, newly elected state's attorney Oscar Carlstrom signed up 152 volunteers from that county to go to France under his command. Carlstrom was thirty-eight years old, the reigning national commander of the United Spanish War Veterans, and an infantry captain in the army reserves. Battery B of the 123rd Field Artillery—"Battery B from Mercer County"—remained intact throughout the rest of the war. All but three of the 152 men returned home safely.

And in Pekin, Mrs. Dirksen's son Everett enlisted for one of the most dangerous assignments, that of an aerial balloon observer for a field artillery unit just behind the front lines. He was said to have done so to quiet local residents who were threatening to burn down the family home because Antje Dirksen would not remove the picture of the kaiser from her kitchen wall.[12]

Government propagandists stirred patriotic spirit. "The Hun" was depicted as an evil villain from whom no one could be safe anywhere in the world. Even before the United States entered the war, civilian organizations were formed to harass potential German agents and radicals generally who posed a threat to war production. One such volunteer group, the American Protective League, enlisted two hundred thousand amateur detectives to identify suspiciously disloyal individuals on the home front. Chicago alone counted more than thirteen thousand card-carrying APL members. At sporting events, they conducted "slacker raids," demanding to see the draft registration cards of young men who were in attendance. Aliens and others who spoke out against the war effort could be charged with a crime under the Espionage Act of 1917 or the Sedition Act of 1918. The federal Department of Justice appointed APL chiefs in each downstate county.

The *War History of Lee County, Ill., 1917–1919,* published later by Dixon Post 12 of the Legion, describes the activities of the APL in a typical Illinois county.

> Each community was provided with an operator and every report of enemy propaganda was traced to its source and the author properly dealt with by the officers of the law. . . . [A few were] lukewarm towards the war who needed to have their viewpoint changed. There were some citizens of Germany whose sympathy for her was entirely too evident. And there were some who while they had become citizens of this country had forgotten the evils of imperialism and only remembered the beauties of the country and the kindly faces of the peasants.

The replacement militia in Sycamore brought one of their neighbors, Danish-born John Hansen, to the town square where a large crowd had gathered. Hansen stood accused of expressing pro-German sympathies. The account in the *Sycamore True Republican* newspaper said the "pale and perspiring" man was instructed to kiss the American flag, which he did after hearing voices in the crowd muttering something about "the end of a rope."[13]

The Illinois Vigilance Association tended another worthy cause—protecting young women from the libidinous instincts of men in uniform. At an appearance in Deerfield, the secretary, Alice Hyatt Mather, warned young women against "accepting courtesies from strangers." She told them to "seek friends through the social channels of the church. Lax associations with men in uniform [are to be] decried. The uniform has not a transforming power, and [yet] young women have gone mad over it. The moral and immoral are called together in promiscuous groups of soldiers. . . . Young people should be sent out into the world with a knowledge of the impulses of the flesh."[14]

Others did their bit on the home front in other ways. Fuel and tires were scarce. A motorist who went driving for pleasure on Sunday might wake up on Monday morning to find his car painted yellow. More Illinois high schools instituted military "pretraining" for students. At Deerfield-Shields High School in Lake County, for example, the boys wore khaki military uniforms to school, while the girls wore nurses' dresses.

The Bolshevists in the meantime had overthrown the Russian regime and made a separate peace with the Germans. Whatever advantage this treaty gave the Central powers on the western front was more than offset by the continuing infusion of fresh American troops and the enormous productive capacity of the United States. What turned out to be the last phase of the war began toward the middle of 1918. The Germans attacked along the Somme River but were thrown back at Cantigny, at Château-Thierry, and in the second battle of the Marne. The tide of battle had turned. Yankee soldiers and marines, 1.2 million strong, went on the offensive at Belleau Wood, Soissons, and Saint-Mihiel, and in the fateful fighting in the Argonne forest. During this final phase of about a month and a half, they died at the rate of six thousand a week.

Wilson's fourteen points or conditions for an end to the fighting called for the creation of a League of Nations, another for an independent Poland. The president was understood to favor a less punitive peace than the other Allies or the commanding general of the AEF, John J. Pershing.

"Black Jack" Pershing wanted no less than unconditional surrender, even if it meant the military occupation of Germany. Because the British and French armies were nearly bled dry by then, he thought the AEF would play a dominant role in the invasion of Germany. Before a united position could be established, however, the war came to an end—with an armistice, not a surrender. Dramatically, and to the considerable surprise of almost everyone, the armistice took effect at the eleventh hour of the eleventh day of the eleventh month.

The guns fell silent along the western front before the great powers were altogether battled out. That had been time enough, in the slightly more than twelve months of AEF combat, for 116,516 Americans to die, either of wounds or illness—forty-nine thousand killed in action. Another 204,002 were wounded, almost two-thirds of them suffering the aftereffects of poison gas.[15] Many others were blinded or lost limbs. The average length of time in the field for an American combat unit was only six months, but for many of these troops, it had been a terrifying, emotionally scarring exposure to bursting shells, poison gas attacks, and hand-to-hand warfare. For all the nations engaged in the Great War, ten million soldiers were estimated to have died of wounds or sickness.

Back home, Illinoisans spread the news of the end of the fighting by parading through town and making noise. Deep in the Shawnee Hills of southern Illinois, in the tiny town of Vienna, Civil War veteran "Uncle" Mark Hankins took from a closet the shotgun that he had captured from a Confederate soldier. He drew a figure of the kaiser on a flag that he ran up the pole on the courthouse lawn. After shredding the kaiser with bullet holes, Hankins and his friends lowered the banner and slashed it to pieces with swords. Then they hauled away the tattered remains in the town hearse. The war was over.[16]

Although the patriotic propaganda had saturated the public consciousness, the troops who were on the ground in France were less impressed. Not a few of the conquering warriors of the AEF still were puzzling over why they were even there. Many of them, combatants and noncombatants alike, were aware only that they preferred not to have made the journey. With Wilson's ideas hanging in the air, anti-imperialists and the many varieties of "hyphenated Americans" knew not whether to rejoice or to despair. None of the important questions were close to resolution. How would the imperial appetites of the European allies be satisfied? How would the spoils of victory be divided? Would the United States exercise its newly acquired power in the world by engagement or withdrawal? And, above all, how would the workers of the world—including those in industrial America—react to Russia's new collectivist economic and political system?[17]

The war was the one great experience of life.

—Major Thomas R. Gowenlock

1 ORIGINS AND DIRECTIONS

When the shooting stopped abruptly at the end of the Great War—what we now know as the First World War—the commanders of the American Expeditionary Force in France were confronted with a new set of problems. There would be no invasion of Germany, no army of occupation, and more than a year before the two million soldiers could all be brought back home. Neither the men nor their officers saw much need for more military training. They were homesick, restless, tired of army discipline, uncertain about the future.

Concerned about morale, the general headquarters staff asked Lieutenant Colonel Theodore Roosevelt Jr. to summon twenty of the most popular "civilian" commissioned officers to a conference in Paris. On the battlefront staff of the First Division—the "Big Red One"—the son of the former president had been gassed at Cantigny and shot through the knee at Soissons. He recovered sufficiently to host a dinner for the invited officers as requested on February 15, 1919, at the Inter-Allied Officers Club on Rue Faubourg St. Honore. Two of Roosevelt's close friends were entrusted with the responsibility of screening out any stray liberals who might have found their way onto the invitation list. The two lieutenant colonels—Eric Fisher Wood and Franklin D'Olier—were both from Philadelphia and well connected in prewar business circles.

Colonel Roosevelt had a personal fondness for one of the men on the list. Major Thomas R. Gowenlock, thirty-one, from Chicago, survived the war in one of the most perilous battlefield positions as commander of the First Division's combat intelligence section. His job was to keep tabs on where the enemy was and what he was planning to do next. In later wars, this task would be accomplished mainly with aerial and electronic surveillance. In 1918 it meant that Gowenlock and the four hundred brave scouts in his unit were detailed to sneak through the barbed wire across no-man's-land at night and infiltrate the German lines. The casualty rate was so high in his outfit that more than a thousand men had filled the four hundred slots by the end of the fighting. Tom Gowenlock's taste for adventure began in childhood. Of English and Scotch ancestry, his family roots were in southern Illinois. Both parents grew up in Jefferson County, where his paternal grandfather had started a railroad car manufacturing company in Mount Vernon. Like so many others during that period, Gowenlock moved to the big city in 1911 at age twenty-four. He made his mark quickly in two growth ventures, first as an investment banker, then in advertising. By the time the war came along, he and his wife already were socially prominent.

Unlike some other newcomers to Chicago, Tom Gowenlock never doubted whose side the United States should be on. He tried unsuccessfully to join the British army in Canada, then volunteered to lead a semi-official civilian force of thirty Chicagoans who were assigned by the Justice Department to disrupt gatherings of potential troublemakers. He was told to follow the suspected German agent Gaston B. Means around Chicago. "I lived almost under his nose for sixteen hours a day," Gowenlock recalled later. He took special pleasure in crashing meetings of "radical agitators"—a class that for him included members of the Wobblies labor movement, anarchists, communists, extreme pacifists, and some he described only as "plain cranks."[1]

"Most of the work of real value accomplished by our squad was breaking up the activities of labor agitators and anarchists, a large proportion of them recently arrived immigrants," he said in his memoirs. "Night after night we maneuvered ourselves into their meetings, usually arresting the leaders. At times a handful of us would have to fight our way through a mob of several hundred." The nightly challenge excited him. He remembered in particular one rally of five thousand men and women in Grant Park. "Three of us worked our way to the speakers' stand. When a particularly vicious orator began to incite the mob with treasonable statements, I jumped on the platform and grabbed him." The meeting quickly deteriorated into a riot. Gowenlock and his companions had to be rescued by police.[2]

In August 1917, he entered officers training at Fort Sheridan, north of Chicago. When later, at Camp Funston, Kansas, a flu epidemic broke out among the men, Gowenlock suspected it might have been the result of a germ warfare attack by German saboteurs. He reported this hunch to his superiors, who concluded immediately that such a suspicious mind should not be wasted. So, after a short course in the rudiments of counterespionage, he was sent to France to lead the battlefront intelligence operations of the Big Red One. There he earned the respect of the West Point graduates in the regular Army officer corps, as well as the troops under his command. After the armistice was signed, units of the First Division marched into Germany, preceded by Gowenlock and his scouts. He had the distinction of being the first American officer to lead troops across the Rhine River at Coblenz on December 12.

Though men in the ranks may have been uneasy about what lay ahead, not many were defying authority, as their officers had feared. "True, we never liked the war," Michael Sullivan of Homewood, Illinois, would remember later. "It was a job to be done. We wanted to go home. We chafed a little as month followed month and our turn did not come. But did we sit idly waiting? Nothing of the sort. After the armistice, whether or not we *were* soldiers, we looked like soldiers. We visited all the old castles and made friends with the mademoiselles."[3] Military police who had been stationed at the doors of brothels during the war to prevent their visitation by U.S. personnel were withdrawn. The French sanctioned separate-but-equal brothels for their own officers and enlisted men. They did the same for the British, and offered to make similar arrangements for the Yanks. Sensitive to the feelings of American mothers, the Secretary of the Army declined, however, and went so far as to try (unsuccessfully) to force the closure of all such facilities at the principal port of debarkation for the AEF. All that changed on November 11. It was estimated later that at least 9 percent of American soldiers returned home with venereal disease.[4]

Their officers were more worried about fraternization with soldiers of other nations, including the Germans, than with friendly mademoiselles. Seepage of Bolshevist sentiment beyond the borders of Russia made the American leaders leery of contacts that could heighten class-consciousness among those who had done the fighting and the dying. Young Americans who had never been very far from home and who lived fairly humdrum lives were sent across the ocean in the company of strangers whom they came to know well and to trust with their lives.

Individuals of diverse backgrounds were drawn together in what the historian Page Smith called the "religion of combat."[5] For some it was a horrifying ordeal from which they would never recover emotionally. For others it was merely an inconvenient interruption in their workaday lives. For most of them it was, in one way or another, an unforgettably new experience. Major Gowenlock went into the oil drilling business after the war and made a small fortune. But he emphasized in his memoirs that, for him, "business could never be what it had been before the war. To me, as with most of the men who had seen any appreciable amount of action in France, the war was the one great experience of life."[6]

Most of the officers who were present at that first morale conference had received their commissions either by political appointment in the National Guard of their state or by their participation in the army reserves. Many of them had been either upwardly mobile politicians or successful business executives. Almost all were, like Major Gowenlock and colonels D'Olier and Wood, conservatives of comfortable financial means who were alarmed by the incalculable specter of working-class revolution. Looking beyond the morale problems of the next few months, they wanted to divert the attention of their restless troops away from anxiety about the future and toward the advantages to be gained by their continued solidarity as veterans of the Great War. Out of that concern was born, on that February evening and at two follow-up meetings in Paris, an organization the founders chose to call the American Legion.

Since the beginning of the republic, American war veterans have organized and been rewarded, upon their return to civilian life, with grants of free land or other benefits. The officers of General Washington's revolutionary army banded together in a club they called the Order of the Cincinnati. The eldest of their sons were made eligible for membership in an effort to give continuity to the exclusive society. After the Civil War, two Illinoisans were instrumental in the founding of an organization of Union veterans, called the Grand Army of the Republic. Governor Richard J. Oglesby and General John A. Logan, the commander of the Army of the Tennessee (and later a member of the U.S. Senate), played a part too in the conversion of the GAR into an adjunct of the postwar Republican Party. In many Illinois courts, the GAR controlled the judicial nominations of both parties after the war.[7]

To avoid the impression that this new fledgling group would be a promotional tool for any political party or presidential candidate, Lieutenant Colonel Bennett C. Clark presided at the second meeting. He was the son of the Democratic Speaker of the U.S. House of Representatives, Champ Clark of Missouri. Roosevelt was his father's son, a Republican. Together he and Clark lent a bipartisan flavor to the organizational planning. On March 15, one month after the initial gathering, about 450 officers filled an old French residence that had been made into the American Officers Club at 4 Avenue Gabriel near the Place de la Concorde. Oscar Carlstrom, from Mercer County in Illinois, attended as a delegate from the Judge Advocate General's section of the army, to which he had been assigned.[8] Carlstrom recalled later that the meeting almost fell apart on the first day. In the absence of a formal chain of military command, to which the men were accustomed, they were reluctant to assume leadership. They suspected—accurately as it turned out—that some of their fellows already were planning to use the organization of veterans to propel themselves into postwar public office. At this stage, none wanted to appear to be overly conspicuous about it.

Prior to Roosevelt's dinner conference, there had been innumerable informal discussions, particularly among the many politicians in the AEF, about the form that a postwar veterans movement would and should take. One such conversation occurred four months before the armistice over dinner at Vergnet's restaurant in Besançon. The two diners were Major Robert R. McCormick, heir to control of the most profitable and powerful newspaper in the Midwest, and his friend, Republican party associate, and military patron, Colonel Milton J. Foreman. Bertie McCormick and Milton Foreman had known one another since their service together as Republican aldermen on the Chicago City Council beginning in 1904. Grandson of the legendary *Chicago Tribune* editor and mayor of Chicago Joseph Medill, McCormick had been wired from childhood into multiple circuits of influence. His father had been ambassador to Russia in the Theodore Roosevelt administration. His older brother was a member of Congress, married to the daughter of one of the most powerful politicians in the land, Senator Mark Hanna of Ohio. As the elected president of the Chicago Sanitary District, Bertie McCormick learned a good deal about how Chicago worked. In 1914, having been made president of the *Tribune*, he toured the Russian battlefront as a sort of journalist-cum-dignitary. Before leaving, he thought the Russians would be more impressed by a military title. So Foreman, who had served in the Spanish-American war, arranged for McCormick to receive an honorary commission in the Illinois National Guard. Governor Edward Dunne, who had to sign off on such a request, balked at first but then changed his mind, whereupon, according to McCormick's biographer, the *Tribune* editorial page "found previously undiscovered virtues" in the Democratic governor.[9]

Within days of his return from Russia, McCormick managed with Foreman's help to become a major in the First Illinois National Guard Cavalry, an elite outfit that supplied its own horses, uniforms, and weapons. Already a self-determined military expert, he wrote to friends, suggesting the construction of massive fortifications protecting cities in the U.S. heartland—including Vicksburg on the Mississippi River—and in mountain passes in the West. He assumed that German invaders would easily crush effete Eastern population centers and were unworthy therefore of elaborate protective measures.[10] Richard Norton Smith, the first biographer given access by the *Tribune* to McCormick's personal papers almost fifty years after his death, found in his subject "a curious balance of aggressive self- regard and almost morbid self-doubt."[11] Through his brief military career, according to Smith, McCormick lived in fear of disgracing himself by succumbing to cowardice. Bertie was, in any event, an unusual soldier. When his Guard unit camped at the state fairgrounds in Springfield, en route to Mexican border duty, the major brought along the *Tribune*'s executive dining room chef as his personal orderly. He thought his outfit needed machine guns to protect the border. The army disagreed. McCormick went ahead anyhow and solicited funds from Chicago meatpacking mogul Ogden Armour and banker Charles Dawes to purchase five machine guns from the Colt firearms firm. McCormick himself paid for a Ford automobile in which to haul the guns and ammunition to the Rio Grande. Meanwhile, the major kept his wife and himself bivouacked some distance away at a rented house with a barn for his polo ponies in San Antonio.

When the United States entered the war in Europe, McCormick's brother, the congressman, approached the commanding general of the AEF, John Pershing, at his club in Washington to offer Bertie's services. Major McCormick sailed with his wife on a French passenger ship and checked into the Ritz Hotel in Paris. A month later, over the protests of Pershing's staff, he was attached to two field artillery battalions in the First Division. He wore a monocle now and carried a walking stick. His units were among those that laid down a covering barrage in one of the decisive endgame battles of the war—at Cantigny, only sixty miles from Paris. His involvement in that campaign profoundly affected the rest of his life, so much so that he would name his country estate in Wheaton "Cantigny." Within days, however, McCormick left for Paris and what Smith described as "three days of strenuous self-promotion in quest of a transfer."[12] He became ill and was treated in a military hospital for sinusitis.

It was around this time that McCormick, thirty-seven, and Foreman, fifty-five, began talking about the importance to the Republican party in Illinois of having an organization of discharged servicemen that would act as a counterforce against radicalism in the state. Foreman was the son of a German Jewish immigrant merchant whose business and home were destroyed in the Chicago Fire of 1871. At age thirteen, Milton worked for four dollars a week as an errand boy for a wholesale hat company, of which he eventually became part owner. He went to law school at night, joined the National Guard in 1895, and chaired Chicago's street railway commission while serving on the city council in 1900. In his McCormick biography, Smith ungraciously describes Foreman as having been "in civilian life an obese Chicago alderman whose defective eyesight and impaired hearing inspired few comparisons to Sergeant York," referring to Alvin York, the famous World War I sharpshooter.[13]

Others, in the meantime, were going beyond discussion and actually laying the groundwork for a veterans organization. The chief chaplain of the AEF, Episcopal bishop Charles H. Brent, put the chaplains to work proselytizing prospective members of a group to be called "Comrades in Service." But the bishop was known to be close to General Pershing. It was widely assumed that the bishop's campaign was a front for Pershing's future presidential candidacy. A graduate of West Point, "Black Jack" Pershing made a wise career move early on by marrying the daughter of the chairman of the Senate Military Affairs Committee. From that point thenceforth, promotions came easily. In the Indian wars, the war against Spain, chasing after Pancho Villa in Mexico, and then in France, Pershing exhibited sound military judgment. But he was an aloof, uncharismatic leader whose personality did not yield the adoration of the men in the ranks. Most of the veterans returned to civilian life with an aggressive dislike of all regular army officers, beginning with their commander. In any case, Pershing did not appear to have a strong appetite for public office. So at the third and last of the Paris caucuses—the one at which the organization acquired its name—Comrades in Service willingly folded into the American Legion.

Roosevelt had already left for the States, but he saw to it that a larger cross-section of the entire force was represented at this final session. Delegates were chosen from all military units and all geographic regions of the United States. About half of the fifteen hundred men who were ordered to Paris for the meeting were enlisted men. Although the meeting took place at the Cirque de Paris, an auditorium for circus and vaudeville shows, most of the enlisted men were diverted by the city's other attractions and did not make it to the conference; at least 90 percent of those who were actually present were officers. Colonel Foreman, one of three delegates from the Thirty-third Division, the old Illinois National Guard, was elected chairman of an executive committee of fifty who drew up this preliminary list of purposes for the new organization:

1. To perpetuate the principles of justice, freedom and democracy for which we have fought.
2. To inculcate the duty and obligation of the citizen to the state.
3. To preserve the history and incidents of our participation in the war.
4. To cement the ties of comradeship formed in the service.

There would be no military rank in this American Legion. No distinction would be made between officers and enlisted men. Or between those who had been in combat and the 60 percent who had not. Or between those who served abroad and those who had remained in the United States. Another important policy decision was nailed down quickly at the insistence of servicemen from the southern states. The state would be the Legion's basic unit, with almost total authority to handle its internal organization. The state departments, as they were called, would be sovereign. They had the power to charter local chapters, or posts, as they saw fit. It was understood that this provision would allow southern states to exclude black veterans.[14]

Both of the other two representatives of the Thirty-third Division at this meeting were Chicagoans—Colonel Abel Davis and Captain John V. Clinnin. For those veterans who were already in the United States, an organizational meeting was set for May 8 in St. Louis. The committee to make plans for the St. Louis caucus included two others from the Chicago area—General Robert E. Wood and McCormick's cousin, Captain Joseph Medill Patterson. McCormick and Patterson were sharing temporary leadership of the *Chicago Tribune* at that time. After Patterson's discharge from the service, the two men agreed that he would start a newspaper in New York, which turned out to be the highly successful tabloid *New York Daily News*. Previously, in May 1918, Bertie McCormick had been promoted to colonel and ordered back to the United States. He was on a training assignment at a camp in South Carolina when the armistice was signed.

The Caucus in St. Louis

All the Illinoisans involved in the planning process in Paris were officers. All but Oscar Carlstrom, who served on the committee on organization, were Chicagoans. Already the dominance of individuals from the big city was beginning to concern ambitious would-be leaders from the rest of the state. Shortly before the St. Louis caucus, a mass meeting was scheduled to be held in Springfield to select delegates from Illinois. But the chairman of the "Advance Illinois Committee"—Major John Callan O'Laughlin, a Chicago advertising man—fell ill at the last minute and the meeting was canceled. As a consequence, any Illinois veteran who was interested and could afford the trip to St. Louis showed up. Illinois sent 112 delegates, far more than any other state. Fifty-five percent of the Illinois delegates were officers. Had the Illinois delegation not been self-appointed, it is highly unlikely that Earl B. Dickerson, an African American veteran from Chicago who was the grandson of slaves in Mississippi, would have been one of the fewer than two dozen blacks in attendance. Besides the 226 lawyers and 63 business owners or managers, newspaper editors and publishers were disproportionately represented in the various state delegations.

Colonel McCormick, however, was too busy to attend. Back now determining newspaper editorial policy, he was shuttling between Chicago and Paris, kibitzing the progress of the peace conference. He did find time to take over O'Laughlin's duties as chairman of the preliminary state American Legion organization.

One of his fellow members of the First Cavalry who made the trip to St. Louis was a polo player who had a bank account bigger even than Bertie McCormick's—Captain Marshall Field III. Field's grandfather of the same name founded the landmark Chicago department store Marshall Field & Company in 1881. Probably the most powerful individual in the city at that time, the senior Field distrusted the immigrant masses and fretted obsessively about social unrest. With that in mind, he contributed financially to the strengthening of the Illinois National Guard and was said to have been the one who prevailed on the army to establish a base at Fort Sheridan. Having troops nearby made him feel more secure. At the beginning of the war, Field III was estimated to have been worth $140 million. Married with two children, he also had medical problems that would have disqualified him from service. But he used his considerable influence to enlist as a private in what was known as "the Millionaires Battery" of the First Cavalry. Transferred later to the field artillery, he was promoted to captain and saw two months of combat action in France.[15]

Captain Field and two other wealthy Chicagoans—Colonel Bion J. Arnold, the president of an interurban electric railroad; and Major Albert A. Sprague, who had inherited the city's largest wholesale grocery firm—dug deep into their pocketbooks to help the Legion get started in Illinois. One Legion historian said the three men "built bridges over the financial marshes" throughout the early years.[16]

Many of the former enlisted men who attended the St. Louis caucus were without jobs. There was much talk of enforcing a veterans preference policy in employment. Cheers greeted the statement from one delegate that "we are a body large enough and representative enough to tell Congress what we want." The mood in the ranks could best be described as restive. A song leader tried to stir the spirit of the assembly with some patriotic tunes, but the men in the ranks had had their fill of that in the army. They hooted him down. A publication called the *Latrine News* had been started by some Chicago veterans to provide a voice for the lowly enlisted men. "The delegates arriving in St. Louis were suspicious," an anonymous buck private wrote. "The gossip around the hotel lobbies and in various delegation headquarters was all of frame-ups. Who was trying to put over what? What political party or what politicians were trying to swing the thing? Prophecy was pessimistic."[17]

Another of the delegates, Chicago lawyer Cornelius Lynde, explained later that "all of us were showing the mental effects [resulting] from the dislocation of ordinary habits inevitably produced by our recent experiences in service. To this day, the members of the Legion are peculiarly sensitive and require in their handling the greatest of tact." Lynde said he was stunned by the "shockingly large amount of suspicion and criticism" directed at the temporary leaders who were chosen by the Illinois representatives in St. Louis.[18] The most serious bickering quickly centered on the competition for dominance between rival factions from Chicago. "A number of free lancers with selfish ambitions came down [to St. Louis] and it was a difficult task to hold them in check at our state caucuses," said John S. Miller, who had been a major in the Army and emerged later as one of the interim Illinois chairmen.[19]

Lynde said some of the conflict reflected different concepts of idealism stemming from wartime experiences. The Chicago faction in control of state affairs at the conclusion of the St. Louis meeting was led by Major John S. Cummings, who had been active in the labor movement and in various liberal causes before the war. A conservative faction led by Tom Gowenlock and Abel Davis, among others, fought Cummings at every turn. A third force consisted of a less doctrinaire contingent allied with the indisputably ambitious Milton Foreman.

Joseph B. McGlynn from East St. Louis described the meetings as "very turbulent."

> Many charges of seeking political aggrandizement were made against some of those who were active in Legion affairs. Factions in the Chicago delegation were so bitterly opposed to each other that it threatened to disrupt our organization. At one meeting the [liberal and conservative] factions began to hurl charges at one another. Things took on a serious aspect for a while. The writer [McGlynn] and [William] McCauley [from Olney] gave them Hell, informing them that unless Chicago factions were able to get it together Downstate would attempt to conduct their own affairs [separately].[20]

It remained to be seen whether, as the correspondent for the *Latrine News* hoped, the American Legion could become "the healthiest, most honest and powerful influence for the promotion of clean, sanely progressive, feet-on-the-ground Americanism."[21]

Resolutions were adopted in St. Louis urging the deportation of "alien slackers" who had dodged the draft by revoking their application for citizenship; opposing clemency for jailed solders; and condemning Bolshevist attempts to take over veterans organizations in other countries. Leaders were able to sidetrack until later a resolution calling for the immediate payment of a cash bonus to all veterans. A Seattle delegate was ejected because of his reputed association with a group rumored to have ties to the Wobblies. There appeared to be considerable sentiment in the hall for the exclusion from the Legion of regular army veterans. Colonel Roosevelt used his influence to fend off that proposal.

Picking a site for the first national convention proved contentious. Because of its central location, Chicago seemed a logical choice. But the

Massachusetts delegation led the resistance to Chicago because of its identification with the famously pro-German mayor, "Big Bill" Thompson. Acting as the new chairman of the Illinois contingent, Chicago lawyer John Miller argued that Thompson's views did not reflect majority sentiment in the state. Anti-Thompson sentiment prevailed. The caucus chose Minneapolis instead.

Until the Minneapolis convention, national policy would be set by a thirty-four-member acting executive committee. Illinoisans on that committee were the seemingly omnipresent Milton Foreman and Albert Sprague. Sprague had been, like Bertie McCormick, a colonel in the field artillery.

By then McCormick had lost interest in Legion affairs, and some of his friends were beginning to wonder what war he had been involved in. The *Latrine News* took note of a speech McCormick made to the Chicago Bar Association in which he referred to the "ignorance and lack of training" of American officers. "Our casualties were two to four times as heavy as they should have been," he estimated, which prompted this comment from the veterans' organ: "Watch your step, Colonel, when you talk about the Great War. Stop, look and listen to the truth about how it was done, and you may learn something."[22] Legion officials would complain often in the next few years about the *Tribune*'s news coverage of their affairs. Given the compatibility of their political goals, this difference was surprising. It probably reflected Bertie McCormick's obstreperous, self-absorbed nature as much as anything else. The Hearst newspapers in Chicago were considered by the Legion to be far more cooperative.

As chairman of the state executive committee, Marshall Field had recommended at St. Louis that the organization wait at least a year before choosing regular officers so that more enlisted men would have time to return from overseas and become involved in Legion affairs. But Foreman would have none of that. A state convention was scheduled for October. Gowenlock appealed meanwhile for help from the national organization in ousting Cummings and his chief supporter, Major C. L. Currier, who was associated with a group called the Training Camps Association. The training camps in question had been organized before U.S. involvement in the war to train junior army officers. Gowenlock complained in a letter to the national secretary, his friend Eric Fisher Wood, that Cummings was "closely allied with the Federation of Labor and spends part of his time making radical talks in halls and in public parks."[23] Wood reported a few days later in a telegram to another national officer, "Illinois situation bad. May cause trouble of national scope." Wood went on to assert that one of the reasons why "the best elements in Illinois [were unable to] rectify the present situation" was that Foreman was deliberately dragging his feet. A man of enormous ego, Foreman felt that he was not being "sufficiently consulted," according to Wood, and that Colonel Roosevelt didn't like him, which may have been true.[24] The infighting proved too much for Field and Arnold—and eventually for Gowenlock—all of whom continued to make their checkbooks available but otherwise withdrew from Legion affairs.

Before dispersing to begin the enrollment of local posts, the Illinois delegates divided the state into regional districts and created a new executive committee of sixteen members. On top of the ongoing struggle for dominance in Chicago, sectional acrimony developed over the composition of statewide organizational committees. Downstaters considered the Chicagoans to be inordinately power hungry. Some of the Chicago activists worried about what they saw as the provincial demands of a few southern Illinoisans.

The southern Illinois representative on the executive committee had enlisted as a private, then advanced to the rank of captain in command of a machine gun battalion. His name was John H. Stelle (pronounced STELL) of McLeansboro. He had been wounded and severely gassed in France. Back home, he bought out the Haw Creek creamery, acquired a local brickyard, and prepared to follow his father into Democratic party politics. His great- grandfather, Thompson Stelle I, who was of French Huguenot stock, came to the Illinois Territory from North Carolina in 1816. He settled on a farm in Hamilton County and fathered fifteen children. One of these, Jacob, fought in General Logan's infantry in the Civil War. Another of his sons, Thompson II, married Judith Farmer, who hailed from the hill country in Tennessee. Thompson Stelle was elected to a judgeship in 1869. He acquired more than two thousand acres of farmland, making him one of the largest landowners in the county. His son John may have been less socially polished than the Chicagoans, but he was no less determined to make his mark in the world, financially and otherwise. A few days after the St. Louis meeting adjourned, Stelle wrote to John Miller in Chicago, vowing to organize Legion posts in every corner of "Egyptian" Illinois. "Say, Miller," he added in his letter, "you might be of some help to me in getting in touch with some people that I can sell some coal lands to. I have some 50,000 acres under option. . . . If you feel interested in same let me know and I will give you a price which I think you might be able to make something out of."[25] Miller replied that he had some clients who might be interested and to send more details. In the years to come, John Stelle would make his presence known often, in the American Legion, the state of Illinois, and beyond. He went on to become governor of Illinois (for ninety-nine tumultuous days), national commander and a "kingmaker" in American Legion politics, and one of the drafters of the World War II G.I. Bill of Rights.

Grumbling over financial affairs divided Legion officials along sectional lines. Because of the long distances involved in traveling from town to town, downstate leaders thought post organizers should be reimbursed ten dollars a day for the time lost from their regular jobs. From his office in Chicago's downtown Loop, Abel Davis objected. He considered this an unnecessary expenditure of scarce resources. For their part, the downstaters resented the unwillingness of wealthy Chicago members to donate their time for organizational work that they expected downstaters to do without pay. "The [Chicagoans] are three-fifths money and influence, men of the highest integrity, prompted by the highest ideals," said the district chairman from Bloomington, Thomas Harwood, not without a touch of sarcasm. "Is Colonel Davis willing to give up his time organizing Legion posts? I am informed that he does not feel inclined to leave his desk to attend meetings of the Chicago committee but rather insists that these meetings be held at his place of business. I am [further] informed that he is being talked of in political circles as a candidate for governor."[26]

Cummings's foes got the opportunity they wanted to displace him at the top when it was discovered that one of his confederates, who had been placed on the Legion payroll as a full-time secretary, was not even eligible to belong. The secretary, Myron Adams, was fired after the disclosure that he had joined, while the war was in progress, a National Guard unit that was never activated for federal service. Adams was an official of two organizations that some of the Chicago Legionnaires thought might merge with the Legion in Illinois: the Fort Sheridan Association and the Training Camps Association. Both ideas were shelved, along with Sprague's proposal for the Legion to affiliate in some fashion with the American Red Cross.

With the date of the Peoria convention drawing near, the most prominent downstater on the most important of the early committees, George

G. Seaman, struck some members as a good choice for state commander. Seaman was from Taylorville, a coal mining town in the central part of the state. The new powers in Cook County—Foreman, Miller, Davis, and Sprague—believed Seaman to be neither well enough known nor a forceful enough personality to lead the organization.[27] Tom Gowenlock attended the St. Louis meeting and chaired one of the temporary committees. But he had no stomach for Legion politicking, preferring thereafter to be active in the association of First Division veterans. Foreman and Davis were suspected by Miller and Sprague of plotting to run for public office. Insofar as possible, many of the foremost figures in Chicago Legion affairs wanted to avoid the divisive manipulation of Legion personnel and symbols that would accompany a partisan campaign by a Legionnaire. Davis and Foreman had both fought in Cuba during the Spanish-American war. Both then became officers in the National Guard, achieved elective office as Republicans and were decorated for their combat service in France.

Both happened also to be Jewish. Abel Davis was born in Lithuania. His command of an infantry regiment on Dead Man's Hill on the approach to Verdun won for him the Distinguished Service Cross. He was destined to become one of the most powerful men in postwar Chicago in his position as vice president and chairman of the Chicago Title and Trust Company. Prejudice and discrimination—against blacks, Roman Catholics, and Jews—existed in Illinois and in the American Legion. Later chapters will examine the experiences of segregated all-black posts; the relationship between the Legion and the anti-Catholic Ku Klux Klan in certain sections of the state; and specific accusations of anti-Semitism in Cook County. There were some special reasons, however, why fewer acts of overt discrimination were reported by the men of the Legion than by those in many other organizations during the same period. These reasons, having to do with (1) their service together in the same causes, past and present, and (2) how their posts were formed, will also be explored later. It might be speculated that the antipathy of enlisted men toward their former officers may have been at least as great as that between ethnic and religious groups.

In due course, the Chicagoans rallied behind Foreman, who wanted the state commander's job as a stepping stone to national commander. He took office in Peoria in October. Franklin D'Olier, the first national commander, wrote to a friend: "Cummings and his crowd were eliminated [in Illinois] in a way which appears entirely satisfactory."[28] The southern Illinois faction put up William McCauley for vice commander. McCauley was elected next in line against divided opposition from Chicago. Delegates in Peoria adopted resolutions favoring universal military training for young men, the payment of a veterans' bonus, and the deportation of certain aliens who had not served. The convention also cast its obligatory vote against Bolshevism.

As more veterans returned to civilian life, the new American Legion made progress but slowly in Illinois. "The men are not falling over themselves to join," Harwood did not need to remind John Miller. "I know from bitter experience." To get started, the new organization solicited contributions from donors. Meatpacking companies in Chicago were among those called upon to help meet the hundred-thousand-dollar Illinois quota. James B. Forgan, chairman of the First National Bank of Chicago, served as treasurer of the Illinois campaign. "We are all interested in the Legion, the results it will obtain, and the ultimate effect in helping to offset radicalism," read Forgan's fund-raising letters written on the stationery of Swift and Company.[29] Workers in the Swift and Armour packinghouses were prime targets of wartime organizing campaigns pursued by Chicago Federation of Labor unions.

Straining to put aside their day-to-day hostility, company executives and union leaders had sat around the same table in Springfield during the war, glowering uncomfortably at one another as fellow members of the State Council of Defense. Governor Frank O. Lowden reminded them that they had an obligation to cooperate during the war years so that the production of essential goods—such as meat and clothing—would not be interrupted by work stoppages. Fitzpatrick's unions took advantage of the emergency to gain not just better wages but also more control over working conditions, especially in Chicago's meatpacking and textile industries. In the postwar era, John Fitzpatrick set out to demonstrate through persistent agitation a new militancy in organized labor. He broke with the national AFL in the autumn of 1918 by announcing plans to form a labor party. A month before the St. Louis Legion caucus, he became a candidate for mayor of Chicago. He did well in the neighborhoods around the stockyards but polled only 8 percent of the citywide vote.

The packinghouse executives and others in Chicago's business community were equally determined to roll back the unions' wartime gains. They saw the men of the American Legion as allies in this mission.

The Boys Come Home

Around the state, meanwhile, many towns and cities were making elaborate arrangements to welcome the returning servicemen home. Don
Kingery, the only contractor in Sullivan, built an arch of wood and wall-
board over a street on the town square. Names of the Sullivan veterans
were inscribed on the arch, which blew down unfortunately in the first
winter windstorm. A large clock was erected at a downtown intersection
in DeKalb as a memorial to the war dead. The town clock obscured the
vision of motorists, however. After being crashed into repeatedly and
disabled by trucks and cars, the timepiece was moved down the street to
a less vulnerable location. The local Legion post, which had taken custody of the memorial clock, painted it red, white, and blue, making what
the *Daily Chronicle* described as a very striking appearance. Farther south,
on the north bank of the Ohio River, the black church parishes in Massac
County turned out to welcome home the men of Company M in the "old
Seventh" all-black infantry regiment. At a citywide dinner in Lake Forest, six local young ladies representing the United States, France, England,
Belgium, Italy, and Romania presented service recognition medals to
returning servicemen. The Illinois legislature did its bit by issuing special medals of honor for all citizens of the state who had been honorably
discharged; and by authorizing a county tax levy for the unreimbursed
burial expenses of the mothers, wives, and widows of veterans.[30]

In some communities, the civic affairs were occasions for the returned
servicemen to talk among themselves about the need for an organization.
Elsewhere, small groups of veterans had already organized themselves
into clubs. There the question became whether they would affiliate with
the American Legion, with some other umbrella organization, or with
no organization at all. The Champaign County Association of Veteran
Soldiers, Sailors and Marines of the World War, and the Sons of Liberty
in Peoria, were among the first to apply for Legion charters in Illinois.
Legion affiliates were instructed in the rituals they were advised to follow. "Nothing holds so well the interests of ex-servicemen as ceremony,"
recommended one of the national organizers. "Refreshments and smokes
should, by all means, be dispensed at all meetings."

Not all veterans took kindly to the regimented ceremony. A group in
Decatur, which called itself "the Chow Club" and which chose not to
affiliate with the Legion, met every Friday for lunch at the Elks Club,

without officers, dues, or ceremony. Another group in Peoria called itself "The Last Man's Club." Each year on Armistice Day, the members gathered in the back room of Donnelly's Shamrock Pub. An unopened bottle of the most expensive cognac they could find rested at ease on the table in front of them. This ritual was to be repeated every November 11 until there was only one man left—"the last man"—who would then uncork and empty the bottle.[31]

Later in 1919, as more veterans returned home, the army recruiter in Peoria strongly encouraged enrollment in the Legion by making it clear that red tape holding up the sixty-dollar mustering-out payment could be made to disappear if two dollars were handed back on the spot for the initial Legion membership dues. At one point in 1920, the Peoria post claimed to have 1,785 members, which would have been more than any other in the entire country. Its treasury was sufficiently plush to permit the purchase of a section in Springdale Cemetery, called "Legion Hill."[32] Posts in Cook County pooled their resources to buy a fifteen-hundred-lot section of Elmwood cemetery for the exclusive use of Legion families.

In the 101 downstate counties, most cities and towns had their separate posts, sometimes more than one. A unit needed at least fifteen members to be eligible for a charter. There were 220 chartered posts with slightly more than fifteen thousand paid-up members at the time of the state convention. A year later, the figures had climbed to 682 posts in all but two counties, with about sixty-two thousand members. Illinois counted about thirty-one hundred more members than did D'Olier's home state of Pennsylvania, of comparable population size and demographic makeup.

Downstate posts often were named after a local member of the armed forces who died in the war. Exceptions to that practice occurred where members could not agree on which of their fallen comrades was most deserving of the honor. In Quincy, enough Legionnaires dissented from the decision to name the post for General Henry Root Hill that a second unit was formed bearing the name of an enlisted man. Subsequently, the units were consolidated in a post named for *both* soldiers.[33]

While some posts were merging, usually for financial reasons, others were subdividing. DeKalb County Post 66 split into DeKalb City Post 66 with Herbert Warren West as commander and Sycamore Post 99 under former captain Cassius Poust. Poust was considered something of a good luck charm by the Sycamore men in his infantry regiment. Less than a month before the armistice, he and several other officers were standing in a dugout near Consenvoye that was struck directly by a German shell. All but Poust were killed. He escaped injury.

If economically possible, rural towns hung onto their own posts, no matter how small. Vermilion County, along the Indiana border, is an example. In a county of only eighty-six thousand population, besides the separate white and black posts in the county seat of Danville (population, thirty-four thousand), Hoopeston, Potomac, Georgetown, Rossville, Oakwood, Ridge Farm, Fairmount, Westville, Rankin, Sidell, and Catlin all had posts named for one or more local men who died in the war.

Some of the posts in Cook County were organized by geographic sections of the city or surrounding towns. But an even more common practice, common only in Chicago, was for Legionnaires to band together on the basis of their occupation or place of employment. The police had their own post, which eventually became the largest in Cook County as more veterans who agreed with the Legion's political agenda joined the police force. Veterans who worked in advertising had their post, too. Armour and the other meatpacking companies had theirs, as did the electric power utility Commonwealth Edison, the Chicago Board of Trade, and the telephone and insurance companies. So did each of the big Loop department stores. Each of the downtown daily newspapers had its own Legion post. This practice, seen much less often in other big cities, had the effect of bringing together men of different ethnic and religious groups (with the exception of blacks, who were expected to maintain their own posts). The practice disturbed labor unions for understandable reasons. It tended to reinforce a Legionnaire's workplace identity, blurring class distinctions between different jobholders, and to tighten bonds of team loyalty, blending military experiences and job experiences.

Some posts were organized by veterans of the same military unit. Chicago's James C. Russell Blackhawk Post 107 was founded by men of the Eighty-sixth Division, nicknamed the Blackhawk Division. Members of that unit had trained at Camp Grant in northwestern Illinois near what had once been the home of the Indian chief Blackhawk. A history of the post emphasized its membership scope: "Diverse elements of American citizenship [belonged], in racial origin, religion, occupation, or degree of educational attainment. Farmers from Northern Illinois, small town mechanics and clerks, workmen from Chicago's teeming west side melting pot, residents of the North Shore Gold Coast, and faculty members and students from Chicago's great institutions of higher learning, civil servants, police, firemen, store clerks, doctors, lawyers."[34]

Generally, it was easier to sign up members in smaller communities than in the big cities. Christopher Post 528 came into being in Franklin County, its founders said later, because they were bored with small-town inactivity after the comparative excitement of military service.[35] Many of the small-town veterans were already acquainted. Some had gone off to war in the same National Guard units or had enlisted together.

Aurora is an example of how this continuity worked. On the morning of September 13, 1917, the 367 members of the Third Illinois National Guard infantry regiment marched from the armory to the Burlington station. They were escorted to the train by the proud mayor and members of the GAR carrying flags. For the five-day train ride to Camp Logan, Texas, mothers of the men had packed two hundred towels and an assortment of foodstuffs, including 150 dozen doughnuts. At the training camp, they joined other Illinois Guard units in what became the Thirty-third Division. On the afternoon of June 2, 1919, those who survived stepped off another train at the same station to march down Main Street and receive the cheers of their townspeople. Then they climbed back on the train and went on to nearby Camp Grant to be discharged. It was natural for them to remain together as civilians in their own Legion post.

Lawyers, insurance agents, car salesmen, morticians, owners of small retail and service businesses, and others whose livelihood would be helped by contacts became the most immediately active Legionnaires. "We thought that all of us fellows could stick together and do business with one another," recalled one member. "It didn't always work out that way, but the business advantage caused some to become professional veterans."[36]

In many parts of the state, the Legion's chief competition for members (and for government attention) came from the Veterans of Foreign Wars. The VFW had been founded before the war and accepted only those veterans who had served overseas. Posts in Chicago had to compete for members with ethnic-specific national veterans' organizations. The Alliance of American Veterans of Polish Extraction merged later, for example, with the Polish Legion of American Veterans. Both were headquartered in Chicago and had as one of their goals to advance the interests of an independent Poland, as provided in the peace treaty. Belgian American War Veterans, the American Yugoslav Legion, and Ex-Italian War Veterans also had chapters in Chicago. Jewish War Veterans of the USA grew out of an organization founded in 1896 as the Hebrew Union Veterans. The latter came into being to counter intimations by Mark Twain among others that Jews had profited from the Civil War while shunning service in the Union army. Actually, a Chicago alderman commanded a volunteer company of ninety-six Jewish soldiers who fought at Gettysburg and some of the other engagements of the war.[37] Occasional disputes between the various veterans groups usually involved complaints, most frequently by the VFW, that the Legion had been recognized as a de facto arm of the government.

Some members in Chicago were sensitive to problems that could occur if Legion posts were based on social and economic class. Jacob M. Dickinson Jr., a former captain and the son of President William Howard Taft's secretary of war, worried about the rumored plans of a few wealthy former officers to form an exclusive post that could be characterized, he thought, as a "silk stocking post." He wrote to a friend, "If it should become the rule in large cities for any considerable numbers of former officers or men of the so-called capitalistic classes to band together and form posts separate and distinct from the ordinary posts, there would invariably arise a class feeling within the organization."[38]

Rank would not have been expected to disappear altogether in an organization of former servicemen—and it didn't. State commanders and other officials, desiring to be recognized, wore white overseas caps. *National* officeholders wore red caps, indicative of their ascendance to the Legion's own college of cardinals. By invitation only, the elite were initiated into a fraternity within the fraternity, which they called the Forty and Eight, after the French railroad boxcar that carried forty troops or eight horses. The super-Legionnaires admitted to the Forty and Eight were issued yet another hat, which resembled the wartime French army headwear. Blacks were not eligible for this august inner circle. Legion conventions were always raucous affairs, and the members of the Forty and Eight were given leave to be particularly hilarious in their public fun making. Through their playful antics, it was intended that the most popular achievers within the Legion would be able to relax and get better acquainted with one another. Some members who had seen frontline combat formed yet another subgroup, which they called the Trench Rats; still others were eligible for the Combat Medal Men. Some years later, in 1933, 350 former Illinois post commanders established a statewide past commanders' club.

All over the state, founders struggled to raise money and keep the members they had signed up. LaGrange Post 41 rented four cold, dark, dingy rooms heated by a single stove over a grocery store on Burlington Avenue. Members grappled with such weighty issues as whether to boycott Nick Pappas's soda fountain for charging twenty cents for a chocolate malt while other stores in town were holding the line at fifteen cents. One member, Howard Walters, was charged with dodging kitchen police duty. He jumped his bail—one box of apples—and was sentenced to pay next year's dues in advance. The LaGrange post also decided, on a vote of sixteen to six, that it would not be a good idea for a "career military man" to be president (General Leonard Wood was a candidate for the Republican nomination. Several former army officers, including Theodore Roosevelt Jr., were working in the Wood campaign). Another resolution denounced the display of a picture of the imprisoned socialist Eugene V. Debs that an alert member reported having seen posted in the village. While in jail, Debs received almost one million votes for president in the 1920 election. He was released in 1921, after serving three years, by order of President Harding. The President also pardoned another prominent radical, William Bross Lloyd, who served only one week of a one-to-five-year sentence for sedition. Oak Park Post 115 told Mr. Harding the pardon was "an insult to each and every man who served the country during the Great War." Ever observant Legionnaires also noticed that the American flags at a new real estate subdivision in LaGrange were left flying overnight and some had been trampled in the mud. A delegation from the post, wearing their blue and gold overseas caps, called on the realtor, who promised to shape up and fly right.[39]

The post in Champaign kept busy that first year bailing veterans out of jail, helping those who were stranded in town without money, and in one case providing a military funeral for a British veteran who died while passing through. Congress had authorized the army to lend rifles to Legion posts for firing squads at funerals. In addition to the many war dead who were being returned for burial, Legion squads were called upon to officiate at an increasing number of Civil War veteran funerals. Peoria Post 2 operated an employment agency for jobless vets, fielded a semipro baseball team, sponsored citywide talent shows, put out a post newspaper, and sought out German army veterans who had migrated to central Illinois for social get-togethers. The chamber of commerce in Aurora raised money for a post clubhouse.

Other units searched for ways to raise funds on their own. The Lombard post organized a basketball team only to discover that local citizens would buy tickets to see high school athletes but not aging Legionnaires. Sycamore sponsored a carnival to pay for an archway at the entrance to the municipal park. The state legislature passed a bill in 1921 specifically permitting veterans to "vend, hawk, and peddle goods, wares, fruits or merchandise." Other posts raffled off radio sets that a member had made, held community dances, and sponsored boxing and wrestling matches. Blackface minstrel shows were popular fund-raising attractions all over the state. The Lake Forest post imported two piano players from Chicago to improve their performances. They were Charles Corral and Freeman Gosden, later to gain fame as blackface radio comedians Amos and Andy. A shoe store owner from Waukegan bought a gift membership in the Lake Forest post for his son. The son, Benjamin Kebulsky, later moved to California, where he changed his name to Jack Benny. The Homewood post featured a blackface singing group known as the "Legion Blackbirds." The Logan post in Lincoln went into the theatrical booking business, sponsoring the "Baby Vamps" road show and other visiting companies at Lincoln's Grand Theatre. LaGrange members paid thirty cents an hour to play pool on a donated table. Dues of nine dollars a year proved too hard to collect, so the figure was reduced to six dollars. When the second commander, Thomas Davis, left office, he reported sadly that "while I have done my best to stop the damnable poker playing [at the post], it is still going strong." LaGrange also was one of the few Legion posts anywhere in the metropolitan area to register its support for the Volstead Act.

It was important to the men in LaGrange, as in other communities, to be seen as more than a poker-playing social club. They helped the Salvation Army with some of its holiday activities. After a federal veterans hospital was opened in Maywood, the LaGrange Legionnaires outfitted the library at a cost of one thousand dollars. On Armistice Day in 1921, the post planted fourteen maple trees in the parkway near the Lyons Township High School football field in honor of the fourteen men from LaGrange who died in the war. Sensing a need for recreational facilities for the young, members of the post in Wheaton persuaded local leaders to form a park district with taxing power.[40] George Alexander McKinlock Post 264 in Lake Forest honored the memory of a young local man who had been an officer in the intelligence service and one of the first Americans to die in France. Organized at a meeting in a local real estate office, the Lake Forest post did not acquire a permanent home until 1935. In the beginning, it had two committees—entertainment and bylaws. By the late 1930s, it had thirty committees.

A Place for the Ladies

One of the questions that all Legion posts had to confront was what to do about a women's auxiliary. Many of the wives who accompanied their husbands to conventions and certain other social activities were eager to organize their own permanent association. Legionnaires tended to be of two minds about this issue. They knew that bringing spouses under the Legion umbrella would enhance their potential organizational voting strength. And they knew that women were good at some of the service functions that were so important in veterans' and children's institutions. But more than a few of the men feared that the women would cramp their merrymaking style and try to dominate Legion activities that they, the men, thought were doing quite nicely as they were.

About 20 percent of Illinois posts established auxiliaries in the first year. Wives, mothers, sisters, and daughters (granddaughters were added later) of Legionnaires were eligible to join the auxiliary in places where the post had requested the chartering of such an organization. Women whose "close male relatives" had died in the war were also eligible. The mother of the dead soldier in whose name the Lake Forest post had been established was one of the founders of its auxiliary. Some of the auxiliaries established separate "junior auxiliaries" later for their young daughters. This meant that when the Sons of the American Legion were added later, entire families were now actively engaged in Legion activities, most importantly beginning with two adult voters.

A few posts declined the opportunity. The LaGrange unit voted again on the proposition in 1934—twenty-four in favor, sixty-one opposed. "So," said historian Larsen, "we're still bachelors."[41] Others delayed as long as they could. Overton P. Morris Post, which had been chartered in Metropolis in 1919, finally got around to establishing a women's auxiliary in 1937. The Harold A. Taylor Post in Chicago discussed the question beginning in 1919 and acted in 1923.

Mrs. W. H. Morgan, state president of the auxiliary, acknowledged at a Legion executive committee meeting in 1924 that there had been problems between posts and their auxiliaries. In some cases, the men had even threatened to revoke their auxiliary charters, she said. "We tell our women that they like to boss and the men like to be bossed, provided we go about it in the right way," she tried to explain. Despite the occasional friction, the presence of the women brought some important advantages to the Legion movement. Mrs. Morgan reminded the committee that woman *were* better at hospital visitation, rehabilitation assistance, and child welfare work. "We do it a little better," she said, "because it is naturally our work to do."[42] A typical auxiliary, of Sycamore's Post 99, gave frequent attention to "making the kitchen neater and easier to keep clean" in the Legion rooms above a downtown tavern. The minutes contained entries like, "It was suggested that the ladies of the auxiliary come up and sew carpet rags for the boys [meaning the men] some afternoon soon."[43] The women served the meals at the father-son banquets but also had their own mother-daughter dinners, played bunco, and held bridge teas. Dues were one dollar a year. Every meeting ended with a penny collection, which seldom raised more than a dollar. The twenty-eight charter members in 1922 grew to 135 by the 1930s. The bulk of their energy was devoted to raising funds by holding bake sales, selling ice cream at Legion picnics, staging a musical comedy (net receipts, $387.07), and collecting the advertising bills for one of the local newspapers. The money was used to buy toothpaste, shaving soap, doughnuts, jelly, player piano rolls, heating pads, and other things for the men they visited regularly in the veterans hospital wards. Like many other auxiliary units in the area, the Sycamore women adopted an orphan child at the institution in Normal. Women in other cities came up with imaginative ways of being of service. Lucille Dowd Cavanaugh, a member of Homewood's auxiliary, which was chartered in 1920, started a State Veterans Craft Exchange in downtown Chicago. Bedridden disabled veterans were able to sell their merchandise at the outlet store on Adams Street.

Women who had been active in the auxiliary for at least three years were eligible to be considered for the feminine counterpart of the Forty and Eight, which the women chose to call the "Eight and Forty Department d'Illinois." Each county with auxiliary units had its Eight and Forty "salon." Although African American men were excluded from election to the inner-circle Forty and Eight, the Eight and Forty imposed no such restriction on black women in Illinois. Olive Leonore Bryden, a caseworker for Sangamon County and the wife of the commander of the black Legion post there, belonged both to the post auxiliary, for which she served as child welfare chairperson, and the Eight and Forty Sangamon Salon.

That the women had a softening effect on the American Legion is unquestioned. One illustration will make the point: When members of the LaGrange post visited the orphans' home at Normal, they donated a punching bag, boxing gloves, a year's subscription to the *Chicago Tribune,* three waffle irons, and a movie projector. When the women from the Taylor post auxiliary stopped by the orphans' home on the way back to Chicago from a lobbying trip to Springfield, they brought three hundred lollypops for the children.

Watch Them.... They're a Live Wire Crowd

Quickly, at the beginning of 1920, Illinois had acquired a national reputation as "one of the most imaginative and productive" of the state departments.[44] One contemporary observer explained the Legion's role in Illinois this way.

> Obviously, in towns [with large memberships] the Legion runs the show. If a veteran wants a job, or a house, or wants to register a claim with the Veterans [Bureau], he needs Legion help. A politician who ignores the Legion in these towns is NO politician. The guy who likes to bowl occasionally winds up at the only alleys in town (Legion-owned). If he'd like to have a beer, well, the Legion post has a fine setup. Add all this up—then look around your own community—and invariably you will find the same situation—even in the big cities. That's why the Legion is so strong. It represents a veritable cross-section of our country.[45]

Passing the torch to new state commander William McCauley at the second state convention in Chicago, Foreman could boast that some downstate communities already were "controlled by this organization—and they are thriving towns too." National Commander D'Olier told the Illinois Legionnaires that "the ex-servicemen soon will run this country. Not because they are heroes of a war. [But because] they were picked men. They were the flower of the country. That is the reason they will run America. They have the health, the youth, the brains, and the ambition. Watch them. They're a live wire crowd. They'll do just about what they wish." Other Legion officials were trumpeting the prediction that those who had "earned the confidence of their comrades"—quoting national adjutant Lemuel Bolles—would soon wish to stand for elective office in the political arena beyond the Legion halls.[46]

Will the Legion have nothing to do with politics? It will have a great deal to do with politics. The Legion will take cognizance of what is sound practice and what is not sound practice in the political readjustment of the country. Its members are not going to wink at political flabbiness and political rottenness. Nor are they going to temporize with public servants or would-be servants whose Americanism is found tainted with suspicion. The word has gone out to 3,500 posts.
—American Legion Weekly, September 12, 1919

2 IN THE POLITICAL TANGLE

And the word did indeed go out to Legion posts in Illinois. When the political readjustment had run its course, the national leadership entertained visions of the American Legion running the country. Legionnaires, in Commander D'Olier's words, would be doing about as they wished. Actually, while these first Legionnaires had their hands full in Illinois raising money, chartering local posts, recruiting dues-paying members, and trying to hold on to the ones they had, a considerable political readjustment was already under way. It began the same month as the armistice with the election of an anti-Wilson Republican Congress. Then in the autumn of 1919, the president suffered a series of disabling strokes while campaigning for American acceptance of the peace treaty. The Senate rejected the treaty in November and with it the League of Nations. Disillusionment over the war and the peace process that followed brought a new national determination to step back from the affairs of the world. This reverse thrust in public opinion gained momentum in the presidential election a year later. Warren G. Harding, an undistinguished Republican senator from Ohio, was elected president by more than 7 million votes. "We seem to be the most frightened lot of victors that the world has ever seen," said the columnist Walter Lippmann.[1]

No one—at the meetings in Paris, St. Louis, or anywhere later—ever thought that the American Legion could not or would not be a political organization. However, the sanctioning charters that were granted by Congress and the various states carried with them the explicit promise that the Legion would not attach itself to any political party nor would it endorse candidates in election campaigns. Even that turned out to be a considerably more controversial policy than might have been anticipated.

Few members objected to the purposes set forth in the preamble to the Legion constitution.

- To uphold and defend the (U.S.) Constitution;
- To maintain law and order;
- To foster and perpetuate one hundred percent Americanism;
- To preserve the memories and incidents of our associations in the Great War;
- To inculcate a sense of individual obligation to the community, state and nation;
- To combat the autocracy of both the classes and masses;
- To make right the master of might;
- To promote peace and good will on earth;
- To safeguard and transmit to posterity the principles of justice, freedom and democracy;
- To consecrate and sanctify our comradeship by our devotion to mutual helpfulness.

Later on, there would be some disagreement about just what some of those terms meant, like "one hundred percent Americanism" and the Legion's duty to "maintain law and order." But for now, the leaders were occupied balancing the budget, signing up members, and jockeying for positions of influence within the state organizations. Various mechanisms that were established to promote interaction among the local posts—such as county councils and district conventions—made it easier to form regional and other kinds of power-seeking coalitions.

Delegations to the first two national conventions brought more younger men, more former buck privates, fewer former officers, fewer public-office seekers. As the membership grew more diverse, the involvement of more ex-enlisted men could be seen in the resolutions that were adopted at the conventions. The rank and file did not leave military service with kind thoughts of professional soldiers. Instead of a large postwar standing army, which they branded in one resolution as "un-American," the Legionnaires endorsed universal military training—but with reservist instructors who were civilians and not army officers. In time of war, local units of a national citizens army would be expected to assemble and march off to defend the nation.[2] The National Defense Act of 1920 provided for the training of reserve officers in summer camps and on college campuses. Subsequently, as this program developed, the Illinois Department of the Reserve Officers Association closely resembled a subsidiary of the Legion.

Much of the debate at the 1919 national convention concerned the political entanglement question. Some members thought the Legion should join hands with candidates and parties that stood for the same things it did. Cornelius Lynde, who had been a chief bosun's mate in the navy, said the Legion is "directly in politics all the time and it would be much better if it were frankly openly and avowedly in politics." But General Pershing among others warned Legionnaires not to let the Legion become "a political tool in the hands of political aspirants." A decisive majority agreed with him. Strong prohibitions were imposed against the endorsement of candidates by any unit of the Legion, giving member mailing lists to candidates, and allowing candidates to address Legion meetings. Probably the most significant provision barred any elected public official or candidate for public office from serving also as a Legion officer. Reopened as an issue at the next national convention, the policy survived numerous attempts at modification, by margins as convincing as nine to one. There would be no way to prevent individual Legionnaires from working in election campaigns, but they would have to leave their blue and gold caps at home.

Before examining how this policy worked in Illinois, here is a brief tour of the state's political and demographic landscape in that period. The figures in the table, from the censuses of 1920 and 1930, chart the population changes that were taking place during the Legion's formative years.

Population Changes in Illinois During the Legion's Formative Years

	1920	1930	Percentage Change
Chicago	2,701,705	3,376,438	+25
Rest of Cook County	351,312	605,685	+72
Cook County total	3,053,017	3,982,123	+30
Downstate	3,405,263	3,648,531	+7
State total	6,485,280	7,630,654	+18
Rural	2,082,127	1,994,927	-4
Urban	4,403,153	5,635,727	+28

The population growth occurred in the cities—by 28 percent—while rural sectors lost 87,200 residents. Chicago grew, but so did the surrounding "country towns" in Cook County—Berwyn, Evanston, Oak Park, Cicero. Chicago became more Catholic and more Jewish in the 1920s. The census documented the movement of many white Protestants to the outer fringes of the city and to the country towns. No fewer than thirty new Catholic parishes were established on the Northwest and Southwest sides. Jews spread out from the inner city Maxwell Street neighborhood into Lawndale and Douglas Park, replacing Scandinavian and German Chicagoans.[3]

Downstate cities—Peoria, Rockford, Decatur—gained population too. Along with German Americans, large numbers of first-generation Americans of Swedish and Italian heritage lived downstate. The Swedes were spread across northern Illinois; the Italians were concentrated in a few towns and in scattered coal-mining sections of southern Illinois.

As in other states, voting in Illinois had been based largely on inherited family tradition, most often on religious affiliation, but was in the process of becoming more class-based. Illinois had gone Republican (as had Chicago) in most presidential elections, except in 1912, when the Bull Moose defection split the Republican vote. President Wilson lost the state by 202,320 votes in 1916. He failed to win Chicago (by twenty-six thousand votes) but did carry thirty-eight of the 101 downstate counties, including the two urban counties of Peoria and St. Clair (East St. Louis).

Entering the election season of 1920, both parties in Illinois were split into reform and antireform wings. Republican Frank Lowden, who was raised on a farm before becoming a lawyer and marrying an heiress to the Pullman sleeping car millions, was elected governor on a reform ticket in 1916. Fifty-nine years old in 1920, he had been commissioned a colonel in the Illinois National Guard during the Spanish-American War. That war ended before his regiment could be activated. While governor, Lowden was harassed at every turn by his fellow Republican, Chicago's Mayor Thompson, who could never have been mistaken for a reformer. The so-called "Poor Swede," Fred Lundin, lurked behind the scenes as the mayor's chief power broker. The Democrats had their regular organization, a confederation of ward bosses that would come to be referred to shortly as "the Chicago machine," and a cast of good-government irregulars identified with former governor Dunne and former mayor Carter H. Harrison II.

Governor Lowden tried for his party's presidential nomination in 1920. He and the other leading candidate, General Leonard Wood, were deadlocked at the Republican convention. The deadlock made it possible for Senator Harding to emerge triumphant from the famous smoke-filled room in Chicago. Lowden chose the son of a Civil War general and three-time governor, John J. Oglesby, to succeed him in Springfield. Business leaders—what today would be called the Republican establishment—were for Oglesby. For its candidate in the Republican primary, the Thompson wing settled on a former state treasurer, Len Small, who owned the newspaper and a bank in Kankakee. Thompson's ethnic neighborhood organizations, which included Bronzeville, the closely confined black neighborhood on the South Side, provided a strong base for Small's campaign in Chicago. The black population had grown due to migration from the South during the war. On the other hand, Oglesby expected to sweep downstate, where Thompson was generally viewed with alarm.

The Political Debut of Oscar Carlstrom

While waiting to be sent home after the war, some of the Illinois servicemen were not thinking about either revolution or the mademoiselles. They were thinking about how their status as a veteran and their association with other veterans could be put to political advantage. Oscar Carlstrom, the commander of Mercer County's Battery B, had friends back in Illinois touting him in absentia (unsuccessfully alas) for the presidency of an organization called the Swedish American Republican Convention. Carlstrom grew up on a farm near the town of New Boston on the Mississippi River. The nature of immigration in Mercer County can be traced by the names of communities settled after New Boston. German settlers decided Berlin would be a good name for a neighboring town, only to see Berlin later renamed Swedona by a fresh wave of Swedish immigrants.

Carlstrom's father, Carl August Carlstrom, came to Illinois from Ostergotland, Sweden, in 1869. Acquiring twelve hundred stony acres that were often flooded by the river, he made a living by cutting wood and selling it for fuel to passing steamboats for three dollars a cord. Oscar was one of seven children born to his father's first wife, who died when he was three. Carl took a second wife, who gave him eight more children. The elder Carlstrom was a man of legendary physical strength. On a dare, he was said to have once carried four sacks of wheat, with a total weight of 480 pounds, up the steps of Kimel's mill—one sack under each arm and one on each shoulder.

Oscar rode a horse five miles to high school. He worked on his father's farm until age twenty. He enlisted in the army in 1899. After serving sixteen months in the Philippines, Oscar returned home to resume reading law in the offices of a local judge. Admitted to the bar in 1903, he went on to become city attorney of Aledo and then state's attorney. By all accounts, Oscar Carlstrom had unbounded faith in himself. He was a world-class joiner. Along with several different veterans organizations, he belonged to the Freemasons, Knights Templar, Shriners, Elks, Moose, Odd Fellows, and Woodmen. He not only became active in any organization that would have him but did whatever was necessary to become a leader of most of them. He knew he had to reach out beyond the small county where he lived by making politically useful friends in Chicago. There, though not musically gifted, he joined a Swedish singing club. On the stump, he was a florid, Chautauqua-style orator who liked to be compared to William Jennings Bryan.[4]

Governor Lowden left as one of his legacies a call for a state constitutional convention. Delegates were elected in 1919 to a convention that drafted the new constitution. Several Legionnaires, Carlstrom and Abel Davis among them, went to the convention as delegates. (The proposed constitution was rejected later by the voters.) Carlstrom got himself made president of the convention, a feat that must have caused him to wonder, Why stop there, why not run for governor? With encouragement from some of his Legion friends, Carlstrom resigned from the constitutional convention and announced his candidacy for the Republican gubernatorial nomination. There is no documentary evidence to clarify the circumstances of Carlstrom's candidacy. It was not unusual in that period, however, for "straw man" candidates to enter a race in consort with an ostensible opponent, not expecting to win but for tactical reasons affecting others in the field of candidates. In this case, the suspicions derived from these facts:

1. Oglesby had to overcome Small-Thompson strength in Chicago by amassing huge pluralities downstate.
2. Any downstate vote for someone other than Oglesby therefore would help Small.
3. Carlstrom had met Chicago's "Poor Swede" Fred Lundin, who was supporting Small.
4. His Legion contacts in heavily Republican counties downstate made Carlstrom a formidable downstate candidate.

Meanwhile, Abel Davis and John Clinnin had organized Cook County Republican Legionnaires into a "Former Servicemen's Club" for Oglesby. "Our Verdun is Springfield," their statement said. "They [referring to the Thompson forces] shall not pass." Oglesby promised to be guided if elected by "what the servicemen in their votes in their American Legion posts determine is best for their needs." American Legion leaders who were involved in the campaign on both sides were identified as such in news accounts.[5] Len Small won the primary by a scant six thousand votes and went on from there to be elected in November. The losing Democratic candidate, former major Barratt O'Hara, had resigned from the Legion when he announced his candidacy. O'Hara, at age thirty-eight, was an impulsive office seeker who had tried a number of different occupations. Before entering the army, he had been a newspaper sports editor, lieutenant governor of Illinois, owner of a movie company, and an unsuccessful candidate for the U.S. Senate. He was only fifteen when he enlisted in the infantry during the Spanish-American War.

Carlstrom polled a disappointing thirty thousand votes in the primary. He carried only one county—his own—but the margin proved instrumental in Small's victory. Then, a few months later, Carlstrom was appointed by the new governor to one of the potentially most lucrative (and thus sought after) positions in his administration, as a member of the state tax commission. The commission determined the tax assessments of commercial properties.

Small arrived in the governor's office with some residual legal encumbrances. His fellow Republican, attorney general Edward J. Brundage, had obtained a grand jury indictment against the governor alleging the embezzlement of funds he had been watching over as state treasurer. Small was acquitted of criminal charges but was hit with a civil judgment of more than one million dollars. Subsequently, in 1924, the governor and "the poor Swede" put up their confederate Oscar Carlstrom against Brundage in the Republican primary for attorney general. It was understood by political insiders that, if elected, Carlstrom would suspend any further criminal investigation of the governor and reduce the civil damages owed to a more manageable $650,000, which he did. After beating Brundage in the primary, Carlstrom won in November by 66,138 votes. Small, who was also reelected, easily raised the $650,000 by assessing state employees and contractors.

These coincidences soured many Legionnaires who believed that the organization had been exploited for selfish political gain. Looking back on 1920, George Seaman, who had been eased out of the leadership, said, "The greatest difficulties were the attempts of various political factions to seize upon the Legion as a vehicle for their own aggrandizement."[6]

Vote for the Soldier Boys

Many of the servicemen who had joined the Legion sharpened their political skills by becoming post and, sometimes, district officers. It was natural for them then to take the next step into a campaign for public office. In this endeavor, they were inclined to seek the help of their Legion comrades. Because the organization was not supposed to be aligned with either party—and Legionnaires were precluded from politicking in their official organizational capacity—the state commanders and state executive committees often had to adjudicate disputes. A post commander of Onarga Post 551 decided to run for Iroquois County treasurer. His campaign literature stated that his campaign had been endorsed by his post, which would have astounded the people of Onarga had it not occurred. But other posts in the county protested, and the post was reprimanded—after the election was over.[7]

Previously invincible candidates were swept under by the isolationist tide of 1920. Henry T. Rainey for one. Henry T., as he was known in Greene County, may have been the most popular public official ever in that reliably Democratic county. He had represented the lower Illinois River valley in Congress since 1903. An admirer of Stephen A. Douglas and later of William Jennings Bryan, Rainey entered politics as a free silver advocate and a progressive Democrat critical of the Cook County party "bosses." The people of Greene County brought their Democratic voting habit from the South, from whence many of their families had come in the reconstruction era. The only union members anywhere in the county were a few railroad workers. Congressman Rainey had been careful to curry the favor of veterans. An officer of the GAR served on his congressional staff. At the end of the war, however, Rainey took the unpopular position of recommending that some American troops be stationed in Europe. And then in the election of 1920, he stood as a resolute defender of the League of Nations, which the American Legion post opposed. The Republican paper in Carrollton, the *Patriot,* ran ads in that campaign like this one:

You Can Vote for the Soldier
Boys Regardless of Party
—
And Your Whole Ballot Will be Counted

The ad then listed the names of the "Soldier's County Ticket," followed by their military pedigree. For example, Dr. Ross Edwards, the candidate for coroner, was a "Medical Det. Field Artillery." The endorsed candidate for county surveyor had been attached to an army motor transport company. "The boys went across for you," the ad declared. "Won't you come across for them?

The ad also included a summary of "Article X of the so-called League of Nations as insisted upon by Mr. Wilson."

"Do you want to send our boys across the water BY YOUR VOTE to be slaughtered in the quarrels of other nations at their command?" the voters were asked. "Vote the Republican Ticket and Keep Our Boys at Home. STAND BY THE BOYS NOW THAT STOOD BY THEIR COUNTRY."[8]

In counties like Greene, it was hard for the Legion to avoid entanglements with the party that stood for the views of most of its members. Henry T. lost that election to Republican Guy Shaw of Beardstown by 3,909 votes. Rainey, who was sixty years old, came home, went about the mending of his Legion fences, reclaimed the seat in 1922, and became Speaker of the House in 1933.

Typically, across Illinois some of the soldier boys were elected and others were not. John Stelle ran for state's attorney as a Democrat in Hamilton County, and then for the state senate, but lost both times. Another Democrat who was active in the Legion, Scott W. Lucas, was elected state's attorney of Mason County in 1920. A tenant farmer's son, Lucas served in the Coast Artillery Corps, a branch of the military assigned to the protection of the coasts against enemy invasion. Returning to civilian life, he married a daughter of the local banker. Then, while promoting Legion membership in his west central Illinois district, Lucas met a city commissioner from nearby Pekin—Everett McKinley Dirksen. After leaving the service, Dirksen was driving a bakery truck for his brothers' wholesale business. With his deep, mellifluous voice, Dirksen aspired to an acting career. If the theater would not call, which it didn't, he took pleasure in the next best thing: making speeches as a political candidate and in American Legion halls. He said later that he had not given much thought to veterans' organizations until meeting Scott Lucas, who urged him to get involved. When he ran for the U.S. House of Representatives, Dirksen said Legionnaires in the thirty-six posts throughout the congressional (and American Legion) district were the deciding factor in his campaign. "Because of the kinship of the uniform and the common purposes to which we were all dedicated," he wrote in his autobiography, "the veterans of World War I became an exceedingly powerful influence at the polls—serving as workers, providing the poll watchers, electioneering day after day and doing all those things that assure a fair and honest election." Like many downstate candidates, Dirksen found it useful to run against Chicago at every opportunity. After letting it be known vaguely that he had received threats from sources he assumed were Chicago thugs, he was accompanied on the campaign trail by "a few friends in the American Legion" who formed "a security guard."[9]

Albert Sprague, one of those who engineered the purge of the liberal John Cummings, had been a Republican by inheritance. But in 1923 he became involved in a nonpartisan committee that searched for a reform candidate to unseat Mayor Thompson. This led to his leadership of an ex-serviceman's club supporting the successful Democratic candidate, a former judge, the Irish Catholic William E. Dever. Sprague then became city public works commissioner in the Dever administration. His appointment proved controversial because of Sprague's antiunion reputation. He had served on a citizens' committee to enforce a judicial ruling that facilitated an open shop in the building trades in Chicago.[10] Nevertheless, Mayor Dever recommended Sprague a year later for the Democratic nomination to oppose the popular former governor Charles S. Deneen for the U.S. Senate. It was assumed by the Democratic leaders in Chicago that Sprague's Legion connections would help him downstate. Sprague adapted awkwardly to his campaigning role. He had to be reprimanded by the mayor for sitting at the same testimonial dinner table with the notorious North Side gangster Dion O'Banion.[11] When the votes were counted, Deneen won easily with 63.5 percent. Sprague carried only twelve rural counties, one of them being Stelle's home county of Hamilton. There was scant evidence of any cross-party assistance based on Legion affiliation. Carlstrom, for example, was of little value to his fellow Legionnaire in Mercer County, where Deneen received almost three-fourths of the vote. Hurt by Dever's enforcement of Prohibition, Sprague tallied 38.9 percent in dripping wet Chicago, even worse (27.4

percent) in the rest of Cook County. If any Legionnaire deserved the support of his fellows, regardless of factionalism, it would seem to have been the generous, unselfish, hard-working Chicagoan Albert Sprague. Yet Deneen ran considerably ahead of the Republican presidential candidate Calvin Coolidge, who received 58.8 percent of the Illinois vote, and Governor Small, who won reelection with 56.7 percent. Big Bill Thompson came back to unseat Mayor Dever in 1927. Candidates competed in that municipal election to see who was more fervently committed to the return of beer and liquor.

Rank-and-file Legionnaires must have been perplexed by the self-promotional zeal of some of their comrades. Were they campaigning for Legion office or public office? Or perhaps both, albeit at different times, since public officials could not also be Legion officers? Systemic contradictions were inherent. How could a prominent member who affiliated with a veterans' committee formed by a political party or candidate appropriately exercise his free expression rights without being identified with the American Legion?

The commander of the Marine Post, made up of former leathernecks in the Chicago area, was a preacher's son from LaSalle County named C. Wayland Brooks. Brooks had joined the U.S. Marines while still in his teens. He was hit by artillery fire at Soissons. Surgeons saved his shattered foot by grafting foot bones from a dead French soldier into the American's foot. His father, the Reverend Jonas Brooks, also served in France as an army chaplain. After the war, young Brooks joined the state's attorney's staff in Cook County. From his rural estate in the Fox River valley, he made the rounds of Legion posts in the country towns west of Chicago, acquiring a reputation as an entertaining public speaker. He also cultivated the friendship of the baron of Cantigny—Colonel McCormick. While Carlstrom represented what could be thought of as the Main Street Legion faction of Republicans, concentrated downstate, Brooks became identified with would later be considered the "Tribune Tower faction," those Republicans who looked to McCormick for their marching orders. Brooks did not seem particularly interested in Legion state politics, though. Listening to his firebrand patriotic speeches, members wondered what else "Curley" Brooks had in mind.[12]

John J. Bullington, a former state legislator from Belleville who had been a major in the quartermaster corps, became state commander in 1924. In his address to the convention, Bullington acknowledged the 1920 gubernatorial experience with these words: "Whatever may have been said in the past about the American Legion of Illinois being engaged in Legion politics or partisan politics, never with my consent shall a politician of whatever party lay his hands on the American Legion."[13] Even with the good intentions of leaders like Bullington, it proved to be almost impossible to police the political entanglement rules in Illinois. Years later, in 1933, the LaGrange post condemned Legionnaires who appeared in full Legion regalia in newspaper photographs "pushing the candidacy of various political figures of both parties, not as individual voters but as Legionnaires."[14] Elected public officials could not simultaneously hold office in the Legion, but that did not mean they could not belong to the Legion. Almost all the veterans in public office belonged to the American Legion.

On through the 1920s and beyond, more returned veterans who were Legion members won local, county, state, and national office. Many of them worked their way up the public office ladder, though not always as successfully as they would have liked. The *Illinois Legionnaire* magazine of March 1930 contained a photo of the Republican candidate for congressman-at-large, Thomas K. Davey, who was identified as a charter member of the Legion and of Voiture 220 of Forty and Eight. "Illinois should send a war veteran to Congress," he was portrayed as declaring. "Some of the states that have sent war veterans to Congress—

Massachusetts—5
New York—8
Pennsylvania—7
Tennessee—3
Michigan—3
Illinois—none."[15]

The establishment of women's auxiliaries appeared to have little effect on the turning out of a unified "Legion vote." Seldom did the wives of Legion members take part in a gender-based campaign organization, with or without an auxiliary roster as a base of operations. Women were generally more interested in the social and service-providing aspects of their Legion affiliation.

Nevertheless, as more and more Legionnaires ran for public office as candidates of both major parties, their election created American Legion coalitions in legislative bodies from county boards and city councils all the way to the U.S. Congress. Republican and Democratic Legionnaires joined hands in the Illinois legislature, for instance, to work for the passage of Legion bills. But their friendships seem also to have had an effect on issues other than Legion issues, more so, evidently, than in other states. Political scientist Daniel J. Elazar has written of the comparative absence of ideological differences in the Illinois political culture. For many years, he asserts, the state's professional politicians were more interested in the personal economic rewards of public service. "These politicians were bound together by various networks of individual loyalty ties and friendships," he says, "ranging from common ethnic backgrounds to association with the American Legion, and cemented by a quid pro quo 'favor' system."[16] Or in plainer language: Political opponents who became trusted friends at Legion conventions, and who shared a bipartisan commitment to the Legion's goals, learned to become more comfortable trading favors on other public business as well, leading to what Elazar and others have characterized as a notably less ideologic two-party system in Illinois.

3 Chicago and Downstate
The Sectional Schism

The United States had been slow getting ready to fight the war. And now that the war was over, the nation was ill-prepared to care for its returned victims. Most of those who served in the armed services were covered by contributory war risk insurance. The widows and children of the dead had financial claims. Soldiers who had been wounded and in some cases permanently disabled needed institutional care. So did those who suffered severe illnesses caused by exposure to poison gas or who developed various forms of psychiatric trauma from battlefield shell shock. The American Legion did not hesitate to assume the oversight responsibility for these obligations. "Before we commit ourselves to a program needing large sums of money for sound men," said Milton Foreman, referring to the call for a cash bonus, "we need to find out how well these people who require our care are being taken care of by the government."[1] As a consequence, much of the organization's attention in the beginning was devoted to supporting relatives of the war dead, finding hospital care for the disabled, and processing benefit claims.

The War Risk Bureau demonstrated at once that it was incapable of coordinating the many disparate federal veterans assistance programs. A new federal agency, the Veterans Bureau, was then established. State departments of the Legion lost no time assembling their own networks of service offices. The Legion's service facilitators thought of themselves as go-betweens who would help members with the paperwork and steer them to the places where they could find assistance. A challenging assignment in the best hands, the enormous flow of casework overwhelmed this government agency, too.

The Veterans Bureau turned out to be not only incompetent but corrupt. The first director, Colonel Charles R. Forbes, compounded his misdeeds by (1) taking kickbacks on the purchase of drugs and medical supplies and (2) intercepting the delivery of some of the same overpriced items and reselling them to others. The colonel was sentenced to the federal penitentiary for two years and fined ten thousand dollars.

Many servicemen returned home to discover either that their old jobs were not available or that they were not yet ready to pick up civilian life where they left off. Draftees and members of federalized National Guard units thought that a social contract existed with the government (borrowing Jennifer Keene's characterization).[2] They thought that in return for their service to the nation, they deserved a job at least as good as and maybe better than the one they left behind. Legion representatives lobbied for rehabilitation and vocational training opportunities beyond what the government was equipped to provide. Many of the returnees reentered civilian life in fits and starts. The Frenchman Erich Maria Remarque put it well when he said, "So life is now too slow for us; we jump at it, shake it, and before it can speak or resound we have already let go again." Waller said returning veterans were "subject to queer moods, queer tempers . . . fits of profound depression alternating with a restless desire for pleasure."

"Hire the soldier," pleaded Illinois state commander McCauley in 1921. "He may have been restless at one time but he is steady now."[3]

At first, most veterans who needed medical care were placed in "contract hospitals" wherever available beds could be found. Legion inspectors said some of the facilities in Illinois were appalling. They intervened to force the decertification of one Chicago hospital and the firing of several Public Health Service physicians. Milton Foreman, Abel Davis, and Albert Sprague all served on various presidential or national Legion commissions that looked into medical care needs. Sprague was especially diligent, arguing for a system of government-operated institutions for the disabled. In one report, he said five thousand men who were suffering convulsive mental illnesses—the frequent aftermath of shell shock—were being "warehoused" in contract hospitals that did little more than collect the daily federal allowance of three dollars per veteran.

In this crucial early period, Sprague could afford to give lavishly of his time along with his money. Both of his parents were descended from the

Puritan settlers of the Plymouth Colony in the 1600s. Ralph Sprague, the first of the New World Spragues, was a captain in the Massachusetts militia and a town constable. His son John fought in the Indian wars as a militiaman. A later descendant, Otho Sprague, Albert's father, founded a wholesale grocery business in Chicago that his son inherited. Albert and his family lived on the Lake Shore Drive Gold Coast and had a summer home at Lake Bluff in Lake County.[4]

The mentally ill were shut away in huge custodial institutions spread around the state. Into these overcrowded state hospital wards were delivered a steady procession of troubled veterans. They were being declared insane at the rate of about twenty a week by the Cook County Court alone. Sprague and other Legion officials believed that war veterans should not be commingled with other psychotic residents in state institutions. The state legislature appropriated funds in 1921 for four separate veterans-only "cottages" at Elgin State Hospital, northwest of Chicago, and four others at Jacksonville in central Illinois. Sprague, in the meantime, continued campaigning for a national system of veterans hospitals that would provide general medical care, not just for the mentally ill. In August of the same year, a new federal hospital for veterans opened on the site of an old speedway in Maywood, just west of the city. By the end of the decade, there were almost seventeen hundred patients in that facility, which had been built on speculation by the wealthy lumber company owner and Legion benefactor Edward T. Hines. Amid allegations of payoffs and kickbacks, Congress refused to reimburse Hines for the cost of construction. But the Legion saw to it that the hospital was renamed for Hines's son, an army lieutenant who died of pneumonia in France.

A few years later, what had been the National Home for Disabled Volunteer Soldiers at Danville was rebuilt and enlarged. Joseph "Uncle Joe" Cannon, the dictatorial Speaker of the U.S. House, used his clout in 1897 to have the facility located in his Danville district. Now the old "soldiers home" was reopened and spiffed up as a twenty-one-hundred-bed neuropsychiatric institution spread over sixty-seven buildings. To run the veterans care system, Congress created yet another reorganized agency to replace the Veterans Bureau. It was called the Veterans Administration. The VA brought programs for Civil War, Spanish- American War, and World War veterans into a single agency combining, besides the Veterans Bureau, the Bureau of Pensions and the National Homes for Disabled Volunteer Soldiers. The American Medical Association, speaking for physicians, objected to the enlargement of what it regarded as a federal socialized medicine scheme. The doctors thought veterans could be treated adequately in regular ("civilian") hospitals.

Still the facilities were considered inadequate. A Legion report estimated in 1924 that one thousand insane veterans were deprived of needed care in Illinois. Two hundred more beds were added to relieve crowding in the veterans' wards at Elgin. The construction was financed in part by a dollar-a-day federal subsidy for each veteran in residence. Legion monitors contended that the federal dollars were specifically intended to buy better food for the veteran population. So the money was redirected thereafter for separate kitchens and improved meals in the veterans' units at Elgin and Jacksonville. The ex-servicemen now had their own barracks, their own mess hall, and supplemental rations not available to other residents. Eventually separate units also were established at state institutions in East Moline, Alton, and Quincy. One survey showed that 89 percent of institutionalized mental patients who were Illinois veterans were being cared for in Illinois at either a federal or a state facility. The comparable in-state-care figure for Pennsylvania at that time was 36.5 percent.[5] Every year around Memorial Day, Legionnaires raised funds by selling artificial poppies made by hospitalized veterans. In return, Legion volunteers sponsored holiday parties and other extras for their disabled comrades.

Many of the long-term patients who had been victims of poison gas showed little improvement over time. Despite the lingering toll, the American Legion lobbied in Washington for the funding of the Chemical Warfare Service and against an international treaty that would ban the wartime use of chemicals in gas. A Legion representative testified, incredibly, that poisonous gases were actually more humane than many other methods of warfare because they were disabling without being fatal. The treaty was never ratified by the Senate. It was revealed later that the Legion lobbyist was also serving as treasurer of an industry association funded by the duPonts and other prospective chemical warfare suppliers.[6]

As the volume of casework increased, Legion service offices screened a variety of requests. A father whose soldier son's body has been returned from France wanted a Legion firing squad for the funeral. A sister wanted to be made the insurance beneficiary after the widow of a dead soldier remarried. A man wanted to transfer into a new vocational training course. A woman wanted a mental examination for her shell-shocked brother. The most troubling cases involved quarrels by relatives of the war dead and of those who had been declared mentally incompetent over the distribution of benefits. In an alarmingly large number of cases, lawyers and other trustees with political influence milked the assets of former servicemen who were wards of the state.

Almost from the beginning, Chicago posts vied with the state department for control over the Legion service operation in Chicago. The Chicagoans believed that their needs were unique and would not be appreciated by the state headquarters. State-level leaders were equally determined not to grant autonomy to the big city because of their fear that the urban Legionnaires would unite and run roughshod over the state administration. Parallels could be seen in other federations of which Chicago groups were a part. Throughout that period, for one example already alluded to, the Chicago Federation of Labor functioned as an insurgent body within the American Federation of Labor. The Irish-led CFL ignored equally the policies of the state and national labor federations.[7]

At the heart of the Legion dispute lay an important difference in the culture of helping people. The political dynamics of doing favors in Chicago were (and are) different from those in the more sparsely settled sections of the state. In smaller communities, residents were generally more reluctant to accept public charity. Not only was there little reluctance in the big city, but the dispensers of public assistance expected to be credited by the recipients. Whenever "benefits" are dispersed in the city with some procedural discretion over their distribution, one of the keys to the operation of any successful big-city political organization has always been to maintain control over the process. Thus it is possible to direct the flow of benefits with particular specificity, as much in the American Legion as in a political party.

Leaders in Chicago did not take easily to directions from above. The Legionnaires Club of Chicago was founded in 1919 by fifteen inner-city posts. Members established their own service center at the Khaki and Blue Club, a wartime servicemen's recreational facility in Grant Park. Plans were made to build a clubhouse downtown. To raise money for the project, the Legionnaires Club sponsored a gala carnival—a typically gaudy Chicago-style entertainment complete with sideshows and beauty queens—at the Coliseum on the South Side. The city government under Mayor Thompson refused to issue a license for the carnival, but the Legion dared the police to interfere, posting a uniformed Legion guard at every exhibit.

Under Commander McCauley, the state officers refused to sanction either the club or its activities, beginning what one Legion historian described as "a period of strife and friction between Cook County and the department which continued for several years. . . . The organization was more-or-less emasculated."[8] Born and raised on a farm in Richland County, not far from the Wabash River, Bill McCauley married into the Yount family who owned the leading newspaper in Olney, the *Daily Mail*. Church-going Protestants, his grandparents had moved north from the Appalachian South. Red-haired and freckled, McCauley was a cocky, gruff, abrasive man; like many southern Illinoisans, he was quick to erupt. He was thirty-eight years old when he was drafted in the army only two weeks before the end of the war. He never left training camp and received his discharge papers at Camp Grant one month after the armistice. At the St. Louis caucus, where he met John Stelle for the first time, McCauley's absence of exposure to combat did not deter him from offering himself as a spokesman for lowly former privates throughout Illinois. Not only did he and Stelle consider themselves the leaders of the "Egyptian" faction in the Legion, but McCauley stood for Legion office as the enlisted man's friend. Unlike Stelle, who was a Democrat, McCauley had always been a Republican. Whatever differences there might have been in their ideological convictions beyond the interests of the veteran were minuscule.

A second version of the Chicago club came into being in late 1920 with the organization of the Cook County Commanders Association. In one way or another, both groups aimed at the centralized coordination of the Legion's service function in Chicago. They wanted to be at the controls of the compensation claims process in the city. They also demanded to be the exclusive lobbying voice of Cook County posts before public bodies in the metro area, to preside over veterans' grave registration, and to have sole responsibility for any Legion public appearances on Memorial Day and other patriotic holidays.[9]

John Clinnin won a bitterly fought intersectional contest for the vice commander's job in 1920. A year later, having become an assistant U.S. attorney, he was ineligible (as a public official) for Legion office. Overcoming Cook County opposition, McCauley was returned to a second term as state commander.[10] While continuing to resist Cook County's efforts to go off on its own, the state department initiated its own service projects in Chicago. A hotel in the Loop was leased for the temporary use of homeless veterans. Early in 1922, the state executive committee met

Cook County leaders at a "summit conference" in Chicago. A negotiated compromise provided for the formation of a fusion body, the Cook County American Legion Association, under terms acceptable to the department. The executive secretary of the association received a monthly salary of $150. Chicago businesses were solicited for a clubhouse that the association wanted to open in the Loop. Later it took yet another title, that of the Cook County Council of the American Legion.

One of the sore points all along had been Cook County's concern that the budget for the Chicago service office would be slashed. The McCauley administration had run an operating deficit of almost seventy-five thousand dollars, due in large measure to the diversion of private contributions meant for Chicago but folded into the state budget and spent. The deficit made it impossible for the Illinois department to pay its dues to the national organization. Just two weeks before the state convention of 1922, Illinois was told that its delegates would not be seated at the upcoming national convention in New Orleans unless back dues were received. McCauley hastily signed promissory notes for the thirty-six thousand dollars borrowed to meet its obligations.

Abel Davis and his friends in Chicago blamed McCauley. Next in line to succeed McCauley waited the senior vice commander, a well-liked Chicagoan, Charles W. "Daddy" Schick. The son of German immigrants, Schick lived in Gettysburg, Pennsylvania, as a boy. He may have been the only Legionnaire anywhere who claimed to remember having watched Pickett's charge from the porch of his home in 1863. A naval officer in the Spanish-American War, he then worked as a life insurance salesman in Chicago while mooring his schooner, the *Glad Tidings,* at the Columbia Yacht Club on the Lake Michigan shore. He instigated the yacht club's reserve officer preparedness program before the war. And then when war came, sixty-one-year-old Daddy Schick volunteered for active duty as a navy enrollment officer at the Chicago Municipal Pier (later Navy Pier). After the war, he helped organize one of the largest Legion posts in the state, the Naval post, which consisted of 812 former sailors living in the metropolitan area.[11] The Naval post chartered a special train from Chicago to support Schick's promotion at the convention in Rock Island. A beloved elder statesman Daddy may have been, but Abel Davis vowed to block anyone associated with the McCauley team.

Oscar Carlstrom presided at a preconvention caucus of downstate leaders who rallied to McCauley's defense. Carlstrom soared to new oratorical heights, pleading for unity at the convention. "Memory paints a wonderful picture of service, fellowship, and experience through which we have passed," he intoned.

> Prophecy points to the ultimate certainty of justice achieved by united action for the men who served our beloved country in its times of stress and emergency. May we lay aside all personal differences in common determination to hasten the fulfilment of that prophecy. May God look down from the stars above to the stars of state here comprising our union and forever bless them and their sons and daughters and perpetuate in their blood and sinews the strength to maintain their institutions of liberty, education, religion, and democracy, and plant in their hearts the clean moral perception of human right and justice to improve them.[12]

As chairman of the state finance committee, Davis accused the leadership team of squandering funds while devoting less than 5 percent of the budget to the needs of disabled veterans. He said the state department had sullied the reputation of the Legion by sponsoring unseemly "raffles and other solicitations in the streets" of Chicago. Demanding a vote of no confidence in McCauley's record, members from Chicago pressed ahead with their opposition candidate, a former colonel named Horatio B. Hackett. More so than before, the politicking broke along sectional lines. Delegates formed regional coalitions. On the first ballot, the five southern Illinois districts cast a unanimous vote for Schick. The count resulted in a 402-to-402 tie. Tempers flared as the various district delegations caucused and recaucused. At one point, the sergeant at arms was deployed to protect one downstate delegation from the "intimidating" tactics of the Chicagoans. On the next ballot, Schick won, 406 to 396.

Daddy Schick proved to be a benign, agreeable leader, ready to reach out and cede more autonomy to the council of Cook County posts. "We firmly believe that the future of America is in the hands of the American Legion," he said. "We propose to overcome class distinctions, eliminate illiteracy and overcome bloc and class legislation. . . . May we be guided in the right path and be supported by all churches and the best elements of America, whereby we may become stronger and better, overcoming all underhanded elements which are now endeavoring to destroy [the nation]."[13]

It was understood further that the commander's position would alternate each year thereafter between Chicago and downstate. Schick won the praise of his fellows for his soothing effect on sectional differences. Ferre C. Watkins, a future state commander from Chicago, reminded the convention a year later that factionalism had threatened to "dismember the Legion in Illinois" at the beginning of Schick's term. "The department is again united," Watkins declared. "Sectionalism is gone, factionalism and old quarrels have vanished as Daddy's term is ended."[14]

All the sectional bickering obviously contributed to the loss of members during this period. Illinois lost 25 percent of its membership—15,683—between 1920 and 1924. During this same four years, the economy slumped across the nation, but in the comparable state of Pennsylvania, membership fell by about eight thousand, a lesser drop of 15 percent.[15] Blue-collar workers were leaving the organization in many big cities. It is impossible to know what part personal finances played in these decisions and how many left because of the Legion's hard-line repressive stand against trade unions and left-leaning thinkers of all stripes. One Chicago member, W. R. Matheny, suggested in a letter to the state commander some other reasons why men were dropping out of the Legion.

- "They think the Legion is largely composed of roisterers."
- "They are afraid of being called upon for too much personal effort."
- "They fear that we will get into politics."
- "They think we are always raising funds and selling tickets."[16]

Whatever the causes, Cook County's share of the statewide membership fell from about one-third in 1920 to 28 percent in 1923.

	1920	1923
Cook County	21,000	14,000
Illinois total	62,000	49,000

The state department appealed to the competitive instincts of the men by sponsoring various intersectional membership enrollment contests. Goals were set for the metropolitan area, the Corn Belt counties, and Egypt. In 1922, two posts—Naval and Rockford—numbered more than eight hundred members each. Twenty-six posts had three hundred or more members: eleven in Chicago (Naval, Hyde Park, Advertising, Logan Square, Commonwealth Edison, Chicago Elevated, Hellenic, Lawndale-Crawford, Bell Telephone, Theodore Roosevelt, Austin); four in the country towns (Elgin, Aurora, Oak Park, Evanston); five in central Illinois

(Sangamon County–Springfield, Bloomington, Decatur–Castle Williams, Peoria, Quincy); four in northern Illinois (Rockford, Freeport, Kankakee, Woodstock); and two in Madison County across the Mississippi from St. Louis (Alton, Edwardsville).

John Bullington of Belleville, who followed Schick as state commander, told the convention in 1924 that the Legion faced a discouraging future—"a decreasing membership, an empty treasury, an indebtedness which must be liquidated, and with some doubt on the part of the public and in the minds of many servicemen that our organization has lived up to its opportunities and responsibilities." Bullington wrote a friend, "I am doing my utmost to bring the Legion out of the woods. Sometimes I become a little blue and discouraged, especially when our earnest efforts to increase our membership fail to meet with success."[17] By the middle of 1926, Cook County membership had fallen to 11,600, from fourteen thousand in 1923. The 647 posts in Illinois now reported forty-eight thousand dues-paying members—about 18 percent of the estimated number of eligible veterans in the state. Attendance dropped so in Homewood that the post had to move one meeting to Bert Heuer's garage in order to have a quorum.

Sectional rivalries continued to plague the organization. J. M. Dickinson complained that the service center in Chicago was being misused by the state department. He said that the staff and facilities had been diverted from their stated purpose and become a branch office of the state headquarters for the convenience of state officials.[18]

Meanwhile, Howard P. Savage, a Chicagoan who had been prominently involved in the efforts to improve medical care and rehabilitation opportunities, succeeded Bullington as state commander. Savage cited figures indicating that the Communist Party USA had more active members in the mid-twenties than did the American Legion. "We must carry on this work of ours," he said, "so that we can hand the torch to the next generation and know that we have stood by our comrades and our country and realize that we have at all times had uppermost in our minds the care of our disabled buddies and the love of our country." Past commander of the Chicago Elevated post, Savage had been one of those striving for a federation of Cook County units. A civil engineer by training, he entered the army engineers with the rank of lieutenant at age thirty-three. Later, in the 1930s, he used his Legion connections to become business manager of the Chicago public school system.

Savage was followed as state commander by Scott Lucas, who resigned as state's attorney of Mason County to take the post. A short time later, the Chicago contingent succeeded in electing Savage, on the twenty-first national convention ballot, to be the first national commander from Illinois. He presided at the convention held in Paris, a memorable opportunity for the twelve hundred Illinois Legionnaires and their wives who crossed the ocean to "storm Cognac Hill in old Paree," as one of them described it. The Illinois legislature appropriated forty thousand dollars for an Illinois drum and bugle corps to make the trip abroad.

When Lucas took over as state commander, he said, "The old breach between Cook County and downstate has gradually disappeared until the time has arrived when harmony prevails almost everywhere." Almost but not quite. Earlier, the Chicago Park Board had approved the construction of a football stadium on the lakefront as a memorial to the World War dead. The American Legion supported the project, of course, and Abel Davis's influence is said to have been responsible for the decision to name the structure Soldier Field. Colonel McCormick, who took a proprietary interest in the lakefront, thought it would be a good idea if the Army-Navy academies football game were moved to Chicago as part of the Soldier Field dedication ceremonies. In its inimitable style, the *Tribune* flooded the successful pressure campaign with publicity, much of it in the name of the Legion. Lucas suspected a Chicago conspiracy, though, when one of the newspaper stories omitted any mention of him and misidentified Savage as state commander. Lucas fired off angry letters to everyone he could think of. Ferre Watkins, his vice commander, replied that Savage had been designated by "the executive committee of Cook County [as the one] with the prestige to properly connect the American Legion with this movement." Lucas cooled off after an irate Watkins reminded him that he (Lucas) had been the Legion personality "out front" in prior Soldier Field dedication affairs. "The papers both before and afterwards left no doubt as to your proper title," Watkins wrote him. The incident demonstrated the importance that ambitious downstate politicians attached to Chicago exposure. (Lucas would some years later be elected to the U.S. Senate from Illinois and serve as majority floor leader of that body.)[19]

Eventually, the give and take between the regional interests produced a tolerable compromise. By 1936 the state department was collecting revenues in excess of one hundred thousand dollars annually: eighty thousand from member dues, twenty-eight thousand from poppy sales. Service offices accounted for $32,845 of the $99,350 budget, including almost seventeen thousand for a downtown Chicago service center and ninety-five hundred for a claims section at Hines hospital.[20]

Profiles of Two Illinois Posts

Most of the irregularities that complicated the administration of the American Legion in Illinois were related to the cultural differences between posts in Chicago and those in other parts of the state. Their similarities and their differences can be examined more closely by looking inside two typical urban posts, one in the heart of the big city, the other a highly successful downstate chapter.

Harold A. Taylor Post 47

In June 1919, Charles Apfel, the proprietor of a rathskeller in one of the several Turner halls on the North Side of Chicago, hosted a banquet to express his gratitude to the returning war veterans who lived in his neighborhood. Alderman Dorsey Crowe, the boss of the Democratic organization in Apfel's ward, took charge of the discussion that followed the dinner. He introduced John Cummings, the labor lawyer who was then in control of American Legion policy in Chicago but, as we have seen, would soon be pushed aside by Abel Davis, Tom Gowenlock, and others. Cummings spelled out why it would be in the best interests of the men to form their own community Legion post.

The north bank of the Chicago River was once a hodgepodge of cheap flophouses, brothels, gambling houses, and other dens of vice, the disreputable playground for patrons of the downtown hotels and businesses. Before Prohibition, German beer gardens and Irish saloons lined Clark Street near the very busy criminal courts building. Now, entering the 1920s, the ramshackle firetrap rooming houses for transients on Clark Street contrasted with the mansions of the superrich on the lakeshore Gold Coast. The Near North Side had become a true polyglot. Around Holy Name Cathedral—the seat of the Roman Catholic Archdiocese—clusters of Germans, Irish, Romanians, Sicilians, Yugoslavs, and other nationalities intermingled. Although a majority of those who lived in the neighborhood were Catholics, some were followers of other faiths. What these families of first- and second-generation immigrants usually had in common was a feeling of satisfaction at having been assimilated into American life. Not all Chicagoans felt that way, to be sure, but the men dining in the rathskeller that night did not come back from the war as prospective revolutionaries.

Alderman Crowe took it upon himself to appoint temporary officers of a post that had not yet been officially chartered. Edward H. Hug, who was close to the alderman, served as the first commander. Cummings saw to it that the formality of chartering followed quickly, with twenty-three charter members. The post was named for a comrade left behind in the American cemetery at the Argonne forest. Harold A. Taylor died there only days before the end of the war. An indication that not all the men who went to war from this neighborhood were candidates for sainthood is seen in the post's long campaign to obtain clemency for Harold Taylor's surviving brother, who was serving a thirty-five-year sentence in the military prison at Leavenworth for a crime committed while in France. Another of the early members of the Taylor post, Joseph L. DeLaCour, was asked later by a Legion historian to describe his most memorable military experience. "Mine was the experience of any private in the AEF," he wrote. "Obedience to orders. One experience I did have was that of being cast into bastile-vile in Gay Paree, just after the signing of the Armistice and having to serve 26 days under the tutelage of Hard Boiled Smith. That was an experience. It is too long a story so will not go into it"[21] (said Smith presumably being the officer in charge of the military stockade). Due partly to his misadventures in Gay Paree, DeLaCour, who was a private in an army motor transport repair unit, did not return to the United States to be honorably discharged until a month after the organization of the Legion post.

Taylor Post's twenty-three members grew to 195 by the end of the year, and to 550 by 1932. A contemporary post historian wrote that "its membership is truly cosmopolitan, claiming comrades of many races and creeds, of all walks of life, from the lowliest to those in high places."[22] Albert Sprague, who lived in the ward on Lake Shore Drive, belonged to the post. So did the chewing gum magnate and owner of the Chicago Cubs baseball team, Philip K. Wrigley. There were no blacks, and most of the Jews who lived on the lakeshore belonged to other posts. Although no statistics were kept, it would appear that the clearly dominant religion was Catholic. In the churning of membership that occurred over the years, many of the relatively few manual laborers dropped out, some to return, sometimes several different times. As in other posts in other places, the leaders were the activists who had the time, money, and requisite interest in public affairs. It is unquestionably true that many labor union members or sympathizers in Chicago made deliberate decisions to stay out or get out of the Legion. One line in a Taylor post account says simply, "The post's relation to labor was discussed and declared neutral."

What is distinctive about the Taylor post in this period, distinguishing it from most other Chicago posts, was its intimate relationship to what (after the ward realignment of 1921) became the Forty-second Ward Regular Democratic Organization. Beginning with Alderman Crowe and the legendary committeeman of later years, William J. "Botsy" Connors, the Irish ran the party and the ward. It was customary throughout the city for gambling proprietors to pay protection money to the ward organization. In the Forty-second Ward, according to one report, 40 percent of this money remained for ward political activities, the rest going "downtown" to party headquarters.[23] An "Irish gang" led by Sprague's inadvertent dinner companion Dion O'Banion controlled bootlegging in the ward, operating out of O'Banion's flower shop across from the cathedral. Until, that is, he was gunned down in a turf disagreement with Johnny Torrio's rival sales representatives. Connors made a nice living for himself and his associates by owning an insurance agency on LaSalle Street that was patronized by those many businesses in his ward that expected to avoid and not be harassed by city inspectors. More than a few of the members of the Taylor post became precinct captains or were active in other capacities on behalf of the Forty-second Ward organization. They could usually arrange to find a place on some city or other government payroll.

Joe DeLaCour is an example. Born in Chicago of French and Irish parentage, Joseph Logue DeLaCour attended the Holy Name Cathedral schools and took night school courses later in real estate law, insurance, banking, and finance. He was drafted shortly after his twenty-third birthday and sent to France in April 1918. Back in Chicago, he became active in the Taylor post and in the Democratic ward organization. DeLaCour advanced from post sergeant at arms to the board of directors, two terms as post commander, then sixth district commander, and finally, in 1933, to the position he most coveted: commander of the Cook County Council. At various times and in various combinations, he worked for Connors's insurance agency, as a civil service examiner for the city of Chicago, as the secretary of the state liquor control commission (after the repeal of Prohibition), and as an elected member of the Illinois General Assembly. (The customary mission of a civil service examiner at that time in Chicago was to secure the public employment of worthy party workers and divert the applications of as many other would-be civil servants as possible.) The membership of Taylor Post also included store clerks, waiters, office workers, schoolteachers, lawyers, chauffeurs, courthouse bailiffs, undertakers, and household maintenance personnel, many of whose jobs were linked in some fashion to the services of local government.

One concern topped Taylor Post's list of concerns from the beginning. For the men of the Taylor post, the social contract called for the expeditious payment of cash bonuses to veterans by the state and federal governments. One resolution specified payments equal to fifty dollars per month of service. By 1921, the post "took issue with the state headquarters on the [urgency of the] bonus question and insisted upon immediate action in favor of a state bonus." Edward Hug filed as a candidate for state commander that year on a give-us-money-now platform but finished fourth. On some other issues of statewide concern—restricting immigration, for example—the Chicago post held back. Members such as DeLaCour who were active in Democratic politics were more interested in helping "foreign stock" newcomers become established (as Democratic voters, of course).

The Legionnaires sponsored a variety of dances, family picnics, and other social activities. Within a year, they were able to acquire a clubhouse at 1358 North Clark Street. The post had a rifle squad, a fife corps, and a drum and bugle corps that won statewide honors the year the state legislature appropriated funds for the winners' trip to the national Legion convention in Paris. Not all the marching musicians were Legionnaires. Legion rules in the early years permitted up to 40 percent ringers.

The men were of two minds about having wives around. As mentioned in a previous chapter, members began talking about authorizing a women's auxiliary at the end of 1919 but did not get around to actually doing so until 1923.

On another matter, repeal of Prohibition, the men of the Taylor post were never the least bit ambivalent. Although drinking alcoholic beverages continued to be officially illegal all through the twenties, beer and whiskey flowed freely at Legion affairs here. In this attitude, the Legionnaires reflected the opinion of their neighbors. On a citywide advisory referendum in 1922, 85 percent of the Forty-second Ward voted wet. Post minutes contained statements such as this one, on January 15, 1926: "A barrel of beverage was donated and the commander ordered the colors retired so that we could proceed with our social functions," meaning that the Stars and Stripes were removed before the beer keg was opened, a gesture of patriotic respect perhaps for the rule of law.

But how typical of the 170 other Legion posts active in Cook County at the end of the 1920s might the Taylor post have been? Various posts were based not only on neighborhood, ethnicity, former military service affiliation, occupation, and place of employment but also in at least one case (to be described in chapter 6) solely on religious conviction. Taylor Post's attitudes on drinking, gambling, sexual gratification ("personal liberty"), immigration, their bonus entitlement, and workers' right to organize were shared by the rank and file, if not always by the leadership, of most other posts in Chicago. Most were, along with Taylor, indifferent to the problems of small towns in rural Illinois. On the other hand, Taylor's membership would appear to have been more vocationally connected to practical politics as something more than a debating society. They were more Democratic, more Catholic, definitely less passionate about ideology among their leadership (though no less outspoken about "Americanism"), less conservative, and less likely to have been an officer in the service and a high-level business executive or professional in civilian life. It is tempting to speculate, but impossible to know, whether and how Albert Sprague's associations in the Clark Street Legion hall influenced his conversion to the Democratic Party.

Curtis G. Redden Post 210

Fifty years or so before the 1920s, long lines of prairie schooners carried fresh farm produce along the main wagon road north from the Wabash valley to warehouses in Chicago. Teams of oxen would turn around then and pull the wagons with their loads of salt and metal implements back to the main agricultural trading center—the town of Danville, seat of Vermilion County, Illinois. At one time, around 1840, the population of Vermilion County exceeded that of Cook County. After the end of the Great War, Danville's 33,776 residents included about twenty-four hundred African Americans and slightly fewer than two thousand foreign-born. More than half the immigrants were of German heritage. Four families of German Jews, recently arrived shopkeepers on East Main

Street, established a reform synagogue in 1909. Later, Eastern European and Russian immigrant tradesmen tried to start their own orthodox congregation, opening what was described as a "deep and bitter schism" between the two groups.[24] The 1920 census counted 3.5 percent of the adult population in the county who did not speak English, compared with 5.2 percent in Chicago.

Although Danville sent two National Guard batteries to France—one white, one black—and was proud of the fact that the number of enlistments precluded the need for a first draft call, local officials tried to hide another statistic. After the United States entered the war, civic clubs circulated loyalty pledge cards throughout the county. More than twenty-three hundred county residents refused to sign the pledges.[25] Many of these dissenters were German farmers in the rural areas.

Danville prospered essentially for two reasons. The first was its location at the junction of three busy railroads. Most of the skilled workers in the railroad shops had come from Germany. They lived together in the community of Germantown. In 1904 the residents of Germantown voted to be annexed by Danville. The coal reserves being strip-mined a short distance from town were the other reason for Danville's prosperity. The easy availability of coal made it possible for Danville to claim what were then the world's largest brick plant and zinc smelter. So here in the midst of the central Illinois coalfields existed in one place a railroad town (the 1920 census counted 117 working locomotive engineers); a mining town (almost one thousand Danville residents worked in the mines); and a factory town (among the 3,343 manufacturing jobs were those in the workforce of the Danville Malleable Iron Works).

Workers on the railroads and in the brickyards, ironworks, and coal mines were much less likely to have had the leftover energy required for drilling in the National Guard in their spare time before the war. The 904 Danville men who were eventually drafted in subsequent calls, not in time generally to see combat action, tended to be less interested in joining the American Legion when they returned home; less interested, that is, than those affiliated with the Guard or who had enlisted. Among the volunteers from Danville, incidentally, were nine army nurses.

The first members of Curtis G. Redden Post 210, chartered October 17, 1919, tended to fall into two categories: (1) lawyers, other professionals, public officeholders, salesmen, business owners and managers, and newspaper editors and ad sellers for whom the contacts were of occupational value; and (2) police and firemen, bookkeepers, clerks and other office workers, postal workers, and others who often were also active in the masonic order or one of the local service clubs. The Masonic Temple stood out as one of the city's more grandiose architectural highlights.

Colonel Redden led his Guard unit, Field Artillery Battery A, to France, where it became one of the many parts of the Rainbow Division. Born on a Vermilion County farm in a family with roots reaching back to colonial Virginia, he received his law degree from the University of Michigan, where he captained the football team in 1903. His promising future was cut short soon after the armistice, when he died of pneumonia in Germany. The downtown public square in Danville also bears the Redden name. The black veterans of Company L of the Eighth Illinois Regiment organized their separate post, named after two privates who were killed in France, Charles Bradley and Raymond Maberry.

It did not take long for Redden Post to become established. Danville might have been one of the communities Foreman had in mind when he suggested that Legionnaires were running the town. The first commander, Casper Platt, had been a lieutenant in the infantry. His parents were among the first Jewish residents in 1877. Before moving to Danville, Louis Platt, Casper's father, had made his living in Chicago dealing in scrap left in the ruins of the Chicago Fire. He started a property insurance business in Danville and, around the turn of the century, was elected to one term as mayor. Casper Platt earned his law degree at the University of Chicago, where he met the woman who would become his wife, Jeanette. He was eased out of post leadership after becoming county chairman of the Democratic Party, which was the minority party in Vermilion County and a still smaller minority in the Redden post. His role in Legion affairs thereafter can best be considered marginal. As a practicing lawyer, he made use of the Legion contacts but took no part in the post's policy-making decisions. In 1933, he was elected a judge of the circuit court and therefore removed altogether from political activity. Although Jeanette Platt was instrumental in establishing Danville chapters of the American Association of University Women and the League of Women Voters, a published history of Judaism in Danville says that Jews were excluded from the Danville Country Club, the Boat Club, the hospital boards, and junior auxiliaries until around 1950.[26] Otto Lesch and then O. K. Yeager succeeded Platt as post commander. Yeager's father had commanded the militia unit that went from Danville to fight in the Spanish-American War. O. K. Yeager was credited with the leadership of the post drum and bugle corps, which started out inauspiciously but went on to win several state titles and to rival the Taylor post for competitive dominance. The post historian gives a humorous account of the corps' debut after the eighty musical Legionnaires had been unable to engage the help of nonmember ringers, due to what was described as a disagreement with the local musicians' union. Appearing at the state fair, the Redden post took to the field.

> [But then] every mother's son of them became so overcome with stage fright that wholesale panic broke out. Governments had decorated many of these men for bravery; many of them had faced the enemy's guns with no sign of fear, but before a friendly audience of fellow Americans all calm left them. Some went east, some went west, and never again did meet! Commander Yeager swore that the only thing that kept them from stampeding into the next county was a high fence. Loyal wives in the grandstand hid their faces and wept. Thus, in utter confusion ended the corps' first attempt to impress the public.[27]

Three weeks later, at the state convention in Rockford, the buglers and drummers of Redden Post redeemed themselves by finishing third in the competition. Redden Post was one of the few Illinois corps to operate without subsidized corporate sponsorship. It was said to have been the only one in Illinois to have its own lighted practice field. The drill field came as part of the Roselawn golf club, which the post purchased in 1936 for a clubhouse. The club's fifty acres of land included a natural amphitheater used for fireworks on Independence Day. Selected non-Legionnaires were sponsored for membership in the "Legion Roselawn Club," where throughout the 1930s, bingo games and Saturday night floor shows were regular events.

Unlike many others, Redden Post continued in strong financial condition throughout the Depression years. The roster in 1931 climbed to 945 members. By this time, peer influence created pressure on more veterans to join regardless of political differences. The Danville post won the Commander's Cup in 1932 for having more activities that year than any post in the state. In addition to its clubhouse, the Redden post maintained a downtown "office" complete with gym equipment, a boxing ring, and bleachers. The Legion took over sponsorship of Danville's Golden Gloves amateur boxing bouts from the local newspaper, the *Commercial News*.

Proceeds from the boxing matches were used to finance the operation of the Sunshine Health Camp, a three-week summer camp for undernourished boys and girls maintained by the Legion ten miles out in the country. Although some black youths fought in the Golden Gloves for the entertainment of spectators, only white children were invited to the camp for tubercular patients and other malnourished youngsters.[28]

All through the 1920s and early 1930s, the dominant leader of Redden Post was a sergeant in the Danville police department—Claude Hart. A corporal in the Rainbow Division, he had received both the U.S. Distinguished Service Cross and the French Croix de Guerre. The French citation described him as "courageous and full of dash . . . a model of bravery and coolness."[29] Legend has it that Corporal Hart deserted officers training camp in order to rejoin his infantry unit in France.

City wards were organized, precinct by precinct, much like a political party, with designated district representatives of the Legion in each subdivision. Not infrequently, the district Legionnaire commander happened also to be the Republican committeeman. Redden's leaders were more conservative, more Republican, better educated, more insular, less understanding of (and sympathetic to) diversity than the Taylor post in Chicago. The *Commercial News* gave front-page prominence to headlines of "crime waves" and other manifestations of social pathology in the evil big city, while ignoring or burying news of local events that would be harmful to the community image preferred by business owners. In this practice, the newspaper and the American Legion reflected the attitudes of the more "respectable" element of Danville society if not those of the lower and manual laboring classes. Mindful of local attitudes, the Redden Legionnaires were less open about their drinking. The presence of the Ku Klux Klan, however, was much more evident in the Danville area than in Chicago. Redden Post was less Catholic than Taylor Post, less representative of conscripted buck privates, and therefore much less insistent about bonus payments from the government. German and Irish Catholics attended their separate churches in Danville. Although their numbers were small in comparison with Chicago, Catholics played a significant part in community life, particularly among blue-collar families, who tended to be less involved in the American Legion. What was unusual about the Danville of that era was that there were enough African American Catholics to maintain their own parish—St. Augustine's—in an unused Protestant church building.

Racial segregation applied equally, of course, to the organization of the Legion in both Chicago and Danville. One incident is especially revealing about the nature of race relations in the Redden post. Three rivers run through or skirt the city of Danville, and in 1939 all three flooded their banks. Legionnaires were summoned for emergency sandbag duty. According to Carl Grove, "flood water was affecting three sides of the city, [but] one side being the colored district it was decided to call for colored Legionnaires to man their own territory. Danville's new radio station, WDAN, called members of Bradley-Maberry Post 736, and about thirty men responded within an hour. This relieved members of Post 210 for duty in other sections, now more threatening."[30] What is interesting about this incident is not that the black post would be asked to help in its own neighborhoods but that communication between the two posts was apparently such that the radio station had to be enlisted as intermediary. Redden Post could not deign to contact Bradley-Maberry Post as an equal in this time of need.

4 THE BRONZEVILLE CHOICE
STRIVER OR REVOLUTIONARY?

Among the volunteers who fought in the Spanish-American War were members of a militia unit that had only recently and very reluctantly been recognized by the State of Illinois. The Eighth Illinois Infantry Regiment consisted entirely of black soldiers. After that war, the regiment continued training but usually not in the taxpayer-financed National Guard armories. It would have been unseemly for white and black outfits to share the same facilities. Company K in Peoria drilled instead on the second floor of a downtown store building. The other black units made do with whatever they could find in their towns.

Even at that early date, military service could be the key to leadership in the black community. Robert R. Jackson joined the regiment in Chicago as a drummer, advanced to the rank of major, and saw action in the war with Spain. Back on Chicago's South Side, he did what was expected of leaders. He joined veterans associations and an array of secret societies, including what was then the pinnacle of leadership in Bronzeville, the Appomattox Club. Jackson went on to be elected to the state legislature and then in 1918 to the Chicago City Council.[1]

The Eighth Regiment enjoyed the distinction of being the only U.S. Army unit to ship to France in 1917 with a full complement of black officers. Most of the other black combat units were led by white officers. Colonel Franklin Denison of Chicago commanded the regiment with a field staff of eight officers. The twelve companies from Chicago consisted of 1,474 officers and men. Four companies originated in Springfield,

Peoria, Danville, and Metropolis with 614 officers and men, bringing the total roster to 2,088, of whom 1,260 returned in good health.[2]

Black combat units were not trusted to fight alongside American battlefront forces. The Eighth Regiment, redesignated the 370th, was attached instead to the French army on the western front. African American troops wore French helmets, carried French rifles, and were issued French rations—except for the wine. Before his unit reached the front, Denison was promoted to brigadier general, replaced by a white commander, and sent back to the states, where he spent the rest of the war in charge of an officers training camp for black men in Iowa.

Some of the reasons why the black soldiers could not join their white compatriots were spelled out in this confidential memo written by a French officer attached to the U.S. Army and directed to the French military command:

> Although a citizen of the United States, the black man is regarded by the white American as an inferior being with whom relations of business or service only are possible. The black is constantly being censured for his want of intelligence and discretion, his lack of civic and professional conscience, and for his tendency toward undue familiarity. The vices of the Negro are a constant menace to the American who has to repress them sternly. . . . We must not eat with them, must not shake hands or seek to talk or meet with them outside the requirements of military service.[3]

The French were further cautioned not to "spoil" the black troops by commending them too highly, particularly in the presence of white Americans. In training camp in Texas, the Illinois regiment marched "with a special rhythmic swagger which only black troops could effect." Their esprit de corps was more racial than military, one of their members acknowledged.[4] A regimental officer from Springfield, Colonel Otis Beverly Duncan, and sixty-seven other members of the unit were decorated by the French with the Croix de Guerre. Colonel Duncan's men wore a shoulder patch with a blue helmet on a field of black. While in France, they acquired the nickname "the Black Devils." It is unclear whether the label originated with the French or the Germans.[5]

Most of the blacks from Illinois who enlisted or were drafted wound up behind the lines, many of them on grave-digging details. Lee Mullin, from Peoria, was commanding an all-black company on burial duty at a cemetery near Belleau Wood on November 11, 1918. He and his men celebrated the end of the war by dropping their shovels and making haste for the nearby village of Fresnes, where they spent the afternoon drinking beer with the Germans.[6]

Sooner or later, black American Legion posts were established in all four of the downstate Eighth Regiment cities. A post in Springfield named for a fallen comrade, Harry Warfield, could not sustain the necessary membership and went defunct. Some of the black veterans who dropped out because of dissatisfaction with Legion policy formed a separate Springfield organization, called World War Barracks, that did not affiliate with the Legion.

Their former commander, Colonel Duncan, died in 1937. The Duncan family had settled in the Illinois territory involuntarily. His father had been taken from his home in the Caribbean and sold as a slave to a family in Kaskaskia, Illinois. Freedom came in time for the father to fight for the Union army in the Civil War. The veterans who had served under the colonel, in Company I of the Eighth Regiment, marched in his funeral procession at the veterans' cemetery near Springfield. Wondering how they could perpetuate Duncan's memory, they hit upon the idea of reviving the Springfield Legion post in his name.

By then the Warfield name had been adopted by a newly established black post in Decatur.[7] Lacking a place to meet, the members of the Decatur Warfield post took turns meeting in one another's house. Decatur also had an active white post, named for infantry sergeant Castle Williams, who died while his unit was taking their position for the battle of Consenvoye.

The black post in Peoria—Roy B. Tisdell Post 537—was not chartered until 1931. Sergeant Tisdell had been mortally wounded while leading twenty men on a mission to wipe out a machine gun nest in the Argonne forest. He walked two miles unassisted to a first aid station. Tisdell Post faced a stormy future. After World War II, its charter was revoked because of the "communist tendencies" of its officers. The crowning offense had been a visit to the post by the great baritone Paul Robeson, who was suspected of harboring subversive thoughts. Later, the post was reorganized and reinstated.[8]

Bradley-Maberry Post 736 in Danville did not begin until 1926. Forty-nine of the 132 who went off to war did not return, many because of influenza and other illnesses.

In deep southern Illinois, the men of Company M, some of whom had also served in the Spanish-American War, did not organize their post—

Neely Fosse Post 760—until even later, in 1934. Prior to statehood, the area had been slaveholding territory. Many of the black people who lived in Massac County worked in the cotton fields around Metropolis. During Prohibition, the sheriff regularly swept the "Black Bottom" swamplands for illegal stills. On one occasion, according to George May's regional history, "mash, liquor and a black man were found, the latter arrested and made to carry his own still to the auto."[9]

Within the strictly segregated black middle class, the American Legion performed an important social function. Legionnaires were looked up to by their neighbors. Wartime service paid off in prestige and sometimes in election to public office. Legion activities tended, more so than in white posts, to be family affairs. Commander Howarth Bryden worked on weekends with the other men of the Springfield post to refurbish a house on South Second Street that they used for a clubhouse. "We [women] would wrap the children up in bundles and take them along," remembered the commander's wife, Olive Bryden. "We would take food for the men and make a party of it. We always did things with the Legion gang. The vacations we took were to Legion conventions. Couples raised money for the post by selling ham sandwiches and then in the 1930s beer at our concession stand at the state fair."[10]

The black post in Chicago that lasted through a series of sometimes disputatious divisions and mergers—George L. Giles Post 87—was founded on August 15, 1919, principally through the efforts of a remarkably gifted man—Earl Dickerson. Earl Burris Dickerson was born in rural Mississippi, the grandson of slaves, in 1891. After the death of his father when Earl was four years old, his mother supported the family by taking in washing. One of the family relatives, a porter on the Illinois Central Railroad, lived in Chicago. When Earl was fifteen, arrangements were made for him to be sneaked aboard an IC train and hidden in the baggage car for the trip north. Once there he had the unusual good fortune of entering the laboratory high school operated by the University of Chicago. Demonstrating a flair for languages, he became proficient in Latin and French. He then attended Northwestern University and the University of Illinois before beginning his studies at the University of Chicago Law School. Upon America's entry into the war in 1917, Dickerson applied for officers training school and was commissioned a lieutenant in the infantry. If the black troops were to fight alongside the French, cool-headed interpreters were much in demand, more so than infantry officers. Lieutenant Dickerson filled the bill perfectly, supervising a platoon of bilingualists who could translate French and African American English under tense battlefield conditions.[11] After the war, he paid his way to the mass organizing meeting of the American Legion in St. Louis. Back in Chicago, he willingly deferred to Colonel Denison, who as past commander of the Black Devils was installed by acclamation to be the first commander of the Giles post. The Giles name belonged to a lieutenant who had been killed in action in France. Deteriorating health soon forced Denison to step down, whereupon Earl Dickerson took over as post commander for the next five years. He would continue for many more years to be one of the senior figures in African-American Legion affairs.

Giles Post operated its own claims assistance branch office for black veterans. No one in the state department office objected to being relieved of this portion of its responsibilities. At one point, the post was processing eight hundred service cases a year, some of them highly complicated estate settlement matters. Its Americanism program emphasized how blacks could unite and use their voting power to elect able representatives to public office. The men in the post and the women in the auxiliary visited patients regularly in Chicago area federal and state hospital wards. The post sponsored, among its other activities, both senior and junior drum and bugle corps, whose lively performances were the pride of the entire community.

Migration from the South did not let up after the war. Between 1920 and 1930, the black population of Cook County more than doubled, from 115,200 to almost 247,000. Chicago's Twelfth Street IC station became a black Ellis Island. The class system differentiated between middle-class blacks, many of them second-generation Chicagoans who had good jobs, and the newcomers from the rural South. Many of the former regimental officers worked in the Chicago post office. Inevitable leadership conflicts developed among the several black veterans, former officers for the most part, who were politically ambitious.

One of the Legionnaires who had plans for himself, William Levi Dawson was a former infantry lieutenant born in Georgia. Giles post had 295 dues-paying members in 1920. A year later, a splinter group broke off to form a new black post called Mont des Singes. Giles membership plummeted to fifty-eight in 1923. The two posts sued for peace and came back together. Another new black post, chartered by followers of former colonel Charles Young in 1924, lasted only a year and a half. Bill Dawson remained loyal to Dickerson's example by staying in the Giles post. Giles entered the 1930s as the sole Chicago black post, with about 250 members on its rolls.

While still in law school, Dickerson drew up the incorporation documents for a company that would make him a multimillionaire. In black neighborhoods, the big national life insurance companies then were selling policies that included a special handling charge. The extra fee was to compensate agents for the risk of coming into what they considered a high-crime zone to collect premiums. Dickerson organized and served as president and general counsel of the Liberty Life Insurance Company (later Supreme Life Insurance Company of America), the first and largest of several black-owned insurance companies for black policyholders. As a lawyer, he argued one of the landmark restrictive covenant cases before the U.S. Supreme Court, which had the effect of opening up an additional twenty-six blocks on the South Side to black residents. He sued and won another case against one of the big downtown hotels that refused to admit his daughter to its dining room.

Most blacks in the North had been voting Republican ever since the Civil War. Dickerson crossed party lines in 1923 (at the same time as his fellow Legionnaire Albert Sprague) to support reform Democratic mayoral candidate Dever. In 1928, and again in 1932, Dickerson participated in the veterans campaign organizations of Democratic presidential candidates Al Smith and Franklin D. Roosevelt. As president of the 40 Club, a gathering place for Bronzeville's most successful politicians and business and professional men, Earl Dickerson now fit comfortably into the social elite. In 1929 he ran for the city council on the Democratic ticket as "the soldier and the statesman" but lost. A fellow Legionnaire who would soon become a political enemy—Bill Dawson—also ran in the same election and lost.

A year later, in 1930, Dickerson encouraged a former Giles post commander, William H. Hughes, to petition for the chartering of a new black post in Chicago. Hughes pointed out that the city's black community had stretched farther south. Some Legionnaires were having to travel considerable distance to meetings and other activities. Representatives from the several dozen all-white posts in the Legion's third district met at the South Shore post with the Giles post delegation to consider the request. District rules provided that any post could veto an application for a new post within the district. A reporter for the black newspaper, the *Defender*, overheard one of the white Legionnaires tell another, "We've got too many niggers in the district meetings now."[12] Much to the astonishment of the white members, Giles Post, not one of the white units, exercised its veto power to block the charter application. The reporter for the *Defender* was appalled. He said the amused whites "were treated to some insight as to how our people feel about each other." Michael H. Browning, the Giles commander, said it had been shown that there were not enough interested black veterans to support two viable posts. He worried specifically that the Giles drum and bugle corps would suffer the loss of good marching musicians.

The *Defender,* which used *race* as an adjective and noun in place of *Negro* and *black,* noted in its editorial that

> many of our veterans [in the South] are kept out of the Legion by the authority of state departments to issue charters. In spite of this Jim Crow policy, we have urged veterans to join the Legion. We believe that the best way to bring about corrective measures in any organization is to get in it and gain power within its ranks. In Illinois last week we were treated to the sorry spectacle of a group of *race* veterans urging the Legion not to issue a charter to another group of race veterans. . . . The veterans were told, in essence, to go out and join the lone Race post or stay out of the American Legion. [There is] no justification for a group of race veterans going before a white group and asking that another race group of veterans be refused a charter.
>
> The act, in itself, shows how far backward we, even in Illinois, are traveling. The American Legion has done very little toward bringing peace among races in America. Instead, it is a militaristic, snobbish organization. It caters to the very prejudices that characterize other organizations composed of 100 percenters. [Yet we ought to] get in and fight for what is necessary to rescue it from Klan influences. . . . [Another post in Chicago would have stimulated interest.] Those dark Legionnaires helped neither the Legion nor their race by opposing that charter[13] [author's emphasis].

Other black posts were organized later. Post office workers formed the Colonel J. R. Marshall Post 829 in 1939, naming it for another former regimental officer. An all-black post was started in Aurora, too. But it took many years for the Giles post to live down the 1930 experience.

Black posts in Illinois participated routinely in meetings with other Legionnaires, as long as they kept "in their place," with only occasional complications. In 1936, for example, Legionnaires from the Giles post joined a delegation of Americans who traveled to Paris for a Christmas reunion with members of French veterans' organizations. According to a report in the *Defender,* one of the African Americans, Luther Walker, ventured to dance with white French women at a party. The white Americans in the Legion contingent went into one corner of the room and "voted" to demand that Luther Walker quit dancing with the French women. The French women told the Legionnaires to mind their own business.[14] (The wartime memo to the French military had ended with this admonition: "Americans become greatly incensed at any expression of intimacy between white women [and] black men. . . . Familiarity on the part of white women with black men is furthermore a source of profound regret to our experienced colonials, who see in it an overwhelming menace to the white race.")[15]

The stage was being set in Chicago, meanwhile, for a series of leadership confrontations in the Bronzeville Second Ward between Earl Dickerson and Bill Dawson. After losing their first campaigns as Republicans, their allegiances diverged dramatically. Dawson tried again. This time he won a seat on the city council. He said his Legion friends from the Giles post made the difference. Toward the end of the 1930s, the two men converted to the Democratic party for different reasons. As a lawyer and businessman, Dickerson became increasingly involved in the civil rights movement. He identified ideologically with President Franklin Roosevelt's New Deal. Running as a Democrat, Dickerson challenged Dawson for the city council and was elected. The new leader of the Chicago Democratic organization, Mayor Edward J. Kelly, did not trust (or understand) the new alderman's liberalism. So Kelly solicited Dawson to take over the Democratic ward organization, the beginning of the latter's long and successful tenure in the Democratic party. Dawson's new ward organization fought Dickerson's renomination for alderman. Dickerson lost. Dickerson subsequently was appointed to the first federal Fair Employment Practices Commission in the Roosevelt administration. Dawson, on the other hand, broadened his control over the entire South Side Black Belt by being elected to the U.S. House. According to some accounts, he and the criminal syndicate ran the "numbers racket" (a form of street gambling not all that different from today's state-run lotteries), loan sharking, prostitution, and the hard drug traffic on the South Side for the next three decades.[16]

Nationally, only about thirty-five hundred of an estimated 380,000 eligible black veterans belonged then to the American Legion.[17] Possibly because the black population was more widely scattered, both Pennsylvania and Oklahoma had more active black posts than did Illinois. Legion meetings remained a vital social and political haven for the Chicago black middle class, nevertheless, on through the 1920s and 1930s. Giles Post held an annual Junior Legion party for the children of members at Christmas. The elected executive board met every month at the commander's home. Often the commander's wife served cake and eggnog.[18]

No Eggnog for the Underclass

Few of the men who served in the Eighth Illinois Regiment before and during the Great War had been blessed with anything like Earl Dickerson's educational opportunities. And few of them, to be sure, were to be found sipping eggnog at American Legion functions. Consider the case of Haywood Hall. He dropped out of school before the war at age sixteen. The only available job was as a dining car waiter on the railroad. He joined the Eighth National Guard Regiment in Chicago, which he thought of as "a big social club of fellow race-men."[19] Shortly after the regiment was ordered for training to Camp Logan, near Houston, Texas, he and his friends heard about a race riot that had erupted in East St. Louis. The black troops at the camp demonstrated in support of the black workers back in Illinois who had been attacked (and some killed) because they had taken jobs in defense plants.

Later, in the first summer following his discharge from the army, Hall stepped off his dining car at the Twelfth Street station one day to see the South Side in flames. A black youth had blundered onto the "white beach" at Twenty-sixth Street and had been stoned to death. For the next six days, armed warfare raged between whites and blacks in that part of Chicago. Hearing a rumor that "Irishmen from west of the tracks" were planning to invade the black ghetto, Hall and a group of fellow veterans confiscated submachine guns and Springfield rifles from the regimental National Guard armory at Thirty-fifth Street and Giles Avenue. Though their show of force in defense of their neighborhood turned out to be unnecessary, before peace could be restored the toll from the six days of combat reached thirty-eight dead, 537 injured, and more than a thousand burned out of their homes.

The confrontation marked a turning point in the life of Haywood Hall, veteran. He and his older brother Otto, who was also a veteran, joined the Communist party and became active in the campaign to enroll American workers. The Halls had nothing but scorn for the "strivers" who sought social status in the American Legion and similar organizations.[20]

Selected officers of the American Expeditionary Force at a caucus in Paris in March 1919. The decision was made at this meeting to begin the organization of the American Legion. (American Legion Library Archives)

Swashbuckling intelligence officer Thomas R. Gowenlock, who engineered the overthrow of the liberal leadership of the Legion in Chicago.
(Chicago Historical Society, ICHi-36147)

Oscar E. Carlstrom.
(Courtesy of the Illinois State Historical Library)

Albert A. Sprague, the driving force behind the Legion's campaign for a system of medical care for disabled veterans. (American Legion Library Archives)

Colonels Milton Foreman *(left, front)* and Abel Davis *(right, front)* wearing their military decorations to welcome visiting French officers to Chicago in 1925. (Chicago Historical Society, DN-0079748; *Chicago Daily News* photo, cropped)

Charles W. "Daddy" Schick.
(American Legion Library Archives)

William R. McCauley.
(Courtesy of the Illinois State Historical Library)

Joseph L. DeLaCour of Chicago, devoted member of Harold A. Taylor Post 47 and the 42nd Ward regular Democratic organization.
(Courtesy of the Illinois State Historical Library)

Claude Hart, a war hero, a sergeant in the Danville police department, and a leader of Danville's Redden Post.
(Vermilion County War Museum)

National commander Howard P. Savage, flanked by General John J. Pershing *(left)* and French Marshal Ferdinand Foch, at the Legion convention in Paris in 1927. (American Legion Library Archives)

Fifteenth national convention of the American Legion, 1933. American Legion parades were spectacular affairs, never more so than when the national convention was held in Chicago.

(American Legion Library Archives; photo by Kaufmann and Fabry Co.)

John H. Stelle.
(American Legion Library Archives)

Scott W. Lucas, 1926.
(American Legion Library Archives; photo
by Charles F. Bretzman, Indianapolis)

[The veteran is] politically dangerous because he has a great deal of hatred to work off. . . . The veteran is accustomed to direct action but not to discussion; he has a pronounced aversion to discussion. He feels intensely but not intelligently, intensely because he has suffered, unintelligently because his political education stopped when he entered the army.

—Willard Waller

5 Taking On the Red Menace

What to do about the Hall brothers and their fellow recruits in the cause of Communism? This question disturbed many Americans who were genuinely alarmed by the anti-American rhetoric. Many of the leading members of the Legion felt intensely, if not always intelligently, that their service in defense of America gave them a special responsibility to stamp out subversive thoughts before they could take root.

But first there was the matter of the "slackers." After the hostilities ended, it was permissible for loyal Americans to believe (as did many Legionnaires in Illinois) that it had been a mistake for the United States to become involved in that or any other "foreign war." However, the men in the Legion would never excuse any lack of commitment to the war effort while it was going on. Milton Foreman said in 1920 that the Legion should never forget or forgive "those who by word, act or deed retarded the vigorous prosecution of the war and thereby became responsible for casualties which might have been avoided."[1]

Civilian patriots made the identification job easier while the war was being waged. In Sycamore, the seat of DeKalb County, citizens were encouraged to post names on a "slacker board" in the town square. A local physician discovered that he had been publicly labeled a slacker for failing to meet his quota of Liberty Bond purchases. The *True Republican*, which kept tabs on the slacker board, reported that the doctor was "reputed to be wealthy." It was not made clear who or what had established the Liberty Bond quotas.[2]

Legion doctrine held essentially that anyone who was not born in the United States and had not become a fully naturalized citizen was more likely than not to be a prospective Communist and therefore dangerous. For the American Legion, the concept of Americanism was more an emotion than an idea capable of precise definition.[3] Beginning with an understandable aversion to any who had been opposed to the vigorous prosecution of the war, the more the Legionnaire activists mulled over the concept of "100 percent Americanism" the bigger their bull's-eye target grew. From revolutionaries and anarchists to aliens who had avoided the draft, to all leftist thinkers and organizers, to all Communists, socialists, and internationalists, to any voices of discontent with the status quo, all were nicely bundled together under the brand name "Reds."

Although fewer than one in ten eligible veterans in Cook County belonged to the American Legion in the mid-1920s, the Legion purported to speak for all veterans of the Great War. The long Chicago tradition of radicalism, social agitation, trade unionism, and preservation of ethnic identity made for considerable commotion during the first few years of the American Legion in Illinois. The most avowedly radical of the labor organizations still in existence in the Midwest—the Wobblies—had about disappeared in the state where it was born. After the war, one of the few remaining IWW strongholds was a long way from Chicago in the lumbering town of Centralia, Washington. On the first national observance of Armistice Day, while delegates were attending the first national convention of the Legion in Minneapolis, the post in Centralia paraded in the direction of the IWW hall. The Wobblies said later they thought the Legionnaires were marching on the hall with intent to do them harm, which the men of the Legion said was not true. Shots rang out from the union hall, and four of the marching Legionnaires fell dead. That night the other Legionnaires removed one of the Wobblies, a veteran wearing his soldier's uniform, from the jail. They dragged him to the edge of town and hanged him under a bridge.

News of the incident transmitted by Morse code over telegraph wires did not have nearly the instant emotional impact that it would have with today's audiovisual communication. But it did have the effect of rallying public support behind the Wilson administration's drive to jail or deport foreign-born people who were accused of various forms of disloyalty. On a single day—January 2, 1920—twenty-seven hundred aliens were arrested, most to be deported to Germany or Russia. Legion posts around the country lent their encouragement on the sidelines by, in one example, demonstrating against concert appearances in the United States by the violinist Fritz Kreisler, who had been an Austrian army officer. "A cloud of suspicion hung in the air, and intolerance became an American virtue," recalled the historian Frederick Lewis Allen. The national commander ordered the Legion to "be ready for action at any time against these extremists who are seeking to overthrow a government."[4]

A year later, in 1921, the *Staats Zeitung* affair had a similar effect on public opinion in Illinois. There were two German-language daily newspapers in Chicago before the war: the *Abendpost* and the *Illinois Staats Zeitung*. Until the United States entered the conflict, both papers supported the German war effort. The *Abendpost* argued that a German victory would "save Americans from Anglo-Saxonism." The *Staats Zeitung*, which had been founded before the Civil War, warned more harshly that "a war of the races" in the United States, meaning Teuton and Anglo-Saxon, would result from American involvement. Considered along with the *Chicago Tribune* as "the leading Republican paper of the Northwest" and a "real power in the Northwest," it had rallied German voters behind Abraham Lincoln's candidacy in 1860.[5] The *Abendpost* thought it expedient to trim its editorial sails after America entered the war in 1917, but the editor of the *Staats Zeitung*, Arthur Lorenz, was less restrained. As a consequence, the *S-Z* lost advertising, converted to weekly publication, and was in precarious financial condition at the end of the war. Lorenz persisted in zeroing in on the American Legion, which he called "an instrument bought with British gold to suppress truth, gag freedom of expression, and betray organized labor."

One day, one of the German-speaking members of James C. Russell Blackhawk Post 107 picked up a copy of the *S-Z* on a newsstand. The Legion pretends that it is the cream of the nation, the editorial read, but actually the veterans were "the refuse of the nation . . . almost without exception tramps, vagabonds, and bums." The incensed Legionnaire translated the editorial and delivered a copy to the *Tribune*, which. reprinted it in English. Blackhawk Post promptly filed a civil complaint seeking one hundred thousand dollars in compensatory damages for libel against the Legion. The publishers requested a meeting to discuss a retraction notice, but the terms were not acceptable to post representatives. John Clinnin, commander of the North Shore post, was consulted in his capacity as an assistant U.S. attorney. A short time later, the paper and its editor were indicted by a federal grand jury for criminal libel.

Clinnin and the Blackhawk Post further demanded the deportation of Lorenz. Clinnin grew up in an Irish Catholic family on a dairy farm near the Wisconsin border. He drove a milk wagon for his father's dairy business at age eleven. An infantry veteran of the fighting in Santiago, Cuba, in 1898, Clinnin came home to start a tailoring business in Chicago. He took law courses, became involved in Republican politics, and obtained a patronage job in the office of the elected county recorder, Abel Davis, when the war broke out. He had some experience with the internal politics of veterans organizations, having served as judge advocate of the Society of the Army of Santiago de Cuba, made up of veterans of that engagement. John Clinnin was a chunky man who had the tough, hard-nosed demeanor of a boxer, which he had been earlier in his life. In France with the rank of colonel, the forty-two-year-old Chicagoan commanded an infantry regiment made up almost entirely of Illinois men who would later join Chipilly Post 310 of the Legion. The name derived from Chipilly Ridge, which the men of the regiment they called the "Dandy First" stormed and took on August 9, 1918, after British and Australian units had tried and failed. Clinnin, Savage, Davis, and Sprague were among those in the forefront of the ongoing movement to establish a semi-independent governing structure for the Legion in Cook County. "Through the American Legion we must grasp such seditionists [as Lorenz] by the scruff of the neck and throw them out of the country," Clinnin declared. "His record during the war gives ample reason for sending him back to Posen."[6] Lorenz was brought to trial, convicted by a jury of libeling the Legion, sentenced to six months in jail, which he served, and fined a token one dollar. The newspaper ceased publication and filed for bankruptcy. Its assets were sold to pay debts. But Clinnin and the Legion never succeeded in having Arthur Lorenz deported.

Most posts had at least one member who specialized in the identification of Americans who bore watching, within and outside the organization. In Homewood, for example, that member was a man named E. Austin Rice. "Comrade Rice's pet quarry is the communist," said the post history. "With the unerring sense of a hunting dog, he can smell him anywhere, even when cloaked, as sometimes he is, in the uniform of the Legion."[7] The tone of this statement suggests that some of Comrade Rice's brethren were amused by his tactics.

Legionnaires monitored closely the words and deeds of native-born but liberal clergy and settlement house workers. Ferre Watkins referred to Jane

Addams's Hull House on Chicago's Near West Side as a hotbed of Communism and of "Pinks trying to sell out America to international schemers for their own advantage." Addams thought it illogical to assume that "a citizen who is against war and wants his country to use non-warlike means to adjudicate disputes is unpatriotic." In 1931 she won the Nobel Peace Prize for her leadership of the women's international peace movement.[8]

The men's club of an Evanston church invited the leftist former missionary Karl Borders to speak, only to withdraw the invitation at the behest of local Legion members, who were pleased to provide a substitute speaker from the state department's Americanism commission. Another committee from the post in nearby Des Plaines paid a call on the Reverend William Bailey Waltmire, the minister of the First Methodist Episcopal Church, to interrogate him about his views after learning that he had participated in the formation of a Chicago branch of the American Civil Liberties Union.[9]

Some units in the Chicago area copied a tactic used in some downstate counties by the Ku Klux Klan. Anonymous in their white robes and hoods, Klan members would march unannounced into a church, carrying lighted candles and an American flag that they would deposit near the altar before marching silently back out the door. In the spring of 1931, the state conference of Congregational churches convened in LaGrange. Six uniformed Legionnaires appeared suddenly at the door. They entered, marching in military fashion to the front of the church bearing U.S. and American Legion flags. Two of the men carried rifles. They placed the flags on the platform, saluted smartly, about-faced, and marched out of the church without uttering a word.[10]

One grievance sure to bring down the wrath of the Legion involved expressions of disrespect for the Stars and Stripes. In one such case, Legionnaires in Chicago protested a speech by a visiting professor from Columbia University that was said to have contained "ironical" references to the flag.[11] The men of the American Legion considered the symbols of patriotism key to national loyalty, especially for young people. The state executive committee proposed the enactment of a state law in 1923 that would require the flag to be flown every day over every Illinois school building. The bill, introduced in Springfield by Legionnaire legislators in both parties, specified also that an American Legion member be present every Wednesday afternoon at three o'clock to preside over appropriate school flag-lowering ceremonies. Unfortunately, the legislation ran afoul of one of the grim realities of the lawmaking process in Illinois. Commander McCauley reported that a lobbyist identified as a representative of flag manufacturers was seen in the statehouse. Whenever agents of commercial interests appeared, legislators would automatically speculate that there was "money on the bill" and then ask, "Where's mine?" The lobbyist evidently did not bring a big enough bag, because the bill died. McCauley told his comrades that the Legion had been used and next time it would be advisable first to "call off" the flag lobby.[12] For whatever reasons, the measure failed to pass on the second try also, but the state leaders took consolation in the organization's distribution of some two hundred thousand pamphlets about the American flag in the public schools.

Later on, while the Depression raged in the early 1930s, the Illinois department's Americanism commission became embroiled in efforts to quell expressions by students that were deemed unacceptable. Three students at Illinois State Normal College, a teacher training institution, gave speeches to service clubs in Bloomington that were said by the Legion to resemble Communist thinking. "Throw them out!" demanded Hayes Kennedy, the state vice commander, noting that one of the accused was the son of a faculty member whose salary was paid by the state. State commander James B. Murphy of Bloomington agreed. "The students' communistic utterances cannot be excused on any grounds," he said. "America cannot tolerate such actions by students of a school supported 100 percent by taxes under a constitutional government."[13]

Another incident involved a mural at a junior high school in Rockford. One of the panels depicted a worker freeing another who was bound in chains. Responding to the Rockford post's demand that the painting be removed, the local school superintendent concurred. "It isn't a painting for children of this age," he said. "It makes one get riled up, stirred up. I didn't look at it very long. Sometimes it is dangerous to look at the same painting too long."[14]

Edward A. Hayes of Decatur, who was state commander in 1930 and became national commander three years later, told the National Education Association in 1934 that the American Legion "has the right to demand that education be constructive for the country's welfare and that it be patriotic in character."[15] Throughout this period, the Illinois department fought unsuccessfully to obtain passage of a law requiring a loyalty oath for teachers. Failing in that objective, the Legion's Americanism commission recommended in 1935, "Subversive teachings to the youth of our land, both from within and without the country, can be fought only by a vigorous campaign of Americanism."[16] Local posts irritated teachers by screening history textbooks for un-American references and by sponsoring countless essay contests prepared to their specifications.

In the national politics of Legion affairs, the Illinois department acquired a reputation for being hard-liners on the Americanism commission. For a time, around 1925, the national director of the Americanism commission was a man named Frank Clay Cross. Illinois officials considered Cross to be excessively tolerant of free expression. When Howard Savage of Chicago became national commander in 1927, Cross was replaced.

Occasional protests against the hard-line policies were lodged in Illinois by Legionnaires who were educators, ministers, or union members. The Reverend Thomas A. Goodwin, chaplain of the post in Winnetka, complained to the national commander in 1928 that it had been wrong for the Legion to organize a pressure campaign against the "evil influence" of lecturer Sherwood Eddy, an official of the YMCA and a pacifist. "There are many ex-servicemen who would be in the Legion if they did not suppose the Legion to be lacking in tolerance," Goodwin asserted. Another clergyman, the Reverend Eliot Porter in Lincoln, said he was "impressed by the contempt in which the Legion is often held at many universities, not by 'pinks' or 'smart young radical instructors' but by sound and intelligent people." The Lincoln chaplain said he had considered resigning from the Legion but that he knew that "this phase of intolerance is not a fundamental expression of its spirit."[17]

Soon after its founding, the organization established a national policy of teaching citizenship to young people through team sports. Professional baseball contributed to the support of a highly successful American Legion summer baseball program for high school–aged youths that thrived for many years in all parts of the nation.

The state executive committee resolved in 1920 that the Legion should cooperate in any way possible with the Boy Scouts of America, which the resolution said "stands for thoroughgoing manhood and Americanism." Several Illinois posts sponsored Boy Scout troops. By the mid-1930s, 157 posts had chartered Sons of the American Legion "squadrons." It was estimated in 1936 that dues were being paid for less than half the more than ten thousand junior members. For their sons and other boys, the Legion also sponsored junior rifle teams and a six-week course in rifle practice.

Attitudes about guns and gun control made an interesting transition in Illinois Legion halls during the decade of the 1920s. One post endorsed a resolution criticizing American Legion publications for accepting mail-order gun sale advertisements. The Legionnaires then presumably feared the arming of revolutionaries. By the end of the decade, however, the same members had come to believe that citizen groups like the Legion should be prepared with superior firepower to put down any insurrection. "[We] condemn the effort to deprive citizens of the right to bear arms, to the advantage of armed criminals," the resolution proclaimed.[18] Later, in the mid-1930s, the Legion advanced proposals for the mandatory fingerprinting of all Americans. Another Illinois resolution would have prohibited political candidates from speaking over the radio in languages other than English.

The most innovative of all American Legion patriotic indoctrination projects originated in Illinois in 1934 as an answer to the Young Pioneer summer camps that were sponsored by the Communist Party USA. It was called Boys State. Posts throughout Illinois selected 217 school-age boys who lived together for a week and governed themselves democratically at the state fairgrounds in Springfield. Hayes Kennedy, a law professor at Loyola University, thought up the idea for Boys State in conjunction with Harold L. Card, a high school teacher and the chairman of the Illinois department's Boy Scout program. The boys formed parties, caucused, elected their leaders, determined their rules of conduct, considered what the rights of the minority ought to have, and practiced the duties of citizenship in a democratic society. The faculty could not resist administering, at Lincoln's tomb on the final day, an oath promising to acquire a thorough flag education and to help make "flag education an essential basic element in good citizenship." One of the Young Pioneers showed up on the first day of the first session to exercise his First Amendment rights by distributing Communist leaflets. He was "arrested" and detained overnight in a cowshed at the fairgrounds before being released.[19] The program, soon copied by other states and renamed Boys' Nation, helped to introduce young people from all sections of Illinois to one another and to the often fractious democratic process.

Legion doctrine did not usually extend to the open exchange of ideas. The Illinois department's Americanism commission recommended "as a general policy that all Legion posts avoid participating in mixed programs, or joint debates, with those of radical views, because such procedures only serve to dignify and advertise the work of the enemy." On another occasion, Gladstone Post 777 on the Northwest Side of Chicago requested the state convention's endorsement of a grant by a philanthropic foundation to establish an endowed chair at a state university for the study of American institutions. The resolution was rejected, 664 to 317, reflecting the leaders' distrust of this sort of inquiry on a college campus.[20]

Posts were expected to perform community service. In Illinois, except in the very smallest communities, most of them did. Each year, beginning in the mid-1920s, the state department bestowed a community service award on one post. Here are some examples of the winning activities:

LaGrange Post 41—for establishing a Sunday evening club for the better understanding of Americanism.

Peoria Post 2—for helping the victims of a flood in East Peoria.

Sarlo-Sharp Post 368, Melrose Park—for sponsoring a safety-first campaign in the schools.

East St. Louis 124th Field Artillery Post 53—for sponsoring a Christmas toy campaign for 3,614 needy children.

Chicago Police Post 207—for sponsoring an essay contest in the schools on law and order.

Some service activities involved the exercise of deputized police powers. Because of their military training, presumably, Legionnaires sometimes made themselves available to augment regular police and fire departments when someone thought they were needed. LaGrange is an example. Once in 1926, the local police walked off their jobs in support of a colleague who had been relieved of his duties by the village trustees. Sixty Legion members were called out of their beds at 2 a.m. and deputized to serve as emergency law enforcement officers. Their only arrest that first night was of a railroad crossing watchman for being asleep on the job. The entire post was mobilized in 1934 to control the crowds who turned out to see the first diesel-driven streamliner, the Zephyr, pass through town on the Burlington railroad. Occasionally the fire department would be called to help fight a big blaze in a nearby town. When that happened, Legionnaires would fill in as backup firemen at home.[21]

The state department considered but did not act on a suggestion by the Marine post in Chicago that a statewide citizen-police reserve consisting of five thousand "carefully selected American Legion members" be organized to aid police in "riots, disasters, or wherever needed."[22] The

Chicago Police post was among the largest in the state. Police and the Legion enjoyed a special relationship throughout the state. Not all Legion police operations were nearly so benign as those in LaGrange, however, as we will see in later chapters. But it appeared, then and now, that the American Legion's perceived role as volunteer enforcer of law and order in troubled times had the support of most local citizens, at least those who spoke out, especially in smaller communities.

One might wonder, looking back now, about the Legion's *authority* to hand down its sweeping judgments of freedom of speech, public education, national security, and so forth. The simple answer would be that it seemed to flow extralegally from "the people," from the force of public opinion at the local level in Illinois. Legionnaires occupied positions of power in community nerve centers—in local government, law enforcement, the judicial system, financial institutions, and the press. The display of this power could be awesome. A bill passed in both houses of the state legislature in 1929 authorizing public bodies to lease government buildings to veterans organizations at "a nominal rent," as happened in some other states. The frugal governor Louis L. Emmerson vetoed the measure. Earlier, in 1921, the legislature adopted a resolution calling for the construction of a new highway—to be called the American Legion Highway—that would run from the northernmost point in Illinois to the southernmost point. The governor chose not to act on the resolution.

Many newspaper editors not only belonged to the Legion but were active members. *Staats Zeitung* notwithstanding, newspapers in all part of the state were almost always sympathetic to Legion interests. Lewis W. Hunt, city editor of the *Chicago Daily News,* served as commander of Marine Post 273. Frank Knox, general manager of the Hearst newspapers, was a Legionnaire. A veteran of the Spanish-American War, he served as an army major in France during the World War. Just after the war, while he was running the newspaper in Manchester, New Hampshire, Knox bankrolled the organization of the Legion in that state. In 1931 he bought controlling interest in the *Chicago Daily News.* Promoted in the army reserves to the rank of colonel, he and Bertie McCormick competed for influence in the Illinois Republican Party—Knox as the "afternoon colonel" (the *Daily News* being an afternoon paper), McCormick as the "morning colonel" (the *Tribune* being a morning paper). No Chicago papers beat the drums for the American Legion with more vigor than the Hearst dailies. Stories of Legion affairs in the *Herald and Examiner* carried a byline without a name: By the Soldier's Friend. William McCauley's newspaper in Olney reported the news of the Rock Island convention without mentioning the criticism of his record as state commander, only that he had been presented with a medal and a ring upon leaving office. Thus, with hands on the public purse strings, the prosecution of crimes, the lending practices of banks and other financial institutions, and the stream of information to newspaper readers, the American Legion could often manipulate mainstream opinion in many Illinois communities.

6 THE LEGION, THE KLAN, AND PERSONAL LIBERTY

The American Legion had a serious rival in the propagation of 100-percent Americanism in some parts of Illinois, and that of course was the Ku Klux Klan. The Legion and the Klan shared certain views, while differing on other questions of lifestyle and morality. This chapter examines their similarities and their differences, particularly as they related to diversity, alcoholic beverages, and what opponents of Prohibition referred to as personal liberty.

Though shrouded in secrecy, chapters of the Klan, or klaverns as they were called, are believed to have existed after the war in every Illinois county. The hooded society was especially strong along the Indiana border from the Danville area south in a belt of Southern Baptist counties, and through the coal-mining counties in the lower one-third of the state. Typical of many downstate cities, the various Masonic orders constituted the base of anti-Catholic Klan activity in that region. The Klan's reinvigoration in the Midwest during the early 1920s is generally understood to have been an outgrowth of religious fundamentalism and the perceived need to remove alien "impurities" in the native American, which is to say white Protestant, stock. The Klan's watchwords were easy to grasp: "The white race must always be supreme," and "Rome shall not rule America."

In Chicago, where Catholics were considerably more numerous and the resistance more aggressive, the movement had been pretty well stamped out by the mid-twenties. A group called the American Unity League, led by Chicago lawyer Patrick O'Donnell, published a newspaper that specialized in "outing" the members of the secret society ("Who's Who in Nightgowns"). O'Donnell"s organization, financed primarily by Chicagoans of Irish descent and endorsed enthusiastically by the *Defender* newspaper, made life miserable for the Kluxers. In April 1923, a bomb destroyed the office of *Dawn,* the KKK organ in the Chicago area.[1]

A warmer reception awaited the Klan in some sections of southern Illinois. With some reason apparently, the impression persisted there that corrupt local police were tolerating bootlegging (making whiskey illegally), gambling, prostitution, and other kinds of vice. Furthermore, it was believed that "foreigners," Catholics for the most part, were responsible for the illegal activity. In the coal town of West Frankfort, about five hundred Sicilians lived in their own neighborhood with their own pool hall, clubhouse, and barbershop. In the summer of 1920, the bodies of two murder victims were found in the town. Rumors spread that the Black Hand, a Sicilian terrorist group, had been responsible for the murders. After advising the mayor and sheriff to leave town, a mob drove the Italian families from their homes and burned their houses and social centers. One man, Louis Carreari, was beaten to death with an axe while his wife and their five children looked on in their own house. A *St. Louis Post-Dispatch* reporter found "a spirit of carnival-like deviltry" in the town before eighteen units of the Illinois National Guard arrived to restore order.[2]

The nearby town of Herrin had its Italian community, too, consisting of miners and their families, and a few who had taken to wine making, bootlegging, and the operation of gambling roadhouses. Ministers denounced "foreigners" in their midst who were linked to vice. Protestant clergy welcomed the arrival in 1923 of the Klan wizard S. Glenn Young. Young led a contingent of white-robed men on horses who said they were going to raid the bootleggers and drive out the gamblers and prostitutes. The Klansmen carried out arrests and put people in jail, usurping the duties of the regularly constituted law enforcement officers.

Major General Milton Foreman arrived from Springfield with a force of seventeen hundred Guardsmen who endeavored to disarm the Klan. The Herrin post of the American Legion pledged to cooperate with an anti-Klan citizens' committee. At one point, Illinois attorney general Oscar Carlstrom made a coolly reasoned appeal to the local pocketbook by raising the specter of martial law, which, he reminded local citizens, would severely dampen property values in all of Williamson County. "I hope we can go back to the day when confidence is placed in the courts and in the processes of the law," Carlstrom said. "Only then can we remove the necessity of an armed camp in this county."[3]

A former Legion post commander, one A. O. Boswell, acted as counsel for the Klan in Williamson County during this period. Boswell claimed that "90 percent of the law-abiding people, or 75 percent of the total population" were supporting the Klan in that county.[4] Many Klan members covered their faces to avoid being identified, so it was impossible to tell how many Legionnaires also belonged to the Klan.

Certain generalizations can be made:

1. Some Legionnaires and some posts, in Williamson among other counties, stood up against the Klan. In an oral history of West Frankfort, L. L. Darnell remembered the Klan coming into town. "After that, a band of 100 citizens, mainly soldiers, organized themselves for the purpose of stopping the actions of the KKK," he said, probably referring here to the former servicemen as soldiers.[5]

2. Some veterans belonged to both organizations. One resident of Massac County told me his father and two uncles were veterans of the Great War. All three both belonged to the American Legion and had hooded white robes hanging in their closets.[6]

3. The social and economic class level of the American Legion in Illinois appeared to be higher than that of the Klan. However, farmers and factory workers were underrepresented in both groups, more so in the Legion than in the Klan.

4. Never did either the national Legion convention or the Illinois state convention formally denounce the Klan by resolution. In Illinois it seemed to be understood that bringing the issue out in the open would be troublesome to some downstate leaders who were candidates for elective office. Whatever critical statements were made by Legion officials in Illinois were couched in terms of the KKK as an instrument of anarchy, to which the Legion was steadfastly opposed. At the national level as well, the Legion tried to tie the Klan to the radical left. "By their example, the hooded Peeping Toms give license to every Red and IWW to continue [their] underhanded operations," one Legion statement reasoned.

The American Legion and the Klan found common cause on one big issue: curtailing immigration into the United States. On this question, the Legion parted company with its friends in big business, the mine owners, steelmakers, and other industrialists who depended on a steady source of inexpensive labor. Conversely, the American Federation of Labor, which had an interest in limiting competition for jobs, supported the bill.

The Klan and the Legion organizations premised their support of immigration reduction on different rationales, however. Convinced of Nordic genetic superiority, the Klan wanted to rid the country of blacks, Catholics, and Jews, in that general order of priority. As we have seen, Catholics and Jews held prominent positions of leadership in the Legion in Illinois. At one point, three of the top figures in the state hierarchy were all named Murphy. If the Klan was more powerful in neighboring Indiana, in both the civil government and in American Legion affairs, as appeared to be so, one of the reasons was almost certainly the larger concentrations of Catholic population in Illinois.[7] Not only were Catholics and Jews who lived in Indiana spread more thinly through the state, but the migration from the southern states had extended farther north than it did in Illinois.

This is not to ignore the presence of anti-Catholic prejudice in some Illinois Legionnaires. Whenever a candidate who was a Catholic ran for state commander, muttering could be heard that his religion was being used against him in some downstate districts. Yet one of the most popular state commanders, Edward Hayes, who went on to become national commander, was a Catholic. After completing his term as state commander, Daddy Schick made the rounds of Knights of Columbus and Masonic lodge meetings to urge a closer relationship between the Legion and mainstream denominations. "The American people must be God-fearing people," he preached, "holding to a standard of morality and pure living."[8]

In the give-and-take of Legion politics, Jewish members were sensitive to attitudes that they regarded as anti-Semitic. The Linenthal affair is an example. Albert C. Linenthal was a Chicago attorney who had been an army infantry officer and was a delegate at the St. Louis caucus. He served as the commander of Ravenswood Post 149 until 1925, after which he transferred his membership to the Lincoln Square post. In 1938, Linenthal believed that Irving Scheyer, a fellow Jew, was in line to be commander of Lincoln Square. According to an account left behind by historian Gustavus M. Blech, "a small but vocal group of members surreptitiously and in a clear spirit of intolerance opposed Scheyer's nomination." Linenthal admonished his comrades to put aside their prejudices.

But Scheyer lost the election. Whereupon Linenthal, Scheyer, and a few others resigned. They looked around for a neighborhood that didn't have a post and found one in Hamlin Park. Chicago Park District commissioners made a meeting hall available. Thus, Hamlin Park Post 817 came into being, with Scheyer as its first commander. Lincoln Square Post challenged the new chartering before the state judge advocate. The department's legal authority agreed that the new post had been improperly established. Linenthal appealed to the state executive committee, which reversed the judge advocate and sanctioned the somewhat unusual beginning of Post 817 on October 16, 1938.[9]

Thanks to the deluge of apocalyptic headlines in their newspapers, many downstate residents tended to think of Chicago as a nest of labor agitators and bomb-throwing revolutionaries, many of them with Jewish-sounding names. It would be naive to suppose that none of this prejudice spilled over into the Legion halls. Toward the end of the 1930s, the national Legion lobbied in Washington against a bill to admit twenty thousand refugee children, most of them Jews, from Hitler's Germany. The Legion argued that some of the children would surely be followed by their parents, who were probably Communists and who would only swell the ranks of the unemployable.[10] Unlike the Klan, the American Legion theretofore had willingly accepted naturalized citizens who were eager to become good Americans. But this was not the time, its leaders argued, for unassimilated ethnic blocs to threaten America's national unity. It was an antiradical, as opposed to the Klan's eugenic, argument. It was clearly true in Chicago, as Donehower has pointed out, that "the Legion contained many urban members who disagreed strongly with the tone and spirit of Legion policy" on immigration.[11]

One of the interesting similarities between the Legion and the Klan was the frequency of the word *virility* in their public pronouncements. The Klan, many of whose members hid behind masks, justified its cowardly atrocities by invoking the manhood of white America against threatening (nonwhite) alien influences. Legionnaires, on the other hand, together away from home in the company of their fellows, were acting out for others to see, through their convention displays of unruly bravado, what they presumably thought was expected of the poet Walt Whitman's Perfect Soldier. Leaders sometimes cloaked their vigilantism in terms of their virility. When, for example, leftist demonstrators were reported to have trampled on the American flag, Edward Hayes, the Legionnaire from

Decatur who was then national commander, said this: "If we catch them doing that, I think there is still enough virility in the American Legion personnel to adequately take care of that type of person."[12]

Waller tells us that veterans tended more to direct action than to prolonged discussion. Boxing had been included in the physical training of soldiers preparing for combat. It was quite normal then for an organization of former soldiers to enjoy boxing matches, even in the 1920s, when prizefighting was officially still illegal in Illinois. The Naval post in Chicago, which grew out of a Navy reserve athletic association, sold tickets at fifty-five cents for boxing exhibitions that it sponsored in the winter of 1920. Tests of physical combat in the form of boxing bouts were popular entertainment at Legion posts throughout the nation.

By the end of the decade, Illinois counted itself among twelve states that changed their laws to permit boxing, largely as a result of Legion pressure in each case. According to Waller, the Legion in Mississippi had complete control of all boxing in that state.[13] In South Dakota, the Legion collected a percentage of receipts as a commission on all professional boxing matches. Every two years beginning in 1919, the Illinois house of representatives voted to legalize boxing, only to have the bill fail in the senate, where rural and small-town districts had greater representation. The issue was seen as yet another confrontation between ethnic Catholic urban interests and rural constituencies for whom prizefighting was associated with gamblers, immigrants, organized crime, and other evils of the big city. Discovering that their readers of both sexes were interested in news of boxing, the *Tribune* and other Chicago newspapers "needed no special prodding to serve as propaganda outlets for [the American Legion] and all the other groups interested in promoting boxing."[14] Eventually, in 1925, Legion posts in Peoria and Rockford convinced their legislators to support the boxing bill, giving it enough votes to pass and become law. The American Legion became identified thereafter with the Golden Gloves tournaments and other amateur boxing events in many Illinois cities.

Legion and Church

The concept of 100-percent Americanism was, as one historian has observed, "a normal corollary of 'old-time religion.'" The fundamentalist Protestant sentiment that had given rise to the Klan was "not unrelated to the sweeping tide of hyper-patriotism."[15] On some propositions, the Legion and the Klan agreed wholeheartedly: There can be no deviation from an absolute unity of purpose among all Americans, who are or should be one indivisible people. Alien forces breed evil and cannot be tolerated.

Remarkably tolerant of religious diversity, everything considered, most Illinois Legionnaires who were Protestants rejected the "modernism" influenced by the scientific method and what had become known as the Christian Social Gospel. Many of them belonged to denominations such as the northern Illinois district of the Lutheran Church, Missouri Synod, which denounced liberal theology, unionism, lodgism, dancing, the theater, birth control, gambling, and—needless to say—the very idea of drinking alcoholic beverages.[16] They watched with trepidation as clergymen who had been affiliated with the Anti-Saloon League prior to the enactment of Prohibition were drawn into the Klan's orbit. Fundamentalist Protestant ministers marched, usually without masks, in the front row of many KKK parades.

Most Legionnaires were content to keep their faith separate from the activities of the Legion hall. An exception occurred in June 1935 when Jens Olsen met with two other members of Gladstone Post 777 on the Northwest Side of Chicago. They talked about breaking off into a new post "of Christian veterans organized for the purpose of carrying the Gospel to ex-servicemen." A month later, fourteen Legionnaires attended the first meeting at Moody Memorial Church of what came to be called Aaron Post 788. "The spiritual welfare of our former comrades-in-arms is sadly neglected and seldom considered by any veterans organization," Commander Olsen declared. "Our first object is to spread the Gospel of Christ among our former comrades." The post went ahead with plans to place Bibles in every veteran's hospital room and to hold evangelistic services one Sunday every month at Hines VA hospital. Eighteen members were present for an Armistice Day supper, at which, according to the post history, "some testimonies were given" of God's goodwill and mercy. Thirty-six attended the post's Mother's Day service at the Chicago Gospel Tabernacle. "Two speakers spoke on motherhood from the hygienic and spiritual standpoints," the historian recorded. The youngest and oldest mothers were honored, one twenty-nine, the other eighty-two. Aaron Post grew in size, adding members from throughout the city and establishing an auxiliary and a squadron for sons of members.[17]

Not all Christian sects were treated so kindly. On one occasion, a delegation of sixty members of Jehovah's Witnesses journeyed from St. Louis to solicit followers in the Illinois city of Litchfield. Edgar Bernhard tells us in his study of civil liberties in the state that the Litchfield police chief deputized fifteen men, "some of whom were members of the Legion." The deputies escorted their visitors to the county jail, where some were forced to kiss a large American flag. State police arrived to protect the missionaries, who boarded a bus for the return to St. Louis. A short time later, George Hart Post 167 called on the city council in Harrisburg, Saline County, to bar the Witnesses from distributing literature or playing recordings of their teachings in and around Harrisburg.[18]

With some exceptions, however, Aaron Post being one, Legionnaires in Illinois could not in good conscience join in the Klan's crusade against drinking, gambling, and a freer and more open sexuality. To do so would have been hypocritical in the extreme. Alcoholic beverages were an important, nearly universal feature of Legion hall fellowship. Legion conventions often degenerated into drunken displays. For almost fourteen years—from 1920 to 1933—rural America managed to suppress the drinking habits of the immigrants in the cities (and Legionnaires in their clubhouses) by outlawing the commercial traffic in liquor. Opposition to the Volstead Act began the melding of the various ethnic voting blocs into what became the Chicago Democratic machine. On this issue, downstate Legionnaires parted company with their neighbors at home by working with the Cook County members for repeal of Prohibition.

When someone suggested at a meeting of the state executive committee in 1923 that maybe the Legion ought to curtail "public drinking" at conventions, John Stelle said, "You all drink and what the hell is the use of denying it." To pacify downstate churchgoers, delegates at Legion conventions urged compliance with Prohibition laws while trying as quietly as possible to upset them. The sectional politics of Prohibition required the same finesse that applied to questions involving the Ku Klux Klan. "Wet" Legionnaires who were opposed to the Klan did not want to put fellow member politicians on the spot. At the national level, the Legion waited until 1931 before endorsing a national referendum on the question of repeal—and until 1932 before supporting outright repeal.[19]

A Time for Merriment

The spirit of alcoholic conviviality present at all American Legion conventions had two equally important effects: Legionnaires of different backgrounds—from inner-city Chicago and hamlets in the Shawnee Hills;

Protestants, Catholics, Jews; Democrats and Republicans; the DeLaCours and the Yeagers—were able to become better acquainted and to recognize their common interests. But their often drunken, reckless, and childish behavior created an image that was amusing to some onlookers, less so to others.

Legion gatherings were relatively subdued the first few years. Battlefront memories were still fresh. Returning veterans were careful to defer in their patriotic holiday observances to the few surviving veterans of the Civil War. One of the initial rituals called for the elderly members of the Grand Army of the Republic to present to the charter members of the new American Legion post the tattered remains of one of their battlefield flags.

In a typical Memorial Day parade in Quincy in 1924, the marchers proceeded through the business district to the cemetery, where the GAR's "men in blue" were seated on a flatbed wagon. Tears tumbled down the wrinkled cheeks of the old men while a high school student read the Gettysburg Address. Marching units included, besides the drum and bugle corps of various veterans organizations, the Quincy College band, officers of the reserve army corps, two infantry companies of the National Guard, and several Boy Scout troops.

One or more parades were high points of any Legion event. Legionnaires appreciated the importance of martial music, the sound of brass bands and beating drums, to stir patriotic feelings. Later, Legion posts involved young people in their musical activities. Some Legion-sponsored Boy Scout troops had drum and bugle corps. The post in Aurora tried to identify "patriotic musicians" in the high school band whom they enlisted in a Legion cadet band. The women's auxiliary in Ottawa organized a dozen girls, aged three to ten, in a junior rhythm band. Everything went well until a measles epidemic hit the Ottawa schools.

Policy in the Legion originated, theoretically, at county and district get-togethers. Resolutions advanced from there on to the state and national conventions. Between conventions, decisions were made by the state (or national) executive committees over which the state (or national) commander presided as the public voice of the organization. Several state commanders from Illinois served later on the supreme governing body—the national executive committee.

Legion conventions were more or less equal parts debates over policy questions raised by the resolutions, politicking for leadership positions, parades and other public exhibitions, and carousing. The devotion to carousing increased with the passage of time as the Legionnaires grew more comfortable in the company of strangers who had become close friends. The second state convention at the Medinah Temple in Chicago was a sedate affair, climaxed by a watermelon barbecue and dance at the Khaki and Blue Club. The inclination to carouse generally varied in proportion to a delegate's distance from home. The farther away, the more outrageous were likely to be his (and sometimes his wife's) fun-making proclivities. Groups of conventioneers designated hotel suites as "dugouts," where liquor and conversation were available. The historian of Marine Post 273 left this description of the former leathernecks at one Legion reunion: "Several milk cans of Harrison's orange juice were used to dilute a liquid dynamite sometimes called alcohol. The result was stirred a bit and poured down the throats of Marines who had been places and done things. The stirring splashed over on other residents of the hotel, on the police force, and on the street."[20] Men and women hanging out of hotel windows singing, cursing, hurling water-filled paper sacks and pillow feathers onto the sidewalks below were a familiar scene. Delegates enjoyed turning in false fire alarms and waiting to watch the confusion. Another favorite pastime, according to the LaGrange historian, was applying "shocking machines to ladies' fleshier parts."[21] Physician delegates were available to attend to the inevitable casualties in local hospitals. At one convention, in Danville, for example, Harry "Hot Dog" Dahlin, from Three Links Post 361 in Chicago, fell and broke his leg while trying to hop nimbly aboard a passing truck.

Downstate cities competed for the honor and the economic benefits of hosting a state Legion convention. Host cities had to promise not to allow merchants to raise their prices outlandishly and to remove any distractions in advance. The Danville paper reported that police were ridding the city of "undesirables who want to prey on Legionnaires" at an upcoming convention there. "Moochers, professional beggars and strangers who cannot give a good account of themselves must vacate Danville at once," announced the *Commercial-News,* adding that four "suspects" had already been locked up.[22] Another of the willingly negotiated conditions required the temporary nullification of minor criminal statutes as they related to the behavior of the visiting delegates. Local authorities vested police powers in the Legion's own "military police," who were stationed in the various hotels and other gathering spots to watch for excessive public displays of drinking, gambling, destruction of property, and the fallout from the playful games indulged in by the frolicking visitors. MPs issued summonses for the perpetrators to appear before special panels of American Legion judges. The point of the whole business was to keep the administration of Legion justice for these few days within the Legion family.

In Quincy, for instance, the law against slot machine gambling was suspended while the Legionnaires were in town for their state convention in 1935. The Quincy convention was fairly typical. About a thousand voting delegates attended, plus some fifteen hundred drum and bugle corps musicians and several other musical groups, led by Colonel Armin F. Hand's perennial prize-winning Chicago Board of Trade Post 304 band and now including a well-received German band from Macomb, Illinois. The Quincy contingent included a mandolin and guitar marching team. A flyover by six observation planes of the Illinois National Guard began the festivities. One hundred twenty-five state police roared by on motorcycles. Participants included delegations from the Chicago Police Post 207, which with 1,185 members ranked then as the biggest of all Illinois posts; and the Chicago Firemen's post, which was quartered at the Quincy fire station. The firemen packed their fire boots in case they were needed.

In addition to the three-mile-long main parade, the Grand Voiture d'Illinois Forty and Eight had their separate laugh-a-minute torchlight parade, which featured a French taxi, miniature locomotives and boxcars, Leapin' Lena trick cars that would buck and rear up on their hind legs, and a brigade of six-inch cannon. "Wrecking crews" of the superelite Forty and Eight were given special license to stage mock train wrecks that sometimes caused damage to local businesses. New members of the Forty and Eight were initiated in a special ceremony at the Quincy Eagles club hall.

Some of the Legionnaires competed in a trap and skeet shooting contest at the Quincy gun club, one of several martial side events during convention week. Many of the posts sponsored entries in a statewide bathing beauty contest that always attracted the close scrutiny of aging warriors. Local residents were expected to look away while the pranksters were busy. On this occasion, a stuffed bear that stood in front of a Quincy store was abducted and left by the departing conventioneers in the lobby of their hotel.[23]

National conventions were larger, noisier, and more diverse. Wherever they went, delegates from the western states liked to bring along a menagerie of steers, mules, coyotes, and other indigenous critters that they turned loose in the streets and sometimes the hotel lobbies of the convention city. In Boston in 1930, Legionnaires played craps on the Common; 358 revelers were hospitalized for alcohol poisoning. "When ex-soldiers get drunk at their conventions, when they whistle at women and dress in ridiculous costumes and throw furniture out of hotel windows," Willard Waller said, "they are merely trying in a stupid way to recapture their youth and vanished comradeship."[24]

In his book *For God and Country,* William Pencak printed a collection of Legion poetry that included this anonymous work about a Chicago convention:

Goodbye Legionnaires

O! The Legion has departed
And as down the Loop I roam
I wonder what those roguish lads
Are doing back at home.
. . . the gink who tossed the mattress
Twenty stories—all afire,
Is tossing gems of harmony
In the Sunday morning choir.
And that kissing guy on State Street
Had the time of his young life,
But I bet he asks permission
When he wants to kiss his wife.
And the cannoneers on Randolph
With a yen for shot and shell,
Don't even slam the door at home
For fear of catching hell.[25]

7 THE QUEST FOR THE SOLDIERS' BONUS

While American troops were overseas, waiting to be called into battle, they speculated often about the money Uncle Sam might provide for them after the war. This payment was something many of them considered an essential part of the social contract, due the men of a conscripted army to make up for wages lost during their military service. "Adjusted compensation" struck them as an apt term. But the press and public nomenclature settled on simpler words—"the soldiers' bonus."

The people of Illinois did not wait for the national government to act. By a decisive vote, the electorate approved a separate state bonus in 1922. The federal bonus proved to be much more controversial and was not fully realized until 1936. Some generalizations can be made about the politics of the issue.

- Big business opposed the soldiers' bonus, as did the presidential administrations in both parties. A poll of Illinois members of the American Legion in 1920 registered 96 percent in favor of both a federal and state bonus.[1] However, the level of support declined later in the 1920s as the economic status of the membership became more clearly differentiated. Those who were well-off financially and those who invested in the stock market were more sensitive to the effects of a large federal outlay on economic conditions and the value of the dollar; they tended to be relatively indifferent to the need for a general bonus. In the 1930s, however, as the economy deteriorated drastically and jobs were scarce, demands for federal payments to veterans became more widespread and more insistent.

- Throughout this period, the pressure for a federal bonus was considerably stronger among veterans who did not belong to the American Legion. Within the Legion, it was greater in Illinois than in the populous states of the Northeast; more demanding in Chicago than downstate; stronger among the rank-and-file than in the leadership of the state department. Because upper-income members had the time and desire to play Legion politics, they influenced Legion policy disproportionately on the bonus question. With the passage of time, the issue became one of the few matters in which the American Legion in Illinois divided along class rather than sectional lines, and one of the few on which the national rank-and-file eventually overrode the leadership.
- Membership in the Legion increased whenever the bonus issue was heating up. Many veterans came to believe that their political pressure could be brought to bear more effectively as part of a large organization.

Many of those who joined the Legion resented the opposition of business groups to the bonus because of their suspicion that business had profited excessively from war contracts. The typical Legionnaire viewed large corporations with considerable ambivalence. In one survey, almost one-fourth of Legion members nationally were owners of small businesses whose interests often differed from those of big companies.[2] (The same survey estimated that unskilled laborers composed only 4 percent of Legion members but as many as half of the national workforce.) Few in the retail merchant class entertained kind thoughts of labor union leaders, who they believed represented a threat to the control of capital and social stability, and might very well be subject to foreign influences. Many veterans were especially critical of unionized workers who had walked off their jobs during the war, because, in Waller's words, "the striker is a man from his own world, a man with whom he can compare himself, while the profiteer remains a rather shadowy figure." Through the shadows, John J. Bullington echoed the opinions nonetheless of many of his fellow Illinoisans when he made this statement after taking over as state commander in 1924:

There were 7,000 millionaires in America when the fire alarm rang round the world and the scourge of death struck humanity. When the war was over and there were 70,000 sleeping from the Channel to the Alps, maintaining the line of dugouts that shall ever be the vigil place of America's love for ideals, there were 31,000 millionaires in the United States. . . . They say they bought bonds.... [The millionaires club] is the only club that I can't get into, and yet I esteem you [fellow Legionnaires] more because you don't let anyone in who didn't serve.[3]

Looking ahead, Legion committees devised several different plans for universal service in time of war. Citizens would be trained to take up arms in the national defense. An additional feature of the system provided for compulsory "service" by contractors and suppliers, whose profit margins would be regulated. One approach called for 95 percent taxation of wartime profits, an idea seconded by the AFL. Besides being of dubious feasibility, the proposals smacked of socialism. As memories of the war faded into the past, the Legion shifted its focus from compulsory service, which had little public support, to voluntary training.

The first five national conventions of the American Legion adopted resolutions calling for the payment of a federal bonus to all who served. The Legion's original plan consisted of three options: the gift of farmland, money to help buy a home, or a one-time cash payment of up to $625. A bonus bill in some form passed the U.S. House five times and the Senate three times. President Harding, who had endorsed the Legion plan as a candidate, now opposed the legislation because he said it would break the federal budget and bring on disastrous inflation. The U.S. Chamber of Commerce, the Industrial Conference Board, the National Economy League, and other business organizations lobbied against any mass federal payment to veterans. The lobbyist for the Legion characterized the dispute as being between Main Street and Wall Street.

The simplified measure that finally passed both houses of Congress in 1924 by enough votes to override President Calvin Coolidge's veto had been rewritten by the Senate. Instead of an immediate cash payout, it provided paid-up, interest-earning life insurance to all veterans. Benefits based on length of service and time spent overseas were to be payable at death or in a lump sum after twenty years. Veterans could borrow on their insurance certificates after two years. With accumulated interest, every veteran who lived that long was promised a cash payment in 1945 computed to average one thousand dollars.[4] At the time of its enactment, the projected average bonus amounted to about half the average annual wage in the United States.

Many rank-and-file Legionnaires in Illinois would have liked the money now, not twenty years from now. But that would have doubled the federal budget. Deficit spending of that magnitude terrified the business and investment communities. Anyhow, times were good. Jobs were plentiful. Many Americans were buying shares in the stock market. The future looked bright.

In the meantime, an American Legion committee headed by William D. Knight of Rockford had drafted a state bonus bill that cleared both houses of the Illinois legislature without a single dissenting vote in 1921. Knight was well known. He had been a Big Ten conference football referee beginning in 1912. After the war, he volunteered (without pay) to help organize Legion posts throughout northern Illinois. In 1924 he resigned as commander of Rockford's Walter R. Craig Post 60 to be elected state's attorney of Winnebago County. The proposition submitted to the voters of Illinois in November 1922 recommended payment of fifty cents per day of wartime service up to a maximum of three hundred dollars. Widows of the war dead would also be eligible for payments of up to three hundred dollars. Voters were told that the state would finance the bonus by borrowing $55 million through the sale of bonds.

The outcome of the statewide referendum was more decisive than Legion officials expected: 1,220,315 (70.8%) for and 502,372 (29.2%) against. About half the favorable votes were cast in Cook County: 575,253 (76.6%) for and 175,939 (23.4%) against. A steady drumbeat of publicity by the Chicago newspapers surely affected the margin of approval. The *Herald and Examiner* assigned one of the Legionnaires on its staff to promote the bonus full-time. Even before the referendum had been held, that newspaper printed, as a public service, application forms that could be clipped and mailed in. The vote was also an illustration of the difference in cultural attitudes between Chicago and downstate—referred to in an earlier chapter—concerning "handouts" from the government.

The proposition did even better, however, in the four fringe metropolitan counties surrounding Cook County (DuPage, Kane, Lake, and Will): 73,530 (81.7%) for and 16,483 (18.3%) against. In the other ninety-seven downstate counties, the vote was closer but still one-sided: 572,032 (64.9%) for and 309,950 (35.1%) against. Overall, urban voters were much more supportive than rural voters. The five major downstate urban counties produced big majorities for the bonus: Madison (Alton), 75%; St. Clair (East St. Louis), 74.3%; Peoria (Peoria), 71.5%; Winnebago (Rockford), 71.4; and Sangamon (Springfield), 65.7%. The proposal failed to carry a majority in only eight counties, all of them small and rural. Six of the eight were in Bill McCauley's corner of southeastern Illinois, an agricultural sector known as the Wabash Slope. Here the glacial till of the Wabash River bottomlands deposited a more fertile soil than in the Shawnee Hills to the west, but it was still much less productive than in northern Illinois. On the day before the election, the newspaper that McCauley was associated with in Olney, the *Daily Mail*, exhorted voters in large type across one whole page: "Remember 1917–18 and Vote Yes on the Soldier Bonus Tomorrow." Yet the proposition barely carried that county (Richland) with 51 percent of the vote. John Stelle's nearby upland county of Hamilton also gave the bonus only a 51-percent majority. By contrast, in the two coal-mining counties that were the scene of the Klan-inspired insurrection described earlier, almost 77 percent of the voters favored the bonus. Rural voters throughout the state were less likely to support the bonus. That reluctance undoubtedly reflected the lower ratio of veterans in the male population. It was estimated nationally that only about 4 percent of Legionnaires were engaged in farming. In Oscar Carlstrom's Mercer County, the majority vote registered about 57 percent in favor.

In the first half of 1923, 236,043 Illinois veterans and widows happily filed claims for their state bonus. Membership in the Legion started to climb soon after, as the economy boomed. Between 1924 and 1931, Illinois gained almost thirty-nine thousand members—a remarkable increase of nearly 84 percent. Enrollment in Pennsylvania rose during the same time by twenty-three thousand, an increase in that state of about 45 percent.[5]

The economy continued to perk along nicely all over the state. The Red scare had subsided. The sectional feuding within the state department appeared to be in remission. Divisional membership quotas set by the state administration were difficult to meet only in Chicago. While statewide membership was climbing, Cook County's share of the total dropped from 36 percent in 1925 to about one-third in 1931. (The principal reason for the difficulties in the big city—namely the Legion's opposition to organized labor—will be examined in detail in chapter 9.) For the time being, however, with membership up, most Illinois communities thriving, one bonus in hand, and another one due down the road, the future looked bright for the Legion.

8 HARD TIMES IN THE LEGION HALL

One bedrock theme underlay the mission of the American Legion: helping one another. Legionnaires would take care of their needy. They would work to their mutual advantage in the world of business. They would band together. They would march in step to save their country in peace as in war. Then, in 1929, the good times shut down hard. The stock market crashed. Banks closed their doors. People lost their savings. Farms were sold for back taxes. Men were without jobs, their families without food. Fathers abandoned their children. The economy spiraled wildly out of control. The nation plunged into chaos. If the "Red menace" of the early twenties had been a mindless reflex response to international Bolshevism, the Depression of the 1930s presented the western world with a genuine threat to the established order. The men of the Legion reacted, first, by trying to help one another; second, by claiming preferential access to publicly financed employment; and, third, by remobilizing as they had ten years before to head off the "Reds" who they thought were exploiting the misery.

Employers who were Legionnaires and who had a job opening or knew where a job was available were expected to think first of Legion members who needed work. At the peak of the Great Depression, one national survey indicated that 7.1 percent of Legion members were unemployed or "on relief" (receiving public assistance).[1] If accurate, that figure would have been considerably under the estimates for jobless veterans as a class and for job seekers in the general population.

More than half the Illinois posts set up some type of unemployment relief bureau for their members. More so than in the big city, downstate Legionnaires considered it demeaning for veterans to have to depend on public assistance. A Crawford County post drafted a resolution in 1930 deploring the fact that "several veterans and their families are now receiving financial aid from the County Board of Supervisors, which relief is raised by direct taxation, thus making objects of charity of our buddies." Posts in all sections of the state were losing members who could no longer afford the dues. George M. Nelms Post 446 in Centralia announced that it would begin accepting farm products in lieu of dues.

Statewide membership fell by twenty-four thousand between 1931 and 1933, a decline of about 28 percent. Pennsylvania's membership dropped in the same period by fourteen thousand, or about 19 percent. It was estimated that in Illinois, more than twenty-two thousand active Legionnaires were delinquent in their dues in 1932. The impact on the women in the auxiliary was even greater. In many households, the women dropped out first. The treasurer of Sycamore's auxiliary said she had no financial report at one point because the local bank had closed with its $231 balance.

At a meeting of post adjutants in Chicago, a Legionnaire named Bill Murray from the South Shore post advised the others on the meaning of "mutual helpfulness."

> Mutual helpfulness. What does it mean? Your doctor, your lawyer, anything you need in your daily life, you will find a Legion man in that line of work if you go a block further and look for him. . . . You don't realize the type of organization that we have in this Legion. There isn't anything you need that you can't buy from a Legionnaire. If you go into a store, ask if there is a Legion man there—if not, don't buy. It will open the way to more employment [for our members]. I have gone into a store and asked if there was a Legionnaire employed there, and if there wasn't I would say I'm sorry and walk out even though they had something on sale that I wanted.[2]

Murray said he had sometimes demanded that a store manager trot out an employee from the back room who was made to produce his Legion card with a paid-up dues notation, no less.

Neighborhood social action organizers received more cooperation and encountered less resistance from Legion posts in Chicago now than they did in the rest of the state. One of them, Saul Alinsky, concentrated his organizing efforts in Back of the Yards, the neighborhood south of the livestock slaughterhouses. "I'm going around organizing, agitating, making trouble," he told Studs Terkel. "At the end of three months, I had the Catholic Church, the CIO [a new federation of industrial unions], and Communist Party working together. It involved the packinghouse workers union. I even got the American Legion involved, because they didn't have a God-damned thing to do. They all had one thing in common: Misery. Powerlessness."[3]

Legion officials knew that Alinsky and the other organizers of the poor could best be countered by creating the public impression that the Legion was successfully engaged in a strenuous economic revival. An Associated Press news story reported with a Chicago dateline in early 1932, "Legion in State Makes Jobs for 6,000 in Month." Frederick Ashley, identified as chairman of the state department's employment committee and "special agent" for the state Veterans Employment Service, explained in the story that the Legion had been involved in some make-work project plans recommended to the state. Legion posts were themselves operating wood-cutting yards in Danville, Mattoon, and Gibson City. But most of their activities consisted of persistent, well-publicized persuasion. In Ottawa, the Legion post "has just secured work for 210 persons in the [Illinois River] deep waterway project underway there," the news story said.

Needless to say, the Legion was hardly alone in its endorsement of more job-creating economic activity. Danville's factories were hit hard by the loss of jobs. The *Commercial News* tried to link the Redden post to recovery efforts, reporting, for example, that it "has secured 43 permanent jobs during the past fortnight by influencing the larger local employers to make additions to their personnel."[4] The Legion was portrayed as an energetic community force that used its influence to increase job availability. Virtually every day, the newspaper pointed to hopeful signs—a furniture store is planning to redecorate, the Danville Malleable Iron Works expects to be rehiring. By playing such a prominent role in the confidence-building campaign, the newspaper commented editorially on February 11, 1932, that "the Legion will itself find a more grateful place in the heart of America."[5]

Two weeks later, notices were posted of a public meeting in Danville to discuss the formation of an organization that would be called the Unemployed Council. The leaflets did not mention that the Trade Union Unity League, an arm of the Communist party, had been facilitating collective action by unemployed workers around the country through the establishment of such councils. One historian of that period said, "The Communists brought misery out of hiding in the workers' neighborhoods. . . . They raised particular hell." In Chicago, some of the demonstrations had become increasingly violent as the unemployed citizens clashed with police.[6]

On Friday evening, February 26, just as the meeting was about to begin in a hall on North Walnut Street in Danville, a group of fourteen organizers were taken into custody by police and sheriff's deputies. Although local authorities gave the impression that the intruders were Communists from Chicago, one turned out to be an ex-serviceman from Danville; the other thirteen were from Decatur, about an hour's drive away. None were from Chicago. All fourteen were lodged in the Vermilion County jail and charged with unlawful assembly and conspiracy to advocate the overthrow of the government. The case was assigned to a judge other than Casper Platt. Bail was set at one thousand dollars each. No jury trials were possible until September, more than six months away. The defendants were warned that they faced a long wait in jail unless they waived the right to a jury trial, which they refused to do.[7]

The *Commercial-News* reported it had learned on good authority, unidentified in the news story, that the fourteen men had appealed for legal aid to the Chicago headquarters of the Communist party but that there had been no response. Rumors then started to spread that more outsiders were expected to try to spring their comrades from jail. "All efforts of organizers from other cities to bring any socialistic activities here will be resisted," the city fathers declared.[8]

To prepare for the invasion from the north, 250 members of the Redden post of the American Legion were sworn in as special police. With 780 paid-up members, down forty-five from the year before, Redden Post still ranked as one of the largest in the state. About fifty of those in the Legion's anti-Red squad were said to have been unemployed themselves. Carl Grove, author of the post history, tells what happened next.

> The Legionnaires, summoned by pre-arranged signals, were ready for them. They were assembled in Redden Square [the courthouse square]—a young army with a collection of the strangest ammunition ever used to win a battle—ball bats, sticks, billiard cues, lengths of rubber hose and pipe. When the police and deputy sheriffs found, while searching suspicious-looking

strangers, Red literature in their possession, these persons were turned over to groups of Legionnaires. Then, with none of the hospitality for which Danville is noted, they were escorted to the city limits and "eased" out of town, with nary an invitation to return. . . . Twelve cars of Legionnaires patrolled the city all night. In addition, every school, some churches and the children's home had an armed guard. After about two months of this, the Communists evidently decided that Danville wasn't a very desirable place and their activities died down.[9]

Delegations of would-be protesters "were not permitted to assemble," the newspaper said, but were being "expelled . . . in a not-too-gentle manner." Some were charged with disorderly conduct. A truckload of visitors spent the night in jail because their vehicle lacked a blowable horn as required by law. "Driver of 'Red' Truck Is Fined," read the next day's headline in the *Commercial-News*. Another story reported, "Red Literature Seized by Police," the incriminating evidence being a boxful of Unemployed Council enrollment blanks removed from the home of a Danville family.[10]

Two lawyers from Chicago who represented the jailed defendants at a later hearing were struck in the face with canes as they left the courthouse. They said they were told by the Legionnaires to "drive north and keep going." When the attorneys complained to the judge about their treatment, he was too busy to look into the matter. Still later, two other lawyers who arrived from Chicago to defend a would-be organizer in another case were told by a deputy sheriff to leave. "We don't want outsiders stirring things up," they said they were warned. "The American Legion here is against them [the organizers]."[11]

Most central Illinois newspapers took all this in stride. One exception, the *Decatur Herald,* found it "ironic that American Legion members fought a war to preserve liberty and are now fighting their fellow countrymen to prevent the exercise of their First Amendment rights."[12] The next time Leslie Davis, the reporter for the *Herald,* returned to Danville for one of the legal proceedings, he was greeted by a committee of Legionnaires who shoved him around and relieved him of his notebook.

For "protecting not only the political institutions of the community but its very hearths and homes," the Redden post received the state department's highest public service honor—the 1932 Hall of Fame award.[13]

Sitting Out the Bonus March

The war had been over for ten years when the stock market crashed in 1929. Most of those who returned from military service with medical or neuropsychiatric disabilities had been cared for. The widows and orphans of the war dead were receiving financial support. Insofar as possible, the government had done what it could to ease the transition to civilian life. Jobs in the federal civil service were made available first to veterans and the wives and widows of veterans. Vocational training was available at no cost.

Nevertheless, as the nation spun deeper into the Great Depression, the veterans of the Great War stepped forward with new, more persistent demands for privileges due them as a class. The American Legion put its weight behind these claims selectively. A Legion committee proposed pensions for the dependent widows of veterans who died *after* leaving the service. The national convention in 1930 declined initially, however, to endorse one of the most controversial new benefits voted earlier that year by Congress: free hospital care in Veterans Administration institutions for partial disabilities that were not connected to military service and did not occur until several years later. President Hoover's administration succeeded in removing several irrational distinctions in the bill as they related to certain illnesses "of a constitutional nature." The measure, reluctantly approved by the president, established a means test for eligibility based on income tax liability—which both the Legion and the VFW denounced as "a pauper's oath"—and limited the new benefits to veterans who had served at least ninety days. But its enactment marked a significant move toward free medical care for all veterans, who were of course entering middle age, substantial numbers of them without jobs.

On this matter as in some others, Legion officials and delegates who could afford to attend national Legion conventions proved unrepresentative of the overall veteran population, which applauded the new VA eligibility standards and called for still more financial assistance. Disability pensions doubled in number—from 370,000 to 850,000. Former servicemen who suffered from gout or other afflictions of their advancing years were now covered by the 25-percent-or-more disability provision. News stories reported the case of one man who fell off a ladder in his basement and entered a VA hospital for treatment of his broken leg, for which he was then declared eligible for a disability allowance.[14] To accommodate the increased patient load, Congress appropriated funds for forty-five hundred additional beds in VA hospitals.

Sensing that it was in danger of being overrun by the galloping senti-ment of its members, the American Legion jumped to its feet and joined in the applause for the expansion of benefits. A few years later, only 20 percent of the patients in VA hospitals were there with service-connected ailments. Hospital and dental services were available in fifty-four VA hospitals with 26,307 beds. In 1938 the facility at Danville housed 1,805 patients, only about one-third of them with wartime disabilities. It was said to have become the second largest of all VA institutions.

All along, the issue that most emphatically separated the leadership elite of the Legion from its constituency at large was when the federal bonus should be paid. Veterans who were in dire straits financially did not understand why an obligation entered into in 1924 would not be fulfilled until 1945. The commitment had been made. So why not now? Nevertheless, the delegates to three consecutive Legion national conven-tions—in 1929, 1930, and 1931—rejected resolutions demanding imme-diate payment. In 1930, the vote wasn't even close—244 for, 967 against.

The case for waiting had to do with fiscal policy. It was easy for veter-ans and nonveterans alike to understand. Payments to veterans (who were 4 percent of the population) already exceeded $800 million a year, the largest single item in the federal budget. As of February 1932, according to a tabulation by the *New York Times,* federal benefits for veterans had totaled $5,475,505,520. In fiscal year 1932–33, federal expenditures for vet-erans relief represented 26.1 percent of the federal budget, compared with 16.9 percent for national defense. In France, by contrast, payments to veterans and their families were consuming 17.5 percent of the national budget; in Britain, only 5.8 percent.[15] Immediate payment of the bonus would cost an additional $2.4 billion, and maybe more, in an overall fed-eral budget of about $3.7 billion. President Hoover considered that un-thinkable. Congress did pass a bill, over his veto in 1931, raising the loan value of bonus certificates, which resulted in new loans averaging $377 and additional federal outlays that year of $680 million. The pressure on the leadership of the Legion continued to rise. Meeting in emergency session later that year, the national executive committee reversed the convention's opposition to immediate payment of the bonus.

Meanwhile, in May of 1932, several dozen bedraggled veterans scrambled aboard empty boxcars in an eastbound train at Portland, Oregon. They said they were going to Washington to petition their government for imme-diate payment of the bonus. The group grew larger as it reached St. Louis, where the Baltimore and Ohio Railroad told the men they could no longer ride the rails for free. This was exactly the kind of uprising of former soldiers that had worried the army officers who founded the American Legion in Paris thirteen years before. It was, Colonel McCormick's *Chicago Tribune* now warned, the "nucleus of a destructive mob."[16]

As the group marched across the Mississippi River bridge onto Illinois soil, President Hoover was running for reelection. Only three months earlier, the Redden post of the American Legion had armed themselves with improvised weapons to forcibly expel a few outsiders who wanted to organize the unemployed in Danville. Legionnaires by and large were determined to stamp out the tiniest spark of radicalism before it could burst into flames anywhere in Illinois.

Nowhere had the Legion been asked to sanction the mass movement of veterans toward Washington. When necessary, Legion lobbyists were capable of producing on short notice large numbers of men in blue and gold caps. But this was not one of those occasions. Few of the travelers belonged to the Legion. In Illinois as elsewhere, most Legion officers regarded the traveling group as Communist-inspired and ipso facto a threat to public safety.

Some of those who joined in along the way were Communists or Communist sympathizers. But as the ragtag outfit that called itself the BEF—Bonus Expeditionary Force—grew in size, an effort was made to impose some semblance of military discipline. Three hundred of the men were designated a military police force. One of the freight car riders, a former field artillery medic, was recognized as the "regimental commander." He and the other spokesmen made an effort to purge the Reds from positions of visibility.

On the Illinois side of the river, the veterans defied the railroad by swarming aboard boxcars in the yards at East St. Louis. The train would not leave, nor would the poachers. The bonus march had reached a crisis. As news of the impasse in Illinois spread, ex-servicemen in other parts of the country decided to come along. Hundreds of veterans without jobs were living in flophouses in Chicago, some of them in the Forty-second Ward. One day, a group assembled in Bughouse Square, well known as a forum for sometimes wildly free speech not far from the Taylor post clubhouse. "We got to talking about the bonus," one recalled, "and the next thing we knew we were on our way." The Bughouse Square gang hopped its own freight train en route to Washington. Haywood Hall said in his memoir, *Black Bolshevik,* that Communists helped organize the march from Chicago. I am unable to determine whether any of these protesters from Chicago were affiliated with the Legion. If they were, they were few in number.

What to do in the rail yards of East St. Louis? Louis Emmerson, a mild-mannered older Republican from Bill McCauley's corner of Illinois, had been elected governor in 1928. Emmerson knew that he could not cave in to what the press was portraying as a rebellious mob. Nor did he want to use force against men who had risked their lives to defend the Stars and Stripes. He wanted only to divert attention beyond Illinois as rapidly as possible. So the governor directed units of the Illinois National Guard to escort the visitors out of the railroad yard and onward into Ohio in trucks. The other states furnished trucks of their own to carry the BEF the rest of the way to Washington.

Other groups converged on the capital by boxcar, truck, automobile, and thumbing their way on foot. A caravan of 131 automobiles came all the way from Los Angeles.[17] Although President Hoover remained convinced (for the rest of his life) that Communist organizers had instigated the whole affair, he ordered the government to provide food, clothing, and supplies at a makeshift campsite on the mudflats of the Anacostia River within marching distance of the Capitol. By the middle of June, more than twenty thousand veterans were on the scene, living—some of them with their families—in lean-to shelters made of packing crates and cardboard boxes.

Floyd Gibbons, a writer for the Hearst news service, described the vigil at the Capitol.

> Tonight they marched in the dark like ghosts out of the forgotten past. Four abreast they marched—five thousand strong. Few uniforms tonight, and those ragged and wear-worn. The grease stained overalls of jobless factory workers. The frayed straw hats of unemployed farm hands. The shoddy elbow-patched garments of idle clerks. All were down at the heel. All were slim and gaunt and their eyes had a light in them. There were empty sleeves and limping men with canes.[18]

A few made the trip from downstate Illinois, including a group from Danville. Some of the residents of the huge VA facility were living there because they were without work, had nowhere else to go, and could not take care of themselves. The people of Danville still referred to the original section of the facility as "the soldiers home." Just before the Fourth of July holiday, Robert George, who lived at the soldiers home because he was destitute, began soliciting fellow veterans there and in the vicinity to join with him in their own odyssey to the nation's capital. None in the delegation, some of whom were from Indiana, were Legion members. The men of the Redden post, who were preparing to host the state convention in August, looked on the Washington scene with a wary, generally disapproving eye. The *Commercial News,* groping for something positive, made fleeting reference to George's departing band of men, quoting its leader to the effect that cashing in the bonus, were it to happen, would inject nearly $2 million into the Danville economy.[19]

While the veterans from the soldiers home were packing to go, two other activities of interest occurred on that Independence Day in Danville. Farmers of Vermilion County, many of them of German or Lithuanian heritage, observed the holiday by staging a two-mile-long protest parade through the city streets and on to the county fairgrounds. No sheriff's deputies or Legionnaires armed with baseball bats interfered with the march. In fact, the farmers were escorted by two companies of the Illinois National Guard and a contingent representing the local post of the Veterans of Foreign Wars. (The VFW was now vociferous in its demand for immediate payment of the bonus.) At the fairgrounds, the farmers burned in effigy symbols of "the enemies of agriculture"—high taxes, low farm prices, and "Old Man Depression."

The second event was a picnic attended by an estimated two thousand members of the Ku Klux Klan and their families at a park in Danville. The unhooded picnickers from Vermilion, Iroquois, Champaign, and Edgar Counties played softball and other games. The pastor of the First Christian Church spoke on "America at the crossroads."[20]

In due course, a bill granting the veterans' demands passed the House but failed in the Senate, ending any possibility of payment in 1932. Some of the veterans went home then with train tickets supplied by the federal government; others stayed. The hard core of protesters, including what were later estimated to have been "a couple of hundred" Communists, threw bricks, created disturbances, and endeavored to occupy some vacant government buildings.[21] A decision was made in late July to bring in a force of army infantry, cavalry, and tanks. Under the command of Major General Douglas MacArthur, who was later shown to have exceeded his orders, the troops used tear gas and bayonets to rout the protesters and drive them out of Washington. The camp at Anacostia went up in flames. Tanks leveled the burned-over ruins. The bonus march was over.

Thomas R. Henry, a reporter for the *Washington Star,* offered his epitaph: "The bonus march may as well be described as a flight from reality—a flight from hunger, from the cries of starving children, from the humiliation of accepting money from worn, querulous women, from the harsh rebuffs of prospective employers."[22] Except for the Hearst chain, newspaper opinion had been almost uniformly critical of the bonus marchers. The *Chicago Daily News* referred to the BEF camps as "nurseries of sedition." As the press historian Louis W. Liebovich has documented, even liberal voices praised the Senate for refusing to yield to the demonstrators. The Catholic magazine *Commonweal* said Congress had never been "more emphatically obligated to ignore pleas of this character than it is now."[23]

In the aftermath, however, there were signs that rank-and-file Legionnaires in Illinois were incensed by the violent overreaction of MacArthur's regular army troops against their former comrades. In Chicago, Legion members regarded the Hearst newspapers almost as their house organs. Vivid reporting of the bonus march by Gibbons and others had an effect on public opinion. One of several Illinois posts that adopted critical resolutions, the Homewood unit condemned "such extraordinary brutality against harmless, hungry, jobless men, the same men that the Nation depended upon in the battles of the World War."

Historian Donald J. Lisio said the Legion nationally "was close to open revolt against Hoover."[24] The Cook County Council adopted by voice vote a resolution censuring the president specifically. The matter had now become a troublesome issue for Hoover's reelection campaign. Democrats in the Chicago delegation made plans to embarrass the administration further at the state convention. VA director Frank Hines was dispatched from Washington to quell the uprising. This he did by forcefully reminding Illinois Legionnaires of the many service-related favors he had bestowed upon them individually and collectively over the years.

A censure resolution failed at the convention in Danville by a vote of 946 to 110. State adjutant William C. Mundt summed up the entire experience by saying it had been a "trying year [because of] the bonus agitation." The delegation from nearby Hoopeston marched in the Legion parade behind an old horse-drawn hearse driven by a Legionnaire in top hat and swallow-tailed coat. "Death Ride for Old Man Depression," read the hopeful sign on the back of the hearse.[25]

The plight of the bonus army undoubtedly influenced the votes of some veterans in November. Hoover's overall vote in Vermilion County slipped from 21,616 (62.2 percent of the total) in 1928 to 15,643 (38.5 percent) in 1932. The dramatic increase in the Democratic presidential vote is shown in these figures:

1924	John W. Davis	6,424 (19.7%)
1928	Alfred Smith	12,728 (36.7%)
1932	Franklin Roosevelt	24,032 (59.1%)

(In 1924 Senator Robert LaFollette of Wisconsin, who had been a prominent anti-interventionist during the war, received more votes in Vermilion County, running as a third-party candidate, than did the Democratic nominee. LaFollette had the support of an unusual coalition of farmers and Socialists.)

The new president, Franklin Roosevelt, took office in 1933 with a mandate to take drastic action to revive the economy. Faced with falling revenues, Congress enacted a broad range of spending cuts, including a 25-percent reduction in veterans benefits. A year later, although the economy had gotten worse instead of better, the Legion exercised its power by having almost all the cuts in veterans' programs restored. The only reductions not rescinded were for some non-service-connected payments.

With a Democrat in the White House, national Legion leaders figured to have less executive branch clout. Having been converted to the immediate payment cause, the American Legion put its muscular lobbying shoulder to the wheel in Congress. National convention delegates in 1933, 1934, and again in 1935 called for early payment of the bonus. Each year the congressional vote for the payment bill grew larger. A payment-now measure passed both houses in 1935 but was vetoed by the president as unjustifiably singling out one class of needy Americans. "No one [merely] because he wore a uniform must therefore be placed in a special class of beneficiaries over and above all other citizens," the president said. By 1935 Colonel McCormick's *Chicago Tribune* had become so frothing-at-the-mouth anti-FDR that it reversed its stand on the prepayment question. With so much money "being thrown around recklessly" in Washington, the *Tribune* said, veterans should not be discriminated against.[26] In January 1936, the same bill passed the House, 326 to 61, and the Senate, 76 to 19—more than enough to easily override the presidential veto and become law.

Throughout Illinois, the American Legion played a visible role in the distribution of bonus checks. LaGrange is an example of how this disbursement worked. The local postmaster bundled the checks together and carried them himself to the Legion hall. A cashier from the LaGrange State Trust and Savings Bank, guarded by armed police officers, arrived at the hall with money to cash the checks on the spot. "It was a regular one-two-three affair," remembered the post historian. "The whoopee spirit was very much absent. Most members planned to use the money to pay overdue bills."[27]

"The bonus, when it came, was too little and too late," concluded the veteran Willard Waller; "too little for justice, too late to be of any help in readjustment."[28]

The New Deal Tug of War

The New Deal that the Roosevelt administration laid before the American people featured a series of emergency programs—the Public Works Administration, the Civilian Conservation Corps, the Civil Works Administration, and the Works Progress Administration—all with the same objective: to make work for people who were without jobs. WPA stuck the longest and probably had the most widespread application. Building projects were providing work relief for 2.6 million Americans at the end of 1935.

Once again, however, the American Legion found itself involved in Cook County in a struggle over access to, and in some cases clearance for, the made jobs. The legislation that created the programs usually specified a set-aside quota for veterans. Chicago Legionnaires would sometimes show up at a job site, accompanied by one of their clientless lawyer brethren, and demand to see the discharge documents of those claiming veterans status. At a new school being built on the West Side, the working veterans were found to include three who had served in the German army. They were replaced on the spot. State convention delegates subsequently proposed the deportation of any noncitizen receiving public assistance of any kind.[29]

Political clearance proved to be a harder problem. The Legion complained that job opportunities were restricted to those with endorsement letters from the ward committeeman or another high official in the Democratic party organization. Joe DeLaCour and others in posts tied tightly to the party were quite happy with this arrangement, of course. But many other noninsiders would have preferred a more flexible system of veterans preference, one in which the Legion and not the Democrats acted in a screening capacity.

The problem was made more complicated for the White House (not to mention the American Legion) by raging factionalism in the Illinois Democratic party. Chicago mayor Kelly presided over the regular organization from his office. Henry Horner, a fifty-three-year-old Cook County judge who became the first Jew to be elected governor of Illinois, belonged to the "good government" wing of the party. The two were preparing for a primary election fight in 1936 following Kelly's decision to deny the governor renomination to a second term: Postmaster General James Farley, the Democratic national chairman, lined up on Kelly's side. Secretary of the Interior Harold C. Ickes, who once told the president that at least twenty cents of every WPA dollar was being skimmed for graft in Chicago, was helping Horner. (It was understood that an unofficial checkoff system required the payment of a portion of the WPA worker's wages to the party in Chicago.)[30]

Four years before, two familiar Legion figures, Scott Lucas and John Stelle, had been co-coordinators of Horner's winning 1932 campaign against Len Small. But now the two were on opposite sides. In 1934 Stelle ran for and was elected state treasurer. Then in 1936 he was slated by Kelly's faction for lieutenant governor on the anti-Horner ticket. Using tactics more familiar in Cook County, Stelle did as he was expected in that campaign, working vigorously to organize WPA jobholders downstate, especially those who were veterans, against Governor Horner.

Lucas, meanwhile, had joined the Horner administration. After serving one term as state commander, he maintained his Legion visibility by being appointed national judge advocate. He made his first venture for statewide public office by competing unsuccessfully in the Democratic primary of 1932 for the U.S. Senate. He then volunteered to work in the Horner campaign and was rewarded with an appointment to the state tax commission. In 1933, shortly after being elevated to Speaker of the U.S. House, Henry T. Rainey, the Democratic congressman from Carrollton, died. Thus a seat in Congress was opened for Lucas, who lived upriver in Havana. Lucas ran and was elected.

This turn of events set the stage for a dramatic saga in Illinois politics, one in which American Legion personalities would be front and center—Lucas, Stelle, Oscar Carlstrom, C. Wayland Brooks, and Everett Dirksen among them. Before continuing with that story, the next chapter will bring to resolution, more or less, a perennial conflict that had plagued the Legion all through this period—namely its relationship with organized labor.

9 THE LABOR MOVEMENT
FRIEND OR FOE?

Early in their relationship, the American Federation of Labor sounded out the American Legion about the possibility of their entering into an alliance. Coming from different directions, the two organizations shared certain attitudes, their contempt for Wall Street being one. Both had been critical of wartime profiteering by munitions makers. They both wanted less immigration. Without labor's strong backing, the national origin quotas in the immigration cutback laws of 1921, 1924, and 1929 would never have been enacted. The leaders of organized labor advocated a national soldiers bonus with more conviction at times than the top brass of the Legion. Under President Samuel Gompers, the AFL had done its bit to generate wartime patriotic fervor through the propagandizing of its American Alliance for Labor and Democracy. There was never any question about Sam Gompers's commitment to either international capitalism or the schoolbook meaning of Americanism. After the war, he agreed with several Legion initiatives, including compulsory military training.[1]

Except for the railroad brotherhoods, the national labor federation represented nearly all of organized labor in the 1920s. With rare exceptions, the building trades and other craft unions that dominated the AFL in this period had no taste for radicalism. Nor, however, did the businessmen who were the backbone of the Legion have the slightest interest in a partnership with the labor movement. Many of them were opposed on principle to the basic concept of collective bargaining by workers. They were predisposed, moreover, to characterize as lawlessness any scene involving a bunch of people who ought to be working but were walking around carrying signs instead. During the Legion's first year of existence, veterans friendly to labor unions were driven out of leadership positions in Chicago at the urging of the organization's national leaders. At the national level, the two organizations remained cordial into the 1930s. The climate of cooperation chilled rapidly, though, essentially for three reasons.

- Gompers died in 1924. He was succeeded as president by William Green, an officer in the mine workers' union whose sentiments were less well established.
- Unions began directing more pressure against entire industries—automobiles, steel, coal, textiles, farm implements, the meatpacking houses. In many of the newly emerging CIO unions, members were carrying on a two-front war: against management and against the avowed Communists who were trying to take control of their unions.
- Third and most important, members of the American Legion made themselves available in many parts of the country to chase away organizers, disrupt peaceful picketing, and break strikes.

Several times, when workers walked off their jobs in an effort to force employers to agree to terms, Legionnaires stepped in to do the work temporarily (referred to by unions as "scab labor"), thereby "breaking" the strike. This intervention happened in the coal mines of Kansas in 1919, against longshoremen on both coasts in 1920, in a violent strike by textile workers in Gastonia, North Carolina, in 1929, against cannery workers in California's Imperial Valley in 1933, and repeatedly by truckloads of Legion volunteers at several different steel mills and auto plants in Pennsylvania, Michigan, and Ohio. Vigilante groups were organized at Legion posts in Michigan to help Ford Motor Company rout its sit-down strikers. Much earlier, it became known that the Legion's national Americanism Commission had been involved in the establishment of the Citizens Transportation Committee, "a scab trucking service designed to break a Teamsters strike."[2]

One relatively liberal national commander of the Legion, Harry Colmery from Kansas, provoked criticism from his executive committee by expressing concern that the Legion might be "put under arms en masse for strike duty." He had but limited success in trying to bar Legionnaires from wearing their Legion hats while they were running interference through picket lines.[3] Whenever incidents of this kind were brought up for discussion at Legion conventions, officials explained that none of the strike-breaking activity had been sanctioned by any Legion post and that the members were acting as individual citizens without the Legion's imprimatur.

Illinois had a long, blood-smeared history of workers rising up against what they believed to be the oppression of their employers: as far back as the Chicago anarchists of the 1880s; as recent as the futile months-long strike by the women's garment makers in Decatur. Unions were more plentiful and considerably more militant in Illinois. There were 186 carpenters locals with 39,345 members active in the state in 1928. There were more musicians locals (seventy-five), typographical locals (fifty), barbers locals (sixty-nine), and railway clerks locals (123) than in any other state.[4]

Their militance was personified by the president of the Chicago Federation of Labor, John Fitzpatrick. Born in Ireland, Fitzpatrick came to America as a child and went to work in the Chicago stockyards when he was only eleven. He learned the blacksmith trade, became a union organizer in the yards, and was elected head of the citywide labor council in what had become the most heavily unionized of all American cities. Fitzpatrick thumbed his nose at the timid leadership of the national AFL. He and the other Irishmen on his team involved the labor council in the nationalistic activities of their homeland. Unions had important friends then among the Irish Catholic clergy—the so-called "labor priests"—in the settlement houses, and in the Chicago Police Department. Fitzpatrick advocated the solidarity of the working classes across international borders. He thought workers should have a greater voice in their working conditions and in the collective management of their work product.

In 1918, as mentioned previously, the CFL defied the national federation by forming an Illinois Labor party. After running for mayor of Chicago on that party ticket in 1919, Fitzpatrick tried for a Senate seat from Illinois in 1920. He lost big both times, but Labor party candidates for mayor did win in eight other Illinois cities in 1919, Aurora, Elgin, and Rock Island among them.

Eventually, the CFL's foray into foreign affairs created severe problems for Fitzpatrick. Although not himself a Communist, he called for U.S. aid to Russia and criticized Poland for its postwar demands on Polish territory remaining under Russian control. Polish workers in Chicago, a sizable portion of his CFL constituency, had never been happy with the heavy-handed Irish domination of federation affairs. Now they threatened to rebel. Fitzpatrick's power began to wane.[5]

Paralleling the decline of Fitzpatrick, the political "readjustment" of the 1920s brought a deterioration of unionism in Illinois and elsewhere. The CIO's organization of the big mass industries proceeded slowly. Labor's influence in Chicago continued to rest on the city's position as a railway center, on the big-city clothing markets, and on the construction and printing trades.

Many of the more militant veterans in labor unions were associated with the radical Veterans of the World War, but that organization faded into obscurity by 1922. More often than not, union members who were veterans either decided against membership in the American Legion or dropped out. Some unions in Chicago and New York City endeavored to prohibit their members from also belonging to the Legion.

The previous chapters showed how Legionnaires in all sections of Illinois were capable of moving forcefully against sociopolitical dissent. They did it during the two major Red scare periods, the first in 1921–22 and then again in the Great Depression of the 1930s. The suppression of the *Staats Zeitung* and the defense of Danville stand as exhibits A and B. But the political dynamics of labor-management relations changed in Illinois, particularly after Fitzpatrick's demise and the differences that sprouted between traditional craft unions and the new industrial unions. The American Legion needed more members in Cook County, and the veterans they thought they needed were trade unionists living and working in the central city.

Some of the leaders in Chicago were determined to tame the antilabor sentiments of their downstate comrades. The Illinois department tried repeatedly to assure its urban posts that the Legion in Illinois would insist on a strict policy of neutrality in labor disputes. John Bullington called on state convention delegates in 1924 to enroll "your buddies who are members of trade unions. Many of them have been kept out of the Legion because of the vicious propaganda that the Legion was the policeman's club of Big Business." Another officer, Earle Benjamin Searcy of Springfield, said Gompers and John L. Lewis, the controversial president of the United Mine Workers Union, had both given their "personal endorsements" to the Legion. "There are certain uninformed anti-American elements in this country which have assumed to attack the American Legion chiefly because its members were men who made up an army which helped keep this country safe for just such culprits," Searcy said. "[The Legion] has no quarrel with any right-meaning organization. Organized labor should join hands with the American Legion to rid this country of anti-American influences which, if not checked, will endeavor to undermine the entire system of government. If that happens, the money we are paid as wages won't be worth carrying around."[6]

"Thousands are waiting to be asked," declared Ferre Watkins. While the estrangement between the Legion and organized labor intensified nationally, a small group of building tradesmen in Chicago who were union stalwarts and veterans with friends in the Legion wondered occasionally whether it might make more sense to try to influence that organization from within. These were no followers of John Fitzpatrick. Rabble-rousers they were not. They would never have stormed the barricades in Danville or anywhere else.

To understand the schism in the AFL that led later in the 1930s to the separation of the CIO, one need only be aware of the legislative history of the first national wage and hour act. The leaders of the AFL did not really want, and had to be persuaded that there should be, a statutory floor under wages and a ceiling over working hours. But the union men knew that the workplace-based Legion posts "all had their own particular axes to grind"—gas and electric companies, department stores, newspapers, medical care workers, meatpacking companies, and many others—to the detriment often of the union movement. Most of the commercial posts, as they were called, were in the downtown district.[7]

Given the Illinois department's rhetorical commitment to evenhandedness, why not a union labor post to present the Legionnaires with a different point of view? The Chicago contingent contacted Bill Green, the AFL president, about their plan. After explaining its purpose to the national commander of the Legion, with whom he was friendly, Green gave his approval to the idea. Chicago Union Labor Post 745 applied for a charter in 1927. It was granted in 1928, the first union labor American Legion post anywhere in the nation.[8]

On July 15, 1928, the first officers were installed in the Electricians' Hall on Washington Boulevard. Patrick "Paddy" Sullivan, president of the Chicago Building and Construction Trades Council, AFL, presented the post colors. "Now Labor has a voice in the Legion," he said. "Use it well."[9] The new post thought its voice could be heard most effectively in the same district with the commercial posts. After some resistance from some of the downtown units, which wanted the labor unit farther away in the West Side district, the request was granted.

More than half Chicago's labor force was unemployed at the peak of the Depression, including a comparable fraction of the former servicemen in Post 745. Jack Daly, finance officer of the labor post, still had his job as a sheet-metal worker for the Chicago schools. He arranged with the sheet-metal workers union to make its headquarters available for Legion meetings. Out of his own pocket, Daly paid the dues of enough impoverished members to maintain the post charter through this difficult period.

> At every meeting a quarter barrel of beer was on hand to cheer up the boys. The hat was passed but never enough was raised in those days to pay for it. Jack always saw somehow that the bill was paid. Oh yes, those were still prohibition days. Gee, but that beer tasted good when you didn't have a spare dime for a glass. Many members walked long distances to attend meetings and those with cars saw that they got home okay. Comradeship was the order of the day.[10]

Later, after jobs were created by federally funded WPA projects, the labor post launched a special drive to enlist as American Legion members the veterans who were union men and WPA workers. Here again we see an example of how the Legion wanted to give the impression that it, as well as the Democratic party precinct captain, had shared in the madework beneficence.

Chicago Union Labor Post 745 acted much like a fire department, sounding the alarm and running out the fire trucks whenever some Legion post appeared about to intrude somewhere in a labor dispute. In one case, the news that Legionnaires were threatening to use baseball bats against CIO strikers in Monroe, Michigan, brought a counterthreat from Chicago. Post 745 sent a telegram to the national commander of the Legion advising him and the Michigan department that a motor caravan of members might be dispatched from Chicago in full American Legion regalia to march on the picket lines in Monroe. Such tactics often, but not always, had the desired deterrent effect.

The Runaway Handbag Factory

Local unions in many of the smaller downstate communities could not survive the economic devastation of the Depression. By 1933, unable to meet their dues obligations, many of them simply disappeared. Outside the metropolitan area, public opinion tended in this period to identify industrial unions everywhere with foreign radicalism.[11] In Chicago, meanwhile, the established unions struggled to stay alive. The needle trades constituted an important part of the organized labor force, representing about twenty-three thousand garment workers. As far back as 1865, there had been an organization—then called the Sewing Women's Protective Union—to assist women in the sewing trades in Chicago. Before the Haymarket Square Riot of 1886, some four hundred immigrant cloak makers marched toward the Loop from the Jewish ghetto around Maxwell Street to protest sweatshop conditions—only to be turned back forcibly by police at the bridge over the Chicago River. At that time, the needle trades were the main source of employment for Jewish immigrants in the city. Their employers often were German or Hungarian Jews who had arrived before them. Opposing Communist and Socialist wings fought in the late 1920s for control of what had then become the International Ladies Garment Workers. By ridding itself of the Communist leaders, the ILGWU prepared for a renaissance in 1929, only to crumble along with the others in the economic distress of the early 1930s. Not until passage by Congress of the union-strengthening Wagner Act in 1935 did the various clothing unions regain their foothold in the industry. Many of the biggest—including Amalgamated Clothing Workers of America—lined up with the CIO when it broke away from the AFL in 1935.

One new union affiliated with the AFL, the Pocketbook and Novelty Workers Union, succeeded in organizing many of the small shops in Chicago. As in the other major garment center, New York City, most of the entrepreneurs, subcontracting operators, union organizers, union leaders, union members, and their social worker–supporters in Chicago's West Side immigrant neighborhoods continued to be Jewish. Labor negotiations often were conducted in Yiddish. Like the other garment industry unions, the pocketbook workers had to cope with small operators who ran out on their collective bargaining agreements and relocated in rural areas less friendly to unions.[12]

The four Levine brothers were thinking in early 1936 about doing just that. Their Mirro Leather Goods Company manufactured women's handbags in Chicago. Two of the brothers managed the company; the other two were traveling salesmen. Now they were scouting around for a cheaper labor supply and an escape from union headaches. The Levines found just what they wanted in a Mississippi River town about fifty miles downriver from Oscar Carlstrom's home county of Mercer. Carlstrom was no longer attorney general of Illinois, having been replaced in 1933 by Cook County Democrat Otto Kerner Sr., the son of Czech immigrants.

Warsaw, Illinois (population 1,866), had an industrial past, several empty factory buildings, and a group of seamstresses who were engaged temporarily in a WPA project sewing long white dresses for the high school senior girls' commencement exercises. Located just below Keokuk, Iowa, in Hancock County, Warsaw was settled by German immigrants who grew grapes for what they hoped would resemble the Rhine wine of their homeland. About fifteen miles north of Warsaw, the Mormon prophet Joseph Smith had led his people to another riverside community in Hancock County—the city of Nauvoo. In the 1840s, the Mormons organized an autonomous renegade society of twelve thousand faithful, complete with their own military force, which they called the Nauvoo Legion. The newspaper in Warsaw—the *Warsaw Signal*—stirred the people of the rest of the county with its strident calls for the extinction of the Mormon settlement. The history of what happened next is a familiar story. Joseph Smith was murdered by a mob at the county jail in Carthage, the Mormon temple was destroyed, and in 1846 the entire colony fled west to Utah.

Besides the grape arbors, the stone caves in the hillside next to the river were perfect for aging beer. So the Germans who lived in the Stump Town neighborhood of Warsaw started a brewery later in the 1800s. Closed during Prohibition, the brewery reopened in 1933 as the Warsaw Brewing Corporation. But the shoe factory, a garment plant, and a button factory had shut down permanently, leaving men and women who were accustomed to factory work unemployed. About 165 people were enrolled then in various WPA projects in Warsaw.

A glove manufacturer from Minnesota arrived first to look over the shoe building. City officials promised to pay for the necessary plumbing and wiring improvements. Eventually, however, the glove makers chose another Illinois city—Beardstown. They explained their reasons to the city fathers of Warsaw: Beardstown's "over-abundance of cheap labor and [its being] free from labor entanglements, for we did worry just a bit about your being so close to Keokuk and the recent labor troubles in that city."[13]

Verle Kramer, editor of the *Warsaw Bulletin*, participated in the factory committee's campaign to attract new industry. Mayor Esper Ziegler (who was also the local postmaster) assured the next prospects, the Levines, that

Warsaw would remain an open-shop town. And, said the *Bulletin*, "there was very little likelihood of labor troubles here as the people were not foreigners or subject to outside communistic influences."[14] The factory committee agreed to raise three thousand dollars for a new roof on the garment building and for Mirro's moving expenses from Chicago.

Early on the steamy hot morning of July 3, 1936, two large trucks rolled into Warsaw with the sewing machines, cutting blocks and tables, embossing machines, and other equipment. Men were hired at thirty cents an hour, women at twenty cents an hour. Among the women who were taken on first were several experienced graduates of the WPA sewing project.

Close behind the moving trucks came representatives of the union who said they wanted to enlighten the people of Warsaw about Mirro and the economics of producing and selling ladies handbags. The factory committee published a statement in the newspaper asserting that the company deserved an opportunity to demonstrate its good faith without "any outside disturbances which might thwart their continued success in our community." "Unfortunately agitation and intimidation is being attempted by paid organizers who care nothing for our community and who are schooled and trained in the art of creating unrest," the statement said. "The citizens of Warsaw are capable of handling any situation that may arise without the aid of outside paid agitators."[15]

Fifteen members of Warsaw's Ralph Parker Post 682 of the American Legion met July 13 to draft another statement for publication in the *Bulletin*.

To Warsaw Citizens

Whereas the Mirro Leather Goods Company has located in Warsaw and is now giving employment to a number of our fellow citizens; and

Whereas outside agencies have attempted to foment labor unrest before the company has had a fair chance to become established and train its workers;

Therefore be it resolved that the undersigned go on record as opposing such uninvited outside interference with local problems, and be it further resolved that in event of any threatened intimidation or violence the undersigned groups will gather at a given signal for the protection of property and the preservation of peace.

Ralph Parker Post 682
The American Legion,
The Warsaw Club[16]

In the adjacent news columns, Editor Kramer accurately described the Legion's statement as "scarcely veiled."

"By force and by threats, labor organizers in certain places have forced workmen into unions," his story said. "This will not be the case in Warsaw. There is a *strong probability that force will be met with a stronger force* [author's emphasis] if it becomes necessary in that way to protect the workers' right to work peacefully."

About a month later, the president of the pocketbook workers union in Chicago, Samuel Laderman, notified the state's attorney of Hancock County that he would be arriving on a specified date in the company of Maynard C. Krueger, an economics professor at the University of Chicago and the Socialist party candidate for governor; and a third man, C. H. Mayer of Carlinville. The three men drove up and down the main street of Warsaw looking for a vacant store that they could rent for a meeting "to tell Warsaw people about sweatshop conditions in the pocketbook industry." They headed for the post office to ask Mayor Ziegler whether a permit would be needed for the public meeting. Krueger said later that they noticed that they were being followed: "Five of these men, all tall, strong fellows, approached and told us we had ten minutes to get out of town. Then they changed [their minds] and told us to go at once. One man tried to drag Laderman out of the car. We sought out the town marshal, Guy Bell, and asked him to take us under his protection to see the mayor. He advised us to get out of Warsaw. So we went."

The *Chicago Tribune* reported Krueger's version of this incident under the headline "U. of C. Prof Is Run out of Illinois Town."[17] Noting Warsaw's location high on the east bank of the river, the weekly newspaper in nearby Blandinsville regretted editorially only that the marshal had not chosen to throw the visitors out of town in a westerly direction.[18]

The Chicago Federation of Labor lodged a protest with Attorney General Kerner. Ten days later, the commander of the Chicago Union Labor post asked to appear before the regularly scheduled meeting of the executive committee of the Illinois Department at the Legion's state convention in Danville. Homer Robbins, the post commander, began by reminding the committee that nearly half the veterans in the commercial-labor district of inner Chicago were either union members or on some government payroll. "Several hundred thousand men who are union men and were soldiers and sailors in the last war have felt that the Legion was a scab organization," he said. Laderman, himself a veteran who subsequently joined the union labor post, said Mirro "ran away" from its union contract in Chicago. "With the ringing of the fire bell," he said, "it was understood in Warsaw that the Legionnaires would turn out in force and throw out any Red organizers who molested their local people."

Having announced in the hometown newspaper plans contrary to department policy, the Warsaw post could hardly plead ignorance. James E. Johnston, the post commander, offered this explanation.

> We are just a bunch of rubes living in the sticks. Our post is made up of a bunch of small-town boys and farmers. We do not have any lawyers in that [part of the] country. We will admit that in essence perhaps we may have erred, but down there in the sticks we are just good old-fashioned Americans and we thought we might take a stand against what we thought were unAmerican ideas.[19]

After sending a fact-finding team to Warsaw, state commander J. B. Murphy of Bloomington delivered an official rebuke to the guilty Legionnaires. Satisfied with the state department's policy reaffirmation, the union labor post considered the remedy satisfactory.

Then, back in Warsaw, all seventeen members of the Parker post who were present at the next meeting voted *against* a resolution rescinding its earlier resolution. The post had said what it said, and that was that. "The people of Warsaw are educated, born of American parents, and they cannot be led away by glib talkers," the *Bulletin* reminded them.[20] Unless and until the Legionnaires did something to carry out their threat, Laderman was willing to let the matter rest. He and the CFL tried to buy space in the *Bulletin* for a half-page advertisement explaining the union's position. The newspaper refused to accept the ad "on the grounds that it was contrary to the best interests of Warsaw, and libelous."[21]

Then, in September, Laderman called the mayor to make arrangements for a public meeting in a city park or street. The mayor said he was sorry but could not grant such a request. Why not? Well, obviously, because without the help of the American Legion, the city cannot possibly be sure of maintaining law and order. Our police forces are not sufficient to be sure of protecting you from possible harm, he explained, in effect, and we have been warned against calling on the Legion for help. So what can we do?

At this point, the union officials in Chicago evidently decided that the prospects for ever organizing the plant in Warsaw were exceedingly dim, so why bother?

The Mirro plant continued as an open shop in Warsaw until it closed in 1939. Sales were said to have begun falling off in 1938. "As a consequence," reported the *Bulletin's* retrospective account, "there was not the need for factory help. The employees for the most part worked only at intervals." Business and civic leaders in Warsaw were asked to provide additional capital by buying Mirro stock, which several of them did. At last, A. E. Levine, the company president, moved back to Chicago, where the Warsaw newspaper said Mirro's other operations had been prospering. The plant closure was unfortunate, agreed the *Bulletin*, unfortunate for the investors who lost their money, for the employees who lost their jobs, and for the community at large.[22]

Living with (and Without) Labor Unions

The new political readjustment of the 1930s gave labor unions the tools they needed to organize American industry. The National Labor Relations Act, upheld as constitutional by the Supreme Court in 1937, required that employers recognize and bargain with units authorized by vote of their workers. Yet, as we have seen, the political ethos that prevailed in ethnically diverse Chicago was different from that in much of the rest of the state. Downstate Illinoisans were more insular, more conservative, generally less tolerant of collective movements of any kind. These differences carried over into the affairs of the American Legion. The men of the Legion understood that the Illinois department could not be influential in the national framework of the organization if it were constantly being pulled asunder by internal sectional divisions. Compromise power-sharing accommodations were devised, therefore, to satisfy the various interests involved in, for instance, the service delivery controversy. Union-organizing activities were another matter. Main Street identified unionism with strange and subversive foreign influences. Labor's message continued to be anathema over many parts of downstate Illinois. Nothing the Chicago Union Labor post could do was going to change that. The presence of the labor post had the important effect, however, of neutralizing the public posture of the Illinois department. What cannot be known with any certainty is whether, or how, the pressure to conform to attitudes fostered by a highly visible quasi police organization, such as the Parker post, may have served to stifle whatever expressions of dissent might have been heard in a community like Warsaw.

10 THE UPS AND DOWNS OF THE ALPHA LEGIONNAIRES

The early payout of the soldiers' bonuses, over the opposition of conservative big business and a liberal president, signified the coming of age politically of the American Legion. Not until the Legion decided as an organization that, yes, it *was* indeed time for the bonus, did the sixteen years of sound and fury over this issue come to an end. Although the Legion did not speak for all veterans as a class, it was regarded by policy-making bodies as the representative voice of most politically attentive World War veterans.

Legionnaires were fully integrated now into the affairs of both parties in Illinois. Almost all veterans who sought public office belonged to the Legion. Being able to appear at a Legion conclave wearing the blue cap was an important identifying symbol for a candidate. The distinction between officers and privates faded with the passing years. James B. Murphy, state commander during the Warsaw union organizing episode, had been a private in a menial assignment as an army headquarters clerk. A record as a commissioned officer was of less value now. Sectional bearing and name familiarity mattered now more than the insignia they had worn in the service.

Many of the most successful Legion politicians capitalized on their contacts and experiences to enter the public arena. This use of Legion membership as a stepping stone happened in both parties and in both urban and rural areas. After his two terms as state commander, William McCauley was elected to the state senate as a Republican from the Olney district. John Clinnin entered the Republican competition for lieuten-ant governor twice but lost both times. In Chicago the emergence of the Democratic machine as the dominant force in Cook County politics made it more likely that candidates who were consistent winners would have affiliated with that party. Legionnaires held positions of power in many ward organizations. These were politicians who practiced their craft in two concentric circles: as Legionnaires and as elected public of-ficials. Partisan differences aside, as noted in earlier chapters, their mu-tual interest in Legion affairs gave them a common point of reference on questions of national security and foreign affairs. Men who were in their forties or thereabouts and were veterans had an advantage over candi-dates who were not veterans.

During one span of a few years, four different men represented Chicago's third district in Congress. All four had Irish names; all four were members of the American Legion.[1] Legionnaires in the public arena were birds of a feather (the feather being their blue overseas cap), but they operated in different political cultures—and projected different images—depending on where they lived and what party they represented. The differences stand out in sharp contrast in the stories of two former en-listed men who did extremely well in politics but would probably never have gotten a start without their American Legion connections: Les Arends and Eddie Barrett.

Leslie Arends grew up on a farm in the heart of the Corn Belt in north central Illinois. His parents were German Methodists. Having played the clarinet in the high school band, Arends was assigned to the band when he joined the navy in 1917. Standing tall and straight as a toy soldier, he made a marvelous drum major as the band made the rounds of home-front Liberty Bond rallies. He had sharp, angular features and a ruddy complexion. In later years, people said Les Arends, his long hair draped over his rear collar, moved with the grace and panache of a proud In-dian chief.

Arends had worked with his father in the grain business. When he returned from the navy band circuit, his father bought the controlling interest in the local bank and made him the president. Arends lent money to farmers, bought a farm of his own, made friends, and helped organize the American Legion post in the little town of Melvin in Ford County. In due course, he became the leader of the Legion district that coincided with the seventeenth congressional district around the city of Bloomington.

In 1934, a most unpromising year for Republicans, he won the party nomination against four opponents and went on to be elected to Congress, the only Republican in the entire nation to unseat a Democratic congressional incumbent that year. Fifteen other House seats turned over to Democrats.[2] Reflecting his rural constituency in every respect, the new congressman believed in agrarian self-sufficiency in the face of adversity. He campaigned against New Deal work relief programs, U.S. involvement in the disagreements of foreign countries, and the sinful excesses of the big city to the north. Poor people in the city were probably lazy; their values were suspect. Chicago politicians were corrupt; government wasted the people's money. Les Arends remained in the House of Representatives for forty years, many of them as the Republican whip, or second in command.

Edward J. Barrett came from a different background—the sidewalks of Chicago. An Irish Catholic lad in a city where many of his fellows hungered for fame and fortune, Barrett joined the army when he was seventeen. He wound up in a combat infantry regiment, the Thirty-third Division's "Dandy First" that shed blood at Chipilly Ridge in France. Young Barrett was gassed and wounded in that engagement. Back home, he helped organize the Disabled American Veterans and sought out as many other veteran organizations as he could find. He used the American Legion, the Veterans of Foreign Wars, and the Thirty-third Division War Veterans Association, among others, to make friends and become known. He took a job as secretary to the leader of the street-sweepers' union, which enabled him to meet the important figures in the Chicago and Illinois Federations of Labor. And, lastly, young Eddie Barrett signed up as a Democratic precinct captain in an Irish-American ward.

In 1928 the leader of the Democratic organization in Chicago, George Brennan, died. His death made it possible for the president of the Cook County Board, a two-fisted former coal miner from Braidwood named Anton J. "Tony" Cermak, to take over command of the party. Barrett thought his acquaintances around the state qualified him for state office in the election of 1930. He went to Cermak and asked for the organization's endorsement for state treasurer. As demonstrated a few years before by Len Small, the considerable power of the elected treasurer in Illinois related to his responsibility for depositing and (one would wish) wisely investing state funds. This authority gave whoever occupied the office opportunities to make more friends among bankers and other local dignitaries. Cermak told Barrett he was too impatient and needed more seasoning. Barrett ran anyway against the organization's candidate, a man named Mike Zacharias. Barrett proved to be a better ballot name than Zacharias. His popularity among Democrats in Irish districts, veterans organizations, and organized labor enabled Barrett to win the nomination and subsequently be elected state treasurer of Illinois at age thirty.[3]

Far to the south, John Stelle climbed behind the wheel of his Model-T Ford and started on the long trek to Chicago to pay his respects to treasurer-elect Barrett. "There I was down in southern Illinois," he told me later, "and if I ever hoped to make it in politics I needed to hook up with somebody who was on the way up in Chicago."[4] He and Barrett knew one another slightly in the Legion. They were better acquainted now because of Stelle's campaigning activities for and among veterans. He had taken the lead in the organization of the Illinois Democratic Servicemen's Club in 1928. Then in 1930 he put together another campaign committee to assist Democratic candidates who were veterans, including, of course, Eddie Barrett. It had become routine practice by then for Legionnaires in either party to join together in campaign efforts under the veterans-for-so-and-so rubric, always without any mention of the American Legion. Stelle left Chicago with the job of assistant treasurer. He and Barrett would be partners and important players in Illinois politics for the rest of the 1930s.

In 1932, against his basic instincts, newly elected Mayor Cermak agreed reluctantly to the slating of a "good government" candidate, Judge Horner, for governor. Horner had many friends in the Standard Club, the downtown gathering place for businessmen, bankers, lawyers, and politicians who were German and western European Jews. Fellow members Abel Davis and Milton Foreman, though Republicans, had known and admired the judge for many years. Russian Jews were not welcome at the Standard Club, which provided a bipartisan social center for Jews who were well established in the community and were interested in civic affairs, in much the same way that Legion membership brought Legionnaires of both parties together. Without regard to their partisan differences, Davis in particular made his financial connections available for the advancement of Horner's career.

Cermak suspected that because judges were more accustomed to giving than taking orders from party bosses like himself, he might have made a mistake. Shortly after Roosevelt and Horner were both elected, Cermak was shot and fatally wounded in Miami by a bullet presumably intended for the president-elect, who was sitting next to him.

The death of Cermak opened the way for Ed Kelly to be selected (by the city council) as the new mayor. As chief engineer of the Chicago Sanitary District, Kelly knew and was well liked by *Tribune* publisher McCormick, their friendship dating back to McCormick's presidency of the sanitary district. Governor Horner's progressive bent resulted in immediate policy and patronage clashes with both the mayor and the Barrett-Stelle team.

Kelly, Barrett, and Stelle would never have argued with their depiction in the press as thorough-going spoils politicians. Statesmen they did not pretend to be. "Well, you see," Horner once tried to explain, "they [Barrett and Stelle] are on the other side of the fence and they think it's greener on my side. Whenever they reach their hand over the fence, I slap it."[5]

The rupture in the governor's relationship with Kelly and the regular organization involved more substantial disputes. Their disagreements were variations on a theme familiar to the American Legion: the conflict between state regulatory power and the city's wish for autonomy. Crucial issues reflected the cultural divisions between Chicago and downstate on "personal liberty"—specifically gambling and the regulation of saloons. Three of the four members of the state liquor control commission were Legion officials—DeLaCour, Foreman, and Sprague. But the mayor wanted to be free of any state-imposed controls in the post-Prohibition era.

Horner's downstate following enabled him to survive the party organization's challenge in the primary, with Abel Davis's generous financial assistance. However, the governor's running mate for lieutenant governor, John E. Cassidy, a Legion member from Peoria, lost to the organization's candidate, who was John Stelle. So the top of the state Democratic ticket in the fall consisted of incompatible teammates—the liberal Henry Horner and the pragmatic John Stelle.

The state Republican ticket in opposition to Horner would be headed by one of two familiar experienced figures—Oscar Carlstrom or Curley Brooks. First, some background: On election night in 1924, twelve years before, when Len Small was reelected to a second term as governor, he was reported to have told associates that he and Mayor Thompson would back Carlstrom for governor in 1928. Carlstrom, it will be remembered, had just been elected attorney general with the backing of Small and

Thompson after helping Small win the first time by siphoning off anti-Small votes downstate.

At some point, however, the attorney general apparently had a falling out with his two confederates. Thompson decided to support who else but Small for a third term. Encouraged by the Main Street faction of the Legion, Carlstrom declared that he would run anyhow against Small in the primary. But the anti-Small forces persuaded him to withdraw in favor of Louis Emmerson so that the anti-Small vote would not again be split as it had been in 1920. Emmerson beat Small in the 1928 Republican primary and was, as we have seen, elected in the fall. Newspapers reported rumors that Frank Knox, the new publisher of the *Chicago Daily News*, who was a confidante of President Hoover's, had offered Carlstrom a federal judicial appointment in exchange for his withdrawal. Such an appointment never transpired, possibly because Carlstrom still harbored hopes of one day becoming governor. Again it was widely understood that Emmerson did promise to endorse Carlstrom *the next time*—in 1932.

Unhappily for the ever hopeful Carlstrom, his aspirations ran aground on the shoals of the Prohibition issue. Most Legionnaires favored repeal of the Eighteenth Amendment, the Volstead Act, and the prohibition of the sale of alcoholic beverages. But the several Legion leaders who were active in local politics in dry districts downstate succeeded in deferring a state convention vote on the question. They also prevented a poll of the Legion membership, the outcome of which would not have been in doubt—and would have been hard to explain in some circles. In 1930 the Cook County Council of the Legion, speaking for the approximately thirty thousand Illinois Legionnaires who were from Cook County (among some seventy-six thousand statewide members), passed a resolution endorsing repeal virtually by acclamation. A subsequent motion to consider the resolution at the state convention was tabled by the leadership. Dr. S. C. Bromberg, a past commander of Chicago's Edison Park Post 541, protested in a letter to the *Illinois Legionnaire.*

> Attendance at six state conventions, two recent national conventions, innumerable meetings of posts, districts, and other units of the Legion convince me that a large percentage, if not an overwhelming majority of our membership drink intoxicating liquor. Drunken Legionnaires have infested every convention I have attended. Every one of these men has taken two solemn oaths to defend the Constitution of the United States. . . . Yet [the resolution endorsing repeal] was not allowed to come to a vote in Aurora.

... Past state commander [Ferre] Watkins said the nation stands at a cross-roads and we must wait. Who will lead us out of this morass of uncertainty?[6]

By a margin of almost two to one, meanwhile, the electorate of Illinois supported repeal in an advisory referendum the same year. All this approval of drinking notwithstanding, being a "dry" still remained a litmus test for many downstate Republican voters. Carlstrom not only talked wetter than most of the other Republican candidates but also, due in part to his prominence as a Legionnaire, acquired the reputation of one who enjoyed spirited beverages in the company of his friends. Oscar Carlstrom liked to drink, and the temperance crusaders knew it.

For whatever reasons, Emmerson gave his support in 1932 to a confirmed dry—Omer N. Custer of Galesburg. Custer's selection inspired Len Small to come hurrying back onto the stage. This time, convinced that he had been treated unfairly, Carlstrom refused to step aside. Once again, Small defeated his divided opposition. The results of the 1932 Republican primary were 481,960 for Small; 370,301 for Custer; and 282,741 for Carlstrom. It was hardly a good year for Republicans, regardless of personalities. In the general election, Small was buried in the Roosevelt landslide. The state inaugurated its first Jewish governor. But then, four years later, the disunity in the Illinois Democratic party caused by the split between Governor Horner and Mayor Kelly gave Republicans reason to be optimistic about their chances. Without the continuing cheerleading of a faithful band of Legionnaires, even one so stoical as Carlstrom might have become disillusioned by his frustrating ventures into gubernatorial politics. He decided to try for the Republican nomination yet another time. So did Len Small. And so this time did another Legionnaire with a strong following among conservatives in the northeastern part of the state—Colonel McCormick's protégé, the former marine C. Wayland Brooks.

Among the numerous members of the Legion who were candidates for public office, Curley Brooks probably came closest to being the World War counterpart of Civil War vets who "waved the bloody shirt." Brooks liked to display his war wounds while preaching isolationism and his evangelical brand of Americanism. In one campaign speech, he startled his listeners by tearing off his (unbloody) shirt to show the audience where a German bullet had grazed his back. He tried for state treasurer in 1932 and for Illinois congressman at large in 1934, losing both times.

Facing off for the first time in a statewide Republican primary thus were two of the best-known Legionnaires—the "Main Street candidate" who had tried and failed thrice before and "the *Tribune*'s candidate" from the Fox River valley. Brooks campaigned strenuously throughout the state and won easily. He finished with 596,445 votes to Small's 268,903, Carlstrom's 52,266, and 91,389 for five other also-rans. Carlstrom received only 16,266 votes in Cook County (to Brooks's 290,970) and 37,000 downstate (to Brooks's 305,475). Carlstrom carried only one county, his own. Counting only the votes for the three leading candidates, Carlstrom did only slightly better downstate (receiving less than 7 percent of the vote) than he did in Cook County (a little over 4 percent). It must have been painful for him to read the returns from Bill McCauley's home county of Richland. It had been Carlstrom who rallied downstate Legionnaires to McCauley's defense fourteen years before when the state commander was under heavy attack from Chicago. Now Carlstrom tallied a pitiful 55 votes in Richland County to 1,163 votes for Brooks and 954 for Small.

All this travail Carlstrom endured with a lifelong sanguinity. While attorney general of Illinois, he filled out an autobiographical questionnaire from the national headquarters of the Legion. Noting the absence of any college attendance in his record, he felt compelled to add this handwritten comment: "I consider that my service in the Philippines, with the travel incident thereto, and the same experience, travel and training in France, gave me the experience and breadth of vision which college training might have given me. Not withstanding the hardships, I feel greatly indebted to my government."

The Republican presidential nominee in 1936, Governor Alf Landon of Kansas, chose an Illinois Legion member for his vice-presidential running mate—*Chicago Daily News* publisher Frank Knox. This choice pleased neither Bertie McCormick nor Curley Brooks and proved to be of little help to Brooks in the general election.

Horner appeared with Mayor Kelly at the Legion state convention in September. The governor praised the record of the American Legion. He said Illinois should be proud of its state hospital facilities for veterans, which he said made it unnecessary for the families of patients to travel long distances to distant VA institutions, as in many other states.

Roosevelt and Horner both carried Illinois handily in November, the president by 714,606 votes, the governor by 385,176 votes. Horner had tried various methods of forcing Stelle off the ticket, but to no avail. Stelle took office with Horner as the new lieutenant governor. Stelle told me shortly before his death that Kelly had no intention of trying to elect the anti-Horner Democratic state ticket in the fall, had Horner been beaten in the primary. He said organization Democrats would have surreptitiously "cut" their gubernatorial candidate at the polls, thereby enabling his friend McCormick's friend Brooks to win. Stelle knew that he would also have been a victim of this perfidy. But, as it turned out, he achieved success tagging along behind a governor he hated, a success that surely would have been denied him had Horner lost the primary.

The feud between Horner and the organization regulars continued into the governor's second term. One of the few Legion politicians who had enlisted for the duration in Horner's cause was Scott Lucas. In 1938 Horner supported Congressman Lucas for the U.S. Senate. The Kelly organization put up a federal judge from Chicago, Michael Igoe, who was an Irish Catholic. It turned out to be an unusually bitter primary campaign in which Lucas was hurt by accusations against his older brother, Allen Thurmond Lucas. His brother had apparently distributed anti-Catholic literature as a member of the Klan in the 1920s. Scott Lucas lost in Cook County but won by more than enough votes downstate to be nominated and then (on the strength of a heavy Chicago vote) elected in a close race in the fall.

That same year, William McCauley, the two-term state commander of the Legion who had been in the middle of the sectional firestorm in the early 1920s, won the Republican nomination to oppose another downstater for state treasurer. McCauley lost Chicago by 260,000 votes and lost the election by slightly over 100,000. He did better in Carlstrom's county of Mercer, with 63 percent, than in his own county of Richland, with 60 percent.

Two days before the 1938 election, with more than two years remaining in his term, Governor Horner suffered the first of several severe strokes. His administration then became a crusade to live out his term and prevent the lieutenant governor from succeeding him. For the gubernatorial primary of 1940, Horner's representatives agreed with Kelly on a compromise candidate, a mine workers union lawyer from Taylorville, Harry Hershey. Stelle ran for governor anyway but had no chance without the backing of either faction. So regardless of what happened in the fall election, Stelle would be looking for work in January.

Henry Horner died on October 6, 1940. For the next ninety-nine days, John Stelle governed Illinois. One of his friends, Springfield paint store owner George Edward Day, took over as state purchasing agent. Day stocked up on several years' supply of yellow paint for lines in highway no-passing zones, a safety innovation that was then being used in only one other state but had come to the attention of the suddenly safety conscious new chief executive. The governor's mansion was repainted, inside and out. Groups of Legion friends were invited from southern Illinois to dine at the governor's mansion. Almost five hundred Legionnaires received honorary commissions in the reserve militia, established to replace the recently federalized Illinois National Guard. Contracts were awarded for the purchase of 385,000 tons of coal, some of it at $1.22 a ton higher than the 1939 price. The governor's office was a very busy place, especially during the Christmas season, while Stelle was attending to the pardoning and paroling of an extraordinarily large number of convicts. Governor Stelle's well-publicized antics, along with the disarray in the Democratic ranks, played a part in the election of the Republican candidate, Dwight H. Green, in November. The new governor was a former prosecutor in Chicago, an army veteran, and an inactive Legion member.

Winners and losers, on the way up, on the way down, they all donned their Legion caps and hitched up their belts an extra notch when it came time to address an audience of affiliated veterans. The dance for power went on, with the Legion chorus humming not so softly in the background. John Stelle made it to the governor's office; Oscar Carlstrom did not. Scott Lucas, Les Arends, and Bill Dawson became influential members of Congress. A few, like Everett Dirksen, were waiting for the opportune time. Bill McCauley, John Clinnin, Curley Brooks, and many others had reached and reached and failed.

It seems to me that the whole future defense of America is in the hands of the American Legion.

—Daddy Schick, 1930

11 ECHOES OF THE PAST

Undaunted by his rejection at the polls, Curley Brooks returned to the American Legion speaking circuit, espousing wherever he went a hard-line doctrine of noninvolvement in the disputes of nations across the seas. Legion policy on military preparedness evolved in the 1920s and 1930s along two sometimes contrary themes. The first, the maintenance of a strong armed capability, emphasized a trained reserve of citizen-officers. The Legion preferred a ready reserve to a large standing army and a massive arsenal. Many Legionnaires held on to their unpleasant memories of full-time career officers. A goodly number of Illinois members who had been officers retained their reserve or National Guard commissions. The Illinois department also pressed for reserve officers training in secondary schools and colleges. As national commander in 1927, Howard Savage said, "Those who attack the military training in high schools and colleges as UnAmerican [*sic*], militaristic, and likely to breed war are cracked idealists who do not know what it is to face a blood-lusting enemy without training."[1] Schick, by virtue of seniority a self-pronounced authority on naval affairs, opposed the building of a big fleet of warships. He believed that it would only bring the United States closer to foreign disputes. The best force, in his view, would be a naval reserve consisting of a merchant marine with *Americans only* (his emphasis) in the crews of those ships.[2] The second theme stressed the defensive nature of preparedness by calling on America's leaders to stay out of all foreign disagreements, absolutely. In Illinois, as in other midland states, the second of these policies gradually took precedence over the first. At Illinois conventions, resolutions that advocated a strengthening of the military were always predicated on the contention that a strong armed force would prevent rather than encourage aggressive behavior against the United States.

Statewide candidates like Brooks, Lucas, and Carlstrom were aware of the tidal wave of pro-German and anti-British sentiment in the 1920 election returns. The war had precipitated a hysterical movement to eradicate everything German. Now many German Americans were settling old scores at the polls.[3] How the Legion fit its isolationism into this political dynamic in Illinois is illustrated by the views of Daddy Schick, who happened to be of German ancestry. He said some years before that it was essential for America to remain independent by avoiding all international conferences. Getting sucked into the conflicting interests of European powers would only oblige American leaders to become involved in world problems and therefore to take sides. He described his feeling of "great hesitance regarding our taking an active part in the decisions of European politics." Then the crux of the matter: "It would be very hard for our people to be united on an issue that is purely a European issue." Hard, he apparently meant, because of the many American citizens who emigrated from Germany, Britain, France, Ireland, Poland, Italy, Scandinavia, the Balkans, Russia, and the various other Slavic states, countries whose interests history had shown would be likely to collide. It was the normal course of affairs in the Old World, perhaps, but need it be any business of ours? The ethnic inheritances of the American people were so durable, he believed, as to make it impossible to weigh right and wrong, justice and injustice, independent of those influences.[4]

Disturbing events across the oceans only hardened the Legion's insistence that they were none of America's concern. The Japanese marched into Manchuria in 1931. Adolf Hitler and the Nazi party seized power in Germany the same year that Franklin Roosevelt took office in Washington. Hitler's armies invaded Poland in 1939. Communist Russia jumped in from the east, and the two invading powers worked out a mutual partition of the occupied Polish land. After conquering Norway, Denmark, the Low Countries, and France, Germany surprised the world by turning abruptly around to attack Russia in 1941.

The mood of the nation was receptive to a policy of what some called isolationism (particularly when directed against the views of ideologues on the right) and others called pacifism (usually the expressions of those on the left). A Roper poll of American public opinion reported these findings in September 1939:[5]

Go to war on the side of Britain and France	2.5%
Enter on their side if they are in danger of losing	14.7%
Take no sides but do business with both	37.5%
Have nothing to do with either side	29.9%
Find some way of supporting Germany	0.2%

The core of isolationist sentiment, stronger among women than men, remained fairly constant at about 30 percent. Robert E. Sherwood, a member of the White House staff, said later that the American public would have been "glad to see the European war end on almost any inconclusive terms merely as a guarantee that the United States would not be drawn into it." Sherwood believed the isolationist sentiment was less concentrated among German Americans this time than before the Great War. "Americans in 1939 were fortified with the experience that the previous generation had conspicuously lacked," he said, "the experience of involvement in European war, and they wanted no part of it."[6]

Roosevelt had to be adroit with the assistance provided Great Britain and Soviet Russia for reasons that had become more complicated than those Wilson confronted twenty-five years before. Not only could the president dare not alienate German, Italian (Italy being a German ally), and Irish American voters, but Germany's unexpected invasion of the Soviet Union, which confused many Americans, reinforced the Legion's determination that the United States had no stake in this fight.

Legion members were never of one mind about these matters, in Illinois or anywhere else. Officials in eastern and southern states tended toward a more interventionist stance. Curley Brooks, the leader of the Legion's isolationist wing in Illinois, ran again in 1940, this time for the U.S. Senate. More devoted than ever to keeping the United States out of the war, he defeated a Chicagoan, James M. Slattery, by only 20,827 votes out of 4 million cast. The weakened status of the Democratic party in Illinois (spelled out in the last chapter) unquestionably made his triumph possible. Brooks's election meant that both senators from Illinois were prominent Legionnaires, the Democrat Scott Lucas being the other.

Lucas had taken his Legion credentials with him to Washington. He voted against the administration's Fair Labor Standards Act in 1938. He supported the several neutrality bills that passed Congress between 1935 and 1939. Running through the national debate was the belief, shared now by many Legionnaires in Illinois, that the Great War had been a horrendous mistake. The *New York Herald-Tribune* said the Neutrality Act of 1937 should more accurately have been titled "An Act to Preserve the U.S. from Intervention in the War of 1914–18."[7] The neutrality measures placed restrictions on the shipment of war goods and required that U.S. vessels try to stay out of the way of German submarines.

In one memorable speech to a Legion gathering, Brooks demanded that the United States stop its "provocative acts against Germany" and steer clear of what he continued to characterize as a European war. Cheering him on, the *Chicago Tribune* harangued against "warmongering." At its national convention in September 1939, the Legion resolved to maintain U.S. neutrality, steadfast in the belief that "preserving the sovereignty and dignity of this nation will prevent involvement in this conflict."[8]

During this period, Legionnaires in Illinois were divided over the need for military conscription. The Democrat John Stelle, for one, joined Brooks in criticizing the imposition of a draft, which passed Congress in the autumn of 1940. The Cook County Council of the Legion criticized aid to the Russians and recommended unsuccessfully to the national convention that Congress be prohibited from a declaration of war until it had been approved in a referendum vote by all the American people. Lucas opposed the war referendum resolution while assuring the voters that he did not think the United States should enter the hostilities at that time.

Frank Knox's *Chicago Daily News* spoke for the interventionists in the Republican Party and the Legion. But its advice to the Legion appealed more to the manhood of its members than the rightness of the Allied cause. One editorial referred sarcastically to "the little band who have been trying to put a pacifist petticoat on the American Legion." By 1940 the leaders of the Illinois department were edging toward an interventionist position already accepted at the national level. The *Illinois Legionnaire*, organ for the department, explained, "In the event it becomes necessary to fight in defense of the United States, we prefer to be prepared to do our fighting outside the United States, and should war be forced on us we believe that the initial fighting should take place as far from our shores as possible."[9] At their state convention in 1941, less than three months before the Japanese attack on Pearl Harbor that brought the United States into World War II, the delegates issued a watered-down resolution of national unity and support for the president.

And so the circle of events closed, connecting the end of one world war to the beginning of the next. What part the veterans of World War I who belonged to the American Legion played in the nation's unreadiness before World War II is a matter of dispute. Some scholars contend that the public policy influence of the Legion has been exaggerated all along.[10] The isolationism in the Midwest was not created by the American Legion. Legionnaires were among many voices arguing for strict neutrality. Robert M. Hutchins, the liberal president of the University of Chicago, advocated a policy of noninvolvement. It is only logical, nonetheless, that such a forceful point of view by demonstrated patriots who had experienced the realty of war could not help but influence others.

One must also question why attentive Legionnaires who were Jewish or of Polish ancestry did not protest more vehemently the refusal of their comrades to recognize the genocidal extermination by the Nazis of Jews in conquered Europe; many Poles, considered by Hitler to be subhuman, also were slaughtered or sent to slave labor camps. An anti-Semitic thread ran through much of the isolationist rhetoric in the United States during this period. By disregarding "the decisions of European politics," in Daddy Schick's words, Legion dogma made it uncomfortable for individual members to speak out against individual exceptions. It is true, in Illinois at least, that veterans who were alarmed early in the war by the plight of Jews and Poles in Europe were more likely to belong to associations consisting solely of Jewish American or Polish American veterans. Some of the most active Jewish Legionnaires were no longer on the scene (Milton Foreman having died in 1935, Abel Davis in 1937), were preoccupied with business interests, or as in the case of those associated with Governor Horner, had political reasons not to pursue their cause vigorously in polyglot organizations like the Legion. Leaders of the Legion had to be careful not to be thought of as somehow placing the interests of foreign peoples above those of fortress America, especially after Communist Russia became a victim of Nazi aggression.[11]

Epilogue

The Second World War generated a huge new class of war-weary veterans, many of them young Americans who joined the American Legion or one of the other veterans organizations. Legion membership in Illinois reached 226,000 within three years after the end of the war in 1945. It remained greater than two hundred thousand for the next fifteen years, more than double the peak enrollment in the period between the wars. Only New York and Pennsylvania counted more dues-paying members. Veterans of the first war managed to hold on to most of the Legion leadership positions during the assimilation of younger men into the organization. Spurred on by a prewar state commander, Edward Clamage of Chicago, the Illinois department plunged immediately into a familiar agenda. Sounding the alarm against Communists and "fellow travelers" in positions of public trust, Legionnaires lobbied in Illinois for a law to require loyalty oaths from teachers and other public employees.

Before and after the Great War, Chicago had been a center of radical leftist ferment. Now the city was described by the author John Gunther as "the headquarters and chief breeding grounds of fascism in the U.S."[1] He identified Edward A. Hayes, the former state and national commander of the Legion from Decatur, as the first president of a new "semi-fascist" organization, American Action, Inc.

World War I veteran John Stelle, the ninety-nine-day governor of Illinois, served as the first postwar national commander of the Legion. He achieved national office in considerable part because of his role in one of the historic public policy decisions that affected veterans—enactment of the GI bill of rights, which provided free college educations, job training, low-cost loans for the purchase of a house, and many other benefits for the men and women who had been in the service. It was, as Jennifer Keene has stated, "the most extensive piece of social welfare legislation in American history. . . . For the first and perhaps only time, wartime military service became a stepping stone to a better life . . . a way to enter the middle class."[2] She interpreted the bonus march and the years of prolonged conflict over the rights and privileges of service in World War I as negotiating points in the social contract between veterans and their government. In her view, the GI bill gave final meaning to that contract after the next great war.

There are, of course, many fathers of the GI bill. But one version of its origin begins in Illinois. On November 4, 1943, while the war was still going on, the state commander, Leonard Esper of Springfield, visited Salem, Illinois, to address a meeting honoring Salem's Luther B. Easley Post 128 for having achieved its Legion membership goal. After the dinner, Esper sat around a table with seven other Legionnaires talking about postwar planning. Two of them were close friends who were deeply involved in Legion politicking at the national level—Stelle and James P. Ringley, past commander of Commonwealth Edison Post 118 in Chicago. Bill McCauley was there from Olney. Two others were from Salem: Omar J. McMackin and Earl W. Merritt, both future state commanders. The other two were A. L. Starshak from Jackson Park Post 555 in Chicago and George H. Bauer from Effingham Post 120. Stelle had received a letter from his son, who was serving overseas and who said the men in his outfit were worried about what would await them in civilian life. The eight Legionnaires began exchanging ideas that Stelle jotted down on a paper tablecloth. He was delegated by the others to draft the parts into a coherent whole that could be submitted to the national executive committee of the Legion in Indianapolis. Stelle not only did that but also accompanied the plan through the Legion's bureaucratic maze and on to Congress. Harry Colmery, the former national commander from Kansas, headed the Legion committee that shepherded through Congress a bill closely resembling the original Legion proposal. A marble plaque hangs today on the post wall in Salem commemorating one of the origins of a system of federal benefits that has been universally acclaimed.[3]

Unfortunately, the "old" Stelle resurfaced as national commander. The VA wanted to build a medical facility especially for women veterans. Stelle owned an interest in some property in Decatur that he thought would be just fine for the site. The new VA director, former general Omar Bradley, a war hero and close associate of General Dwight D. Eisenhower, did not take kindly to the pressure from the Legion official. It was no contest. The hospital got built somewhere else.

Other careers came to an end, meanwhile. Oscar Carlstrom realized that he was not fated to be governor of Illinois. He moved to Chicago for a while, made some money practicing law, then returned to Mercer County to be elected judge of the local circuit court. Until his death in 1948 at age sixty-nine, Carlstrom remained a staunch booster of the American Legion and the small-town verities for which it stood. The people in Aledo remember him for the tangible good things he did for Mercer County. The hard road from New Boston to Aledo would not have been built without Oscar Carlstrom, one woman told me, and had he lived longer, there would probably be a bridge there across the Mississippi River.

Senator C. Wayland Brooks's career in public office ended in 1948. The former marine who was wounded in World War I was defeated by a former marine who was wounded in World War II, the liberal University of Chicago economics professor Paul H. Douglas. One of the U.S. District Court judges selected by Senators Douglas and Lucas for appointment by President Harry S. Truman was Casper Platt of Danville, the first Redden Post commander who had been shunted aside because of his Democratic party allegiances.

The political readjustment that followed the war resembled in some respects what had happened in the 1920s. Public opinion in the Midwest turned inward once again. Congressional committees hunted for Communist influences in the government. President Truman made a controversial decision to commit American military force to prevent a Communist regime from overrunning the Korean peninsula, a long way from Illinois.

Truman's "Fair Deal" record and his conduct of foreign affairs were at issue in one of the classic election campaigns in Illinois political history. Two Legionnaire candidates who were from the same section of the state and had been acquainted for many years faced off in 1950 for the Senate seat occupied by one of them, Scott Lucas. The former Republican congressman from Pekin, the incomparably grandiloquent Everett McKinley Dirksen, ran against Lucas, who had become the Democratic party floor leader (and Truman's spokesman) in the Senate. The real leaders of the Senate were the members of the Southern Caucus, headed by

Richard B. Russell of Georgia, who found Lucas's ideology acceptable. Measured by his party's contemporary standards, Lucas was a moderate. He had what the *New York Times* described as a fondness for "plain solid food, good bourbon, and male talk."[4] Despite what must have been misgivings, he stood behind the president's decision to intervene in Korea. He also supported the most unambiguous U.S. entanglement in European affairs—the North Atlantic Treaty Organization military alliance. Dirksen took the position, popular in the midst of such a remote conflict, that the Korean matter could have been handled short of war. He opposed financial aid to foreign nations and spoke out against the federal Fair Employment Practices Commission, one of whose original members had been a left-leaning Legionnaire from Chicago, Earl Dickerson. Lucas lost by 294,000 votes to the former bakery truck driver he had persuaded many years ago to become active in the American Legion and thence into politics.

Earl Dickerson made one further try at the ballot box, a losing campaign on the Henry Wallace Progressive party ticket for Congress in 1948. By that time, he had renounced his association with the Legion, saying "I don't like the American Legion, and I haven't for many years, but that doesn't take away the fact that I was one of its founders [in Illinois]." The remarkable thing about Dickerson, as the author Alan Ehrenhalt has noted, is that he "managed to be a capitalist role model [as a multimillionaire insurance company executive] . . . a pillar of the Bronzeville social elite and an angry radical [as president of the Lawyers' Guild] at the same time."[5] His nemesis, Bill Dawson, became the first African American chairman of a House committee in 1942 and went on to serve twenty-eight years in that body. As chief South Side mechanic in Mayor Richard J. Daley's Democratic machine, which accumulated power exceeding even that of Mayor Kelly's organization, Dawson helped the party deflect its frequent challenges from the militant left during the civil rights era.

One source of irritation for the Chicago machine (and the American Legion) in this period originated, ironically, in the troubled psyche of another of the founders of the Legion in Illinois. In the beginning, the new organization could not have succeeded without the generous financial backing of former captain Marshall Field III. He found the factional bickering distasteful, however, and withdrew from Legion affairs while continuing to contribute his dollars. Along with the money, the Field heirs inherited a family vulnerability to mental illness. His father had committed suicide, and Field III entered psychoanalysis. He voted for Hoover in 1932 but then experienced a profound ideological conversion to liberalism. Legend has it that his analyst suggested, as a method of assuaging the guilt associated with being so rich in the midst of such poverty, that he start a liberal newspaper. Field responded by founding not one but two liberal newspapers—one called *PM* in New York, which did not survive, and in December of 1941, a pro-Roosevelt, prolabor voice in Chicago called the *Chicago Sun*. The *Sun* merged later with the afternoon tabloid *Chicago Times* and exists today under different ownership as the *Chicago Sun-Times*.

The movement of population from central city to suburb affected Legion membership adversely in Illinois. It was hard to maintain either workplace-based or national identity–based posts after Legion families relocated from Chicago into many different outlying suburban communities. Membership in Cook County dropped from sixty-eight thousand in 1962 to fifty-three thousand in 1973, a decline of about 22 percent.[6] The beer fests and weekly bingo and euchre games continued to be a popular social activity in many smaller town posts throughout downstate in the 1970s and 1980s. An aging population of World War II veterans, combined with the disinterest of many Vietnam era servicemen, took its toll on Legion membership in the 1990s. By 1997, membership in Illinois had fallen to 152,000 from 182,000 in 1973. In Sycamore, four veterans' organizations shared a single clubhouse—the American Legion; the VFW; United Veterans (Univets), founded after the Korean War; and VietNow, consisting of Vietnam veterans.

Conclusion

Some of the most important questions about the American Legion in Illinois must be left unanswered. Were the men of the Legion leading public opinion or merely giving voice to the sentiments of their neighbors? Did the presence on Main Street of veterans who returned from the Great War to band together into an organization, who dressed on occasion in semimilitary garb, and who fired rifle volleys into the air and marched to the stirring music of drums and bugles stifle dissent in the community? How did the environment in which their conventions occurred—with discussion of serious issues of public policy in the morning, drum and bugle corps proudly parading in the afternoon, alcoholic merriment in the evening—contribute to their uniformity of expression?

If I think and do as the others, then must it be that I am thinking and doing right?

The conservative identity of the American Legion was clearly and definitively established in the period between the two world wars. The Legion's power, which varied from state to state, was greater in Illinois than in many other large states, less than in some of the smaller, more homogenous states. More so than in some states, the Legion was able to exert a harsh conservative and isolationist pressure on both political parties. There were, to be sure, other rightist organizations active in Illinois, ranging from the Klan, the German American Bund, and the America First Committee to the Elks and the Daughters of the American Revolution. Through solidarity and its highly visible, unsubtle presence, the Legion projected an air of authority at a time when many Illinoisans were more fearful of class warfare than of the gathering storm abroad.

After the divisive governing crises of the early twenties, the Legion in Illinois succeeded in reconciling its sectional differences sufficiently to preserve an appearance of unity in the national affairs of the organization. At the founding caucus in St. Louis in 1919, a former enlisted man writing in the *Latrine News* dared hope for a movement that would promote "sanely progressive, feet-on-the-ground Americanism." It may be that this was an unattainable goal given the spirit of the times and the people in a state with the multiplex social and political structure of Illinois. This study has shown how the Legion contributed positively to the welfare of deserving veterans and the dependents of those who died in the service. It helped in the social and physical rehabilitation of men who were scarred by the horrors of combat. It contributed to the wholesome development of young people through its junior baseball and Boys State programs. Ultimately, however, the leaders of the Legion failed the feet-on-the-ground test by stumbling time and again into behavior destructive of democratic ideals, grossly intolerant of differing points of view, and disdainful of precious civil liberties. That must remain the legacy of the first twenty years of the American Legion in Illinois.

Appendixes
Notes
Bibliographic Essay
Index

Appendix A
State Commanders of the American Legion, 1919–1939

1920	Milton J. Foreman	Chicago
1921	William R. McCauley	Olney
1922	William R. McCauley	Olney
1923	Charles W. Schick	Chicago
1924	John J. Bullington	Belleville
1925	Howard P. Savage	Chicago
1926	Scott W. Lucas	Havana
1927	Ferre C. Watkins	Chicago
1928	Albert M. Carter	Murphysboro
1929	David L. Shillinglaw	Chicago
1930	Edward A. Hayes	Decatur
1931	Arthur G. Poorman	Chicago Heights
1932	Ivan G. Elliott	Carmi
1933	James P. Ringley	Chicago
1934	Charles C. Kapschull	Deerfield
1935	Paul G. Armstrong	Chicago
1936	James B. Murphy	Bloomington
1937	Matthew J. Murphy	Chicago
1938	Leonard Applequist	Aurora
1939	Edward Clamage	Chicago

APPENDIX B
AMERICAN LEGION POSTS AND MEMBERS, ILLINOIS, 1920–1939

Year	No. of Posts	No. of Members
1920	643	62,221
1921	590	59,089
1922	614	54,257
1923	629	49,538
1924	672	46,538
1925	640	47,455
1926	648	57,762
1927	655	70,130
1928	666	67,886
1929	679	72,529
1930	691	76,866
1931	706	85,036
1932	722	72,336
1933	725	60,925
1934	743	68,563
1935	767	70,600
1936	766	79,548
1937	775	80,127
1938	776	79,976
1939	784	85,959

Notes

Abbreviations

ALNHL   American Legion National Headquarters library, Indianapolis
ILHF   Illinois history file, ALNHL
ILBF   Illinois biographical file, ALNHL
CHS   Chicago Historical Society

PREFACE

1. Willard Waller, *The Veteran Comes Back* (New York: Dryden, 1944), 213.

2. Dixon Wector, *When Johnny Comes Marching Home* (Cambridge, MA: Riverside, 1944), 438.

3. Waller, *Veteran Comes Back*, 26.

4. Jennifer D. Keene, *Doughboys, the Great War, and the Remaking of America* (Baltimore: Johns Hopkins University Press, 2001), 7. Nationally, 72 percent of the U.S. Army is estimated to have been draftees. The figure was smaller in Illinois (about 54 percent) because more National Guard units were activated there than in many other states.

5. Samuel Eliot Morison, *The History of the American People* (New York: Oxford University Press, 1965), 886; Frederick Lewis Allen, *Only Yesterday: An Informal History of the Nineteen Twenties* (New York: Blue Ribbon, 1931), 94; Ben Hecht, *A Child of the Century* (New York: Simon and Schuster, 1954), 383.

6. William E. Leuchtenberg, *The Perils of Prosperity 1914–1932* (Chicago: University of Chicago Press, 1958), 68.

THE WAR AS PROLOGUE

1. John Keegan, *The First World War* (London: Hutchinson, 1999), 48; "ill-glued" empire, Jacques Barzun, *From Dawn to Decadence* (New York: Harper-Collins, 2000), 690.

2. Keegan, *First World War*, 70.

3. Elizabeth McKillen, *Chicago Labor and the Quest for a Democratic Diplomacy, 1914–1924* (Ithaca, NY: Cornell University Press, 1995), 4.

4. Thomas J. McCormack, ed., *Memoirs of Gustave Koerner, 1809–1896* (Cedar Rapids, IA: Torch, 1909), 1:307. Elected lieutenant governor of Illinois and later to the state supreme court, Koerner was considered the state's most influential German American leader during much of the nineteenth century. He advocated political unity by Americans of German descent. In an 1870 speech, he said, "We should not abandon our German views, our German manners, as far as they are worthy to be kept up, but should instil them into the American life," 2:582. He lived in Belleville.

5. Leslie V. Tischauser, "The Burden of Ethnicity: The German Question in Chicago, 1914–1941" (PhD diss., University of Illinois Chicago, 1981), 7 (support for Germany), 43 (Rabbi Hirsch). The number of German aliens residing in the city was estimated then at sixty-five hundred. See also Arthur C. Cole, "Illinois and the Great War," in Ernest Ludlow Bogart and John Mabry Mathews, *The Modern Commonwealth, 1893–1918: The Centennial History of Illinois* (Springfield: Illinois Centennial Commission, 1920), 5:453.

6. Antje Dirksen, Frank J. Fonsino, "Everett McKinley Dirksen: The Roots of an American Statesman," *Illinois History Journal*, Spring 1983, 17. The DeKalb sheriff was James Scott; *Sycamore True Republican*, April 21, 1917.

7. McKillen, *Chicago Labor*, 52. For an excellent description of the counter-pressures in organized labor in Chicago during this period, see also Lizabeth Cohen, *Making a New Deal: Industrial Workers in Chicago, 1919–1939* (Cambridge: Cambridge University Press, 1990).

8. Michael Knapp, "World War I Service Records," *Prologue* (U.S. National Archives), Fall 1990, 300.

9. *Illinois Blue Book, 1919–20* (Springfield: Illinois Secretary of State).

10. Cole, "Illinois and the Great War," 461.

11. There was a disposition, Geoffrey Perret, *A Country Made by War: From the Revolution to Vietnam—The Story of America's Rise to Power* (New York: Random, 1989), 316; Vermilion County quotas, Clint Clay Tilton, ed., *Centennial Book of Vermilion County, Illinois* (Danville, 1926), 43; fingerless gloves, *Decatur Tribune*, September 19, 1990.

12. Fonsino, "Everett McKinley Dirksen," 17.

13. Lee County report, *War History of Lee County, Ill., 1917–1919* (Dixon, IL: American Legion Post 12, n.d.); Hansen incident, *Sycamore True Republican*, July 20, 1918. Many immigrants from Scandinavian countries were, like Hansen, outspoken in their support of Germany. Samuel Lubell, who studied isolationism for his book *The Future of American Politics* (New York: Harper, 1952), said Swedish Americans considered Germany "a champion of Protestant and Teutonic civilization," 135.

14. Deerfield, Marie Ward Reichelt, for Deerfield A.L. Post 738, *History of Deerfield, Illinois* (Glenview, 1928), 69. The Chicago division of the APL conducted 99,175 official investigations during the war. Vigilance association, Marguerite Edith Jenison, *The War-time Organization of Illinois* (Springfield: Illinois State Historical Library, 1923), 77.

15. Knapp, "World War I Service Records," 300. The casualty figures are from a report of the U.S. War Department, February 1942, as modified by the Statistical Service Center, Department of Defense, November 7, 1957.

16. Mrs. P. T. Chapman, *A History of Johnson County, Illinois* (Vienna, IL: Johnson County Genealogical and Historical Society, 1997), 204.

17. Burl Noggle, *Into the Twenties: The United States from Armistice to Normalcy* (Urbana: University of Illinois Press, 1974), 137.

1. ORIGINS AND DIRECTIONS

1. Thomas R. Gowenlock, with Guy Murchie Jr., *Soldiers of Darkness* (Garden City, NY, 1937), 40, 41.

2. Gowenlock, *Soldiers of Darkness*, 40; biographical data, George W. Smith, *History of Illinois and Her People* (Chicago: American Historical Society, 1927), 6:247–48.

3. Michael Sullivan, "History of Homewood Post No. 483," n.d., 3, ILHF.

4. U.S. wartime brothel policy, Fred D. Baldwin, "A Social History of American Enlisted Men in World War I" (PhD diss., Princeton University, 1964); 9 percent with venereal disease, William Pencak, *For God and Country: The American Legion, 1919–1941* (Boston: Northeastern University Press, 1989), 40.

5. Page Smith, *America Enters the World* (New York: McGraw-Hill, 1985), 740.

6. Gowenlock, *Soldiers of Darkness*, 284.

7. G. W. Adams, ed., *Mary Logan: Reminiscences of the Civil War and Reconstruction* (Carbondale: Southern Illinois University Press, 1970), 145. The best work on the political activities of the GAR is Stuart McConnell, *Glorious Contentment: The Grand Army of the Republic, 1865–1900* (Chapel Hill: University of North Carolina Press, 1992).

8. Standard sources for the Paris origins of the Legion are Thomas A. Rumer, *The American Legion: An Official History, 1919–1989* (New York: M. Evans, 1990), and George Seay Wheat, *The Story of the American Legion: The Birth of the Legion* (New York, 1919). For the involvement of Illinois officers, see also Palmer D. Edmonds, "History of the Department of Illinois, 1919–1928," ILHF.

9. Richard Norton Smith, *The Colonel: The Life and Legend of Robert R. McCormick, 1880–1955* (Boston: Houghton Mifflin, 1997), 154.

10. Smith, *Colonel*, 170.

11. Smith, *Colonel*, 66.

12. Smith, *Colonel*, 203.

13. Smith, *Colonel*, 170.

14. Pencak, *For God and Country*, 55; Richard Severo and Lewis Milford, *The Wages of War: When America's Soldiers Came Home—from Valley Forge to Vietnam* (New York: Simon and Schuster, 1989), 243–45.

15. Edwin Darby, *The Fortune Builders* (Garden City, NY: Doubleday, 1986), 40. The estimate of Field's prewar wealth is from *Forbes* magazine, March 2, 1918, 635.

16. Charles V. Falkenberg, "The American Legion in Cook County, Illinois, 1919–1929," 7, ILHF. Falkenberg was a member of Logan Square Post 405, Chicago.

17. *Latrine News* (Chicago), June 14, 1919, 6, American Legion Collection, CHS.

18. Cornelius Lynde, American Legion historian's questionnaire, September 22, 1921, ILHF.

19. John S. Miller, American Legion historian's questionnaire, September 23, 1923, ILHF.

20. Joseph B. McGlynn, American Legion historian's questionnaire, October 21, 1921, ILHF.

21. *Latrine News,* 11.

22. *Latrine News,* 11. McCormick was not alone in his opinion that the casualties were higher than they needed to be because of poor training and high officer turnover. See, for example, Timothy K. Nenninger, "American Military Effectiveness During the First World War," in *Military Effectiveness,* vol. 1, *The First World War,* ed. Allan R. Millett and Williamson Murray (Boston: Allen and Unwin, 1988). I tend to agree with John Keegan, *The First World War* (London: Hutchinson, 1999), that "most of the [criticism of] Generals of the Great War— incompetence and incomprehension foremost among them—may be seen to be misplaced" (316). He pointed out that the communications technology had not begun to keep pace with the innovations in weaponry.

23. Thomas R. Gowenlock to Eric Fisher Wood, July 1, 1919, ILHF.

24. Eric Fisher Wood to Henry Lindsley, July 19, 1919, ILHF.

25. John H. Stelle to John S. Miller, May 16, 1919, Miller Papers, American Legion Collection, CHS.

26. Thomas Harwood to John S. Miller, June 25, 1919, Miller Papers, American Legion Collection, CHS.

27. John S. Miller to Albert A. Sprague, October 7, 1919, Miller Papers, American Legion Collection, CHS.

28. Franklin D'Olier to Eric Fisher Wood, October 30, 1919, copy in ILHF.

29. Marcus Duffield, *King Legion* (New York: Cape and Smith, 1931), 8.

30. *Our 70th Year: Moultrie County Post 68, Sullivan* (Sullivan, IL, 1989), 43; *DeKalb Daily Chronicle,* May 29, July 3, August 8, 1929; George May, *History of Massac County, Illinois* (Metropolis: Massac County Historical Society, 1987), 1:91; newspaper clippings, dates and sources unspecified, "American Legion, Lake Forest" main library vertical file, Lake Forest Public Library.

31. "History of Champaign County Post 24," ILHF; military and veterans vertical file, WPA history of American Legion in Peoria, both in Peoria Public Library; speech by Mississippi state commander, 1928 conference of post commanders and adjutants, ILHF; O. T. Banton, ed., *History of Macon County,* (Decatur, 1976); *Peoria Journal Star,* November 12, 1982.

32. Veterans organizations vertical file, Peoria Public Library.

33. Carl Landrum, history column, *Quincy Herald-Whig,* November 9, 1997, Quincy Public Library vertical file.

34. Palmer D. Edmonds, "James C. Russell–Blackhawk Post 107" (unpublished, 1939), 21–22, ILHF.

35. Franklin County War History Society, *Franklin County, Illinois, War History, 1837–1919* (Ziegler, IL, 1920), 225.

36. Willard Waller, *The Veteran Comes Back* (New York: Dryden, 1944), 207; Aurora regiment, J. W. Greenaway, *With the Colors from Aurora, 1917–19* (Aurora, 1920).

37. Irving Cutler, *The Jews of Chicago: From Shtetl to Suburb* (Urbana: University of Illinois Press, 1996), 21.

38. Jacob M. Dickinson Jr. to Noble B. Judah Jr., May 27, 1919, American Legion Collection, CHS.

39. Henry M. Larsen, *LaGrange Post 41: The First Twenty Years, 1919–1939* (LaGrange, 1940), 7, 10.

40. Larsen, *LaGrange Post 41*, 10; Lombard basketball, *A History of Lombard American Legion Post 391* (Lombard, 1967); Jack Benny, *Lake County Legionnaire*, 1935; Lincoln "Baby Vamps," *Lincoln Courier-Herald*, January 8, 10, 11, 25, 1921; Wheaton park district, *DuPage Discovery, 1776–1976* (Wheaton, 1976), 75.

41. Larsen, *LaGrange Post 41*, 131.

42. Mrs. W. H. Morgan, report to state executive committee, June 8, 1924, ILHF.

43. Sycamore Post 99 auxiliary meeting minutes, February 25, 1926, Roberta Wildenradt's personal files.

44. Pencak, *For God and Country*, 67.

45. George C. Danfield, "Did You Know That? A Story of Chicago Union Labor Post No. 745," 2, ILHF.

46. Duffield, *King Legion*, 98; *Chicago Tribune*, September 3, 1920, 3.

2. IN THE POLITICAL TANGLE

1. Page Smith, *America Enters the World* (New York: McGraw-Hill, 1985), 768.

2. Thomas A. Rumer, *The American Legion: An Official History, 1919–1989* (New York: M. Evans, 1990), 92.

3. Paul M. Green and Melvin G. Holli, eds., *The Mayors: The Chicago Political Tradition* (Carbondale: Southern Illinois University Press, 1987), 102.

4. Carlstrom family history is from *Aledo Times Record*, November 4, 1926, 1; *Past and Present of Mercer County Illinois* (Chicago, 1914), 2:78; Daniel T. Johnson, *History of Mercer County Illinois, 1882–1976* (Aledo, 1977), 42; and Oscar Carlstrom, biographical questionnaire, ILBF.

5. *Chicago Daily News*, September 7, 1920, 3. For a journalist's overview of the political shenanigans of this period, see William H. Stuart, *The Twenty Incredible Years* (Chicago: M. A. Donahue, 1935).

6. George G. Seaman, summary of convention proceedings, 16, ALHF.

7. Minutes of state executive committee meeting, 1920, 16, ILHF.

8. *Carrollton Patriot*, October 28, 1920, 4; Rainey biographical material, Robert A. Waller, *Rainey of Illinois*, (Urbana: University of Illinois Press, 1977).

9. *Dispatch* (Illinois State Historical Society), May-June 1989, 8; Everett M. Dirksen, *The Education of a Senator* (Urbana, 1998), 85 (Chicago thugs), 91 (powerful influence).

10. Green and Holli, *Mayors*, 74. The Citizens Committee to Enforce the Landis Award was established in 1921 and disbanded in 1929.

11. John R. Schmidt, *The Mayor Who Cleaned Up Chicago* (DeKalb: Northern Illinois University Press, 1989), 133.

12. Brooks biographical file, ILBF.

13. Summary of proceedings, state convention, 1924, 78, ILHF.

14. Henry M. Larsen, *LaGrange Post 41: The First Twenty Years, 1919–1939* (LaGrange, 1940), 114.

15. *Illinois Legionnaire,* March 1930, 3.

16. Daniel J. Elazar, *Cities of the Prairie: The Metropolitan Frontier and American Politics* (New York: Basic, 1970), 283.

3. CHICAGO AND DOWNSTATE: THE SECTIONAL SCHISM

1. Thomas A. Rumer, *The American Legion: An Official History 1919–1989* (New York: M. Evans, 1990), 130.

2. Jennifer D. Keene, *Doughboys, the Great War, and the Remaking of America* (Baltimore: Johns Hopkins Press, 2001), 1.

3. Subject to queer moods, Willard Waller, *The Veteran Comes Back* (New York: Dryden, 1944), 118; Remarque quoted in Waller, *Veteran Comes Back,* 120; hire the soldier, William McCauley, commander's report to state executive committee, October 10, 1921, ILHF.

4. Sprague biographical data, ILBF; obituary, *Chicago Tribune,* September 17, 1955.

5. Commander's report to state executive committee, May 3, 1921, 52, ILHF; Terry Radtke, *The History of the Pennsylvania American Legion* (Mechanicsburg, PA: Stackpole, 1993), 39.

6. Marcus Duffield, *King Legion* (New York: Cape and Smith, 1931), 154.

7. Roscoe Baker, *The American Legion and American Foreign Policy* (Westport, CT: Greenwood, 1954), 137; Elizabeth McKillen, *Chicago Labor and the Quest for a Democratic Diplomacy, 1914–1924* (Ithaca, NY: Cornell University Press, 1995), 15.

8. Charles V. Falkenberg, "The American Legion in Cook County, Illinois, 1919–1929," 6, ILHF.

9. This account of the disputes surrounding the state convention of 1922 is largely as related in Falkenberg, "American Legion," ILHF, and in *Chicago Herald and Examiner,* September 25–27, 1922.

10. Summary of proceedings, state convention, Decatur, October 10, 1921, ILHF.

11. "History of Naval Post No. 372," Illinois Post Histories, ILHF. See also Schick biographical file, ILBF.

12. "The Illinois Legionnaire: The Official History of the American Legion Department of Illinois, 1919–1923," unpublished, 6, ILHF.

13. "Illinois Legionnaire," 52.

14. Summary of proceedings, state convention, September 18, 1923, ILHF.

15. Radtke, *History of the Pennsylvania American Legion,* appendix.

16. W. R. Matheny to state commander, February 1, 1926, Lucas Papers, box 449, Illinois State Historical Society.

17. Summary of proceedings, state convention, September 3, 1924, box 450; and correspondence file, July 10, 1924, box 448, Lucas Papers.

18. J. M. Dickinson to Herbert Moulton, chair, Chicago Rehabilitation Committee, American Legion, September 3, 1926, box 499, Lucas Papers.

19. The Soldier Field episode is related in boxes 450 and 451, Lucas Papers. Abel Davis's role is described in the Ferre Watkins correspondence file, box 450.

20. Convention proceedings, 1936, ILHF.

21. This statement and most of the other biographic information is from an undated questionnaire prepared by DeLaCour, ILBF.

22. Various post historians prepared undated summaries of minutes for a loose-leaf history of Harold L. Taylor Post 47, now part of ILHF. Chester Woolman, historian for 1924–1929, is the only author identified. The pages are numbered. Titled "History of Harold L. Taylor Post 47," this compilation is the source of most of the information about the Taylor post in this section, including Alderman Crowe's role in its formation, the post's relation to organized labor, and its view on the bonus.

23. Roger Biles, chapter 8, in Paul M. Green and Melvin G. Holli, eds., *The Mayors: The Chicago Political Tradition* (Carbondale: Southern Illinois University Press, 1987), 117.

24. "Congregation Israel Synagogue, 1916–1991," n.d., 21, Vermilion County Museum files, Danville.

25. Clint Clay Tilton, ed., *Centennial Book of Vermilion County, Illinois* (Danville, 1926). Other historical material about the county is from Katherine Stapp and W. I. Bowman, *History under Our Feet: The Story of Vermilion County, Illinois* (Danville: Interstate Printers, 1968).

26. Most of the Platt family history is from "Congregation Israel Synagogue, 1916–1991."

27. Carl Grove, "History of Curtis G. Redden Post 210," April 28, 1939, 52, ILHF.

28. The unpublished Grove history includes photographs and descriptive information about the Sunshine Camp. Most of the other Redden material in this section is from the *Danville Commercial News*, August 14, 1932, 2.

29. A display at the Vermilion County War Museum features biographical information about Claude Hart.

30. Grove, "History," 60.

4. THE BRONZEVILLE CHOICE: STRIVER OR REVOLUTIONARY?

1. Harold F. Gosnell, *Negro Politicians: The Rise of Negro Politics in Chicago* (Chicago: University of Chicago Press, 1935), 110.

2. *Adjutant General's Report, Illinois, Roster of the Illinois National Guard and Naval Militia as Organized When Called by the President for World War Service, 1917* (Springfield, 1929). Number who returned, George W. May, *History of Massac County, Illinois* (Galesburg: Wagoner, n.d.), 1:91.

3. The memo, reported in *The Crisis*, the magazine of the National Association for the Advancement of Colored People, May 1919, 16–17, is quoted in Gail Buckley, *American Patriots* (New York: Random House, 2001), 163. There remains

considerable dispute about the part that Gen. Pershing's staff played in the preparation of the memo. See Jennifer D. Keene, "French and American Racial Stereotypes During the First World War," in *National Stereotypes in Perspective: Americans in France, Frenchmen in America,* ed. William L. Chew (Amsterdam: Rodolphi, 2000).

4. Harry Haywood [Haywood Hall], *Black Bolshevik* (Chicago: Liberator, 1978), 39.

5. Dedication program for new Duncan post facilities, 1981, Black Community Project, Oral History Collections, University of Illinois Springfield. See also Mabel E. Richmond, *Centennial History of Decatur and Macon County* (Decatur: Decatur Review, 1930), 334–35.

6. Mullin was one of the Last Man's Club that met in Peoria every year on Armistice Day. See *Peoria Journal-Star,* November 12, 1982.

7. Dedication program. See also Orville McDaniel memoir, 1978, Black Community Project.

8. *Peoria Penny Press,* June 7, 1973, 10.

9. George W. May, *History Papers on Massac County* (Paducah, KY: Turner, 1990), 144.

10. Oral history memoir, 1978, Black Community Project, 2:76, University of Illinois Springfield.

11. Earl B. Dickerson biographical file, ILBF; Dickerson, speech to the Chicago Historical Society, February 20, 1983, Dickerson Papers, box 75, CHS; and Alan Ehrenhalt, *The Lost City* (New York: Basic, 1995), 57.

12. *Defender,* March 1, 1930, 1.

13. *Defender,* March 8, 1930, 14.

14. *Defender,* January 18, 1936, 10.

15. Buckley, *American Patriots,* 163.

16. For more on Dawson and the Mafia, see Rick Porrello's Web site, *www.americanmafia.com,* John William Tuohy, June 2001. For more on voting trends in black Chicago in the 1930s, see Christopher Robert Reed, "Black Chicago Political Realignment During the Great Depression and New Deal," *Illinois Historical Journal,* Winter 1985, 242–56.

17. Keene, "French and American Racial Stereotypes," 157.

18. *Defender,* January 18, 1936, 9.

19. Haywood, *Black Bolshevik,* 39.

20. Haywood, *Black Bolshevik,* 43.

5. TAKING ON THE RED MENACE

1. Willard Waller, *The Veteran Comes Back* (New York: Dryden, 1944); Milton Foreman, speech to state convention, *Chicago Herald and Examiner,* September 3, 1920, 2.

2. *Sycamore True Republican,* October 19, 1918.

3. Weston Gladding Donehower, "Conflicting Interpretations of Americanism in the 1920s" (PhD diss., University of Pennsylvania, 1982), 106.

4. Centralia incident, *Literary Digest,* November 8, 1919; deportations, Loren Baritz, ed., *The Culture of the Twenties* (Indianapolis, 1970); cloud of suspicion, Frederick Lewis Allen, *Only Yesterday: An Informal History of the Nineteen Twenties* (New York: Blue Ribbon, 1931), 61; commander's quote, John M. Barry, *The Great Mississippi Flood of 1927 and How It Changed America* (New York, 1997), 139.

5. Leslie V. Tischauser, "The Burden of Ethnicity: The German Question in Chicago, 1914–1941" (PhD diss., University of Illinois Chicago, 1981), 7 *(Abendpost),* 30 (war of races); power in Northwest, Thomas J. McCormack, ed., *Memoirs of Gustave Koerner, 1809–1896* (Cedar Rapids, IA: Torch, 1909), 2:84.

6. Clinnin quote, Palmer D. Edmonds, "James C. Russell–Blackhawk Post 107," 27, ILHF; Clinnin biographical information, ILBF; see also Henry M. Larsen, *LaGrange Post 41: The First Twenty Years, 1919–1939* (LaGrange, 1940), 13. For another version of the Lorenz affair, see Rudolph A. Hofmeister, *The Germans of Chicago* (Champaign, IL: Stipes, 1976).

7. Michael Sullivan, "History of Homewood Post No. 483," n.d., ILHF.

8. Watkins quote, Marcus Duffield, *King Legion* (New York: Cape and Smith, 1931), 207; Adams quote, William Pencak, *For God and Country: The American Legion, 1919–1941* (Boston: Northeastern University Press, 1989), 164.

9. Duffield, *King Legion,* 231.

10. Duffield, *King Legion,* 231–32.

11. Pencak, *For God and Country,* 165.

12. State executive committee meeting minutes, July 1923, Chicago, ILHF.

13. Report of annual conference of Americanism Commission, Bloomington, December 1935, ILHF. See also *Chicago American,* December 9, 1935, 12.

14. *Chicago Tribune,* January 29, 1936, 1.

15. William Gellerman, *The American Legion as Educator* (New York, 1938), 224.

16. *Chicago Herald and Examiner,* October 17, 1935, 30.

17. Donehower, "Conflicting Interpretations," 52 (Goodman quotation), 129 (Cross affair), 149 (Porter quotation).

18. Boy Scouts, executive committee meeting minutes, August 31, 1920, ILHF; gun sales, Larsen, *LaGrange Post 41,* 129.

19. Thomas A. Rumer, *The American Legion: An Official History, 1919–1989* (New York: M. Evans, 1990), 253–56.

20. State convention proceedings, 1936, ILHF.

21. Larsen, *LaGrange Post 41,* 62.

22. *Chicago Herald and Examiner,* November 5, 1935, 1.

6. THE LEGION, THE KLAN, AND PERSONAL LIBERTY

1. David J. Goldberg, *Discontented America: The United States in the 1920s* (Baltimore: Johns Hopkins University Press, 1999), 134–35.

2. *St. Louis Post-Dispatch.* The best summary was in the issue of August 9, 1920, 4.

3. Paul Angle, *Bloody Williamson* (New York: Knopf, 1952), 149 (Klan raids and arrests), 195 (Carlstrom), 205 (winemakers and bootleggers).

4. Chicago Civil Liberties Committee, *Pursuit of Freedom: A History of Civil Liberty in Illinois, 1787–1942* (Chicago: Chicago Civil Liberties Committee, Illinois Civil Liberties Committee, 1942), 136.

5. Frankfort Area Historical Society, *History of West Frankfort, Illinois* (Danville: Interstate Publishers, 1978), 78.

6. Wyn Craig Wade, *The Fiery Cross: The Ku Klux Klan in America* (New York: Simon and Schuster, 1987), 202.

7. Richard M. Clutter, "The Indiana American Legion, 1919–1960" (PhD diss., Indiana University, 1974). Clutter estimates that between 20 and 50 percent of Legionnaires joined the Klan in Indiana (85).

8. State convention proceedings, September 9, 1930, ILHF.

9. Gustavus M. Blech, *History of Hamlin Park Post 817,* 1945, ILHF.

10. William Pencak, *For God and Country: The American Legion, 1919–1941* (Boston: Northeastern University Press, 1989), 263.

11. Weston Gladding Donehower, "Conflicting Interpretations of Americanism in the 1920s" (PhD diss., University of Pennsylvania, 1982), 226.

12. *Danville Commercial News,* August 11, 1932, 4.

13. Willard Waller, *The Veteran Comes Back* (New York: Dryden, 1944), 210.

14. Thomas B. Littlewood, *Arch* (Ames: Iowa State University Press, 1990), 37–39.

15. Winthrop S. Hudson, *Religion in America* (New York: Scribner's, 1965), 369–70.

16. Leslie V. Tischauser, "The Burden of Ethnicity: The German Question in Chicago, 1914–1941" (PhD diss., University of Illinois Chicago, 1981), 123.

17. "History of Aaron Post 788," n.d., ILHF.

18. Chicago Civil Liberties Committee, *Pursuit of Freedom,* 17–18.

19. John Stelle, state executive committee minutes, Chicago, July 15, 1923, 85, ILHF. See *Chicago Tribune,* September 15, 1930, for an editorial criticizing the Legion's ambiguous stand on repeal.

20. Frank Hunt Garvin, "History of Marine Post 273," n.d., ILHF.

21. Henry M. Larsen, *LaGrange Post 41: The First Twenty Years, 1919–1939* (LaGrange, 1940), 197.

22. *Commercial News,* August 11, 1932, 4.

23. Quincy conventions of 1924 and 1935, Carl Landrum, local history column, *Quincy Herald-Whig,* November 2, 1975.

24. Waller, *Veteran Comes Back,* 42.

25. Wisconsin American Legion Papers, box 2, Wisconsin State Historical Society, Madison, quoted in Pencak, *For God and Country,* 349.

7. THE QUEST FOR THE SOLDIERS' BONUS

1. The exact numbers of votes, as recorded in the state convention proceedings, Chicago, September 3, 1920, were 12,439 for and 286 against a federal bonus, and 12,264 for and 241 against a state bonus.

2. William Pencak, *For God and Country: The American Legion, 1919–1941* (Boston: Northeastern University Press, 1989), 81.

3. Willard Waller, *The Veteran Comes Back* (New York: Dryden, 1944), 100; John T. Bullington, quoted in state executive committee meeting transcript, Bloomington, 1924, ILHF.

4. Events leading to the approval of the federal bonus legislation of 1924 are as described variously in Thomas A. Rumer, *The American Legion: An Official History 1919–1989* (New York: M. Evans, 1990); Geoffrey Perret, *A Country Made by War: From the Revolution to Vietnam—The Story of America's Rise to Power* (New York: Random, 1989); and Pencak, *For God and Country.*

5. See Appendix B for the year-by-year Illinois figures. Membership increased in Illinois from 46,538 in 672 posts in 1924 to 85,036 in 706 posts in 1931. The Pennsylvania data are from Terry Radtke, *The History of the Pennsylvania American Legion* (Mechanicsburg, PA: Stackpole, 1993).

8. HARD TIMES IN THE LEGION HALL

1. Willard Waller, *The Veteran Comes Back* (New York: Dryden, 1944), 205; Jennifer D. Keene, *Doughboys, the Great War, and the Remaking of America* (Baltimore: Johns Hopkins University Press, 2001), 181.

2. Illinois department conference file, 1936, ILHF.

3. Studs Terkel, *Hard Times: An Oral History of the Great Depression* (New York: Pantheon, 1970), 311.

4. *Commercial News,* February 8, 1932, 3.

5. *Commercial News,* February 11, 1932, 4. See also issues of February 14 and February 16.

6. T. H. Watkins, *The Hungry Years: A Narrative History of the Great Depression in America* (New York: Henry Holt, 1999), 117; Page Smith, *Redeeming the Time* (New York: McGraw-Hill, 1987), 591.

7. *Commercial News,* February 29, 1932, 4.

8. *Commercial News,* March 3, 1932, 1.

9. Carl Grove, "History of Curtis G. Redden Post 210," April 28, 1939, 11–12, ILHF.

10. See *Commercial News,* March 4 and 5, 1932, 1–4.

11. Chicago Civil Liberties Committee, *Pursuit of Freedom: A History of Civil Liberty in Illinois, 1787–1942* (Chicago: Chicago Civil Liberties Committee, Illinois Civil Liberties Committee, 1942), 140–41.

12. *Decatur Herald,* quoted in *Commercial News,* March 8, 1932, 6.

13. Carl Grove, "History of Curtis G. Redden Post 210," 12.

14. William Pencak, *For God and Country: The American Legion, 1919–1941* (Boston: Northeastern University Press, 1989), 191.

15. *New York Times*, June 5, 1932, sec. 10, 1.

16. Louis W. Liebovich, *Bylines in Despair: Herbert Hoover, the Great Depression, and the U.S. News Media* (Westport, CT: Praeger, 1994), 158. See also Watkins, *Hungry Years*, chap. 5; Donald J. Lisio, *The President and Protest: Hoover, Conspiracy and the Bonus Riot* (Columbia: University of Missouri Press, 1974); Jack Douglas, *Veterans on the March* (New York: Workers Library Publishers, 1934).

17. Chicago communists, Harry Haywood, *Black Bolshevik* (Chicago: Liberator, 1978), 380; Los Angeles caravan, Linda Wheeler, *Washington Post*, April 12, 1999, A1.

18. Floyd Gibbons, quoted in Liebovich, *Bylines in Despair*, 162.

19. *Commercial News*, July 3, 1932, 1.

20. *Commercial News*, July 5, 1932, 7.

21. Watkins, *Hungry Years*, 133.

22. Thomas R. Henry, quoted in Wheeler, *Washington Post*.

23. *Chicago Daily News*, quoted in Liebovich, *Bylines in Despair*, 170; *Commonweal*, 163.

24. Michael Sullivan, "History of Homewood Post No. 483," n.d., 41, ILHF; Donald J. Lisio, *The President and Protest: Hoover, Conspiracy and the Bonus Riot* (Columbia: University of Missouri Press, 1974), 244.

25. *Commercial News*, August 14, 1932, 2.

26. *Literary Digest*, October 5, 1935, 7.

27. Henry M. Larsen, *LaGrange Post 41: The First Twenty Years, 1919–1939* (LaGrange, 1940), 153.

28. Waller, *Veteran Comes Back*, 225.

29. George C. Danfield, "Did You Know That? A Story of Chicago Union Labor Post No. 745," 5, ILHF.

30. Ickes, Thomas B. Littlewood, *Horner of Illinois* (Evanston, IL: Northwestern University Press, 1969), 115; WPA checkoff, Paul M. Green and Melvin G. Holli, eds., *The Mayors: The Chicago Political Tradition* (Carbondale: Southern Illinois University Press, 1987), 121.

9. THE LABOR MOVEMENT: FRIEND OR FOE?

1. Gompers's views, Elizabeth McKillen, *Chicago Labor and the Quest for a Democratic Diplomacy, 1914–1924* (Ithaca, NY: Cornell University Press, 1995), 10; AFL overture, William Pencak, *For God and Country: The American Legion, 1919–1941* (Boston: Northeastern University Press, 1989), 216.

2. Pencak, *For God and Country*, 222, 255.

3. Pencak, *For God and Country*, 229.

4. Milton Derber and Edwin Young, eds., *Labor and the New Deal* (Madison: University of Wisconsin Press, 1957), 18.

5. Fitzpatrick biographical information, Barbara Warne Newell, *Chicago and*

the Labor Movement: Metropolitan Unionism in the 1930s (Urbana: University of Illinois Press, 1961); CFL in general, McKillen, *Chicago Labor,* 52, 125, 137, 222.

6. John Bullington, state convention proceedings, 1924 file, ILHF; Earl Benjamin Searcy to Dr. Harry W. Parker, April 29, 1920, ILHF.

7. George C. Danfield, "Did You Know That? A Story of Chicago Union Labor Post No. 745," 4, ILHF.

8. A union labor post was founded in Los Angeles a short time later. By the beginning of World War II, a National Conference of Union Labor Legionnaires had been organized within the Legion by five labor posts representing about fifteen hundred Legionnaires.

9. For the origins of the union labor post, see Danfield, "Did You Know That?," 4.

10. Danfield, "Did You Know That?," 5.

11. Derber and Young, *Labor and the New Deal,* 20.

12. Newell, *Chicago and the Labor Movement,* 58, 63–78; Derber and Young, *Labor and the New Deal,* 16. For the history of needle trades in Chicago, see Irving Cutler, *The Jews of Chicago: From Shtetl to Suburb* (Urbana: University of Illinois Press, 1996), 65, 185.

13. *Warsaw Bulletin,* June 12, 1936, 1. For the history of Warsaw, see County Board of Supervisors, *History of Hancock County, Illinois* (Carthage, IL, 1968).

14. *Warsaw Bulletin,* July 17, 1936, 1; July 24, 1936, 1.

15. *Warsaw Bulletin,* July 10, 1936, 1.

16. *Warsaw Bulletin,* July 17, 1.

17. *Chicago Tribune,* August 13, 1936, 1.

18. *Blandinsville Star-Gazette,* quoted in *Warsaw Bulletin,* August 28, 1936, 2.

19. Minutes of executive committee meeting, August 23–24, 1936 file, ILHF.

20. Minutes of Parker post meeting, August 27, 1936; *Warsaw Bulletin,* July 24, 1936, 1.

21. *Warsaw Bulletin,* July 24, 1936, 1.

22. *Warsaw Bulletin,* January 5, 1939, 1, 4.

10. THE UPS AND DOWNS OF THE ALPHA LEGIONNAIRES

1. The four were Fred Busbey, Emmett F. Byrne, Neil J. Linehan, and William T. Murphy.

2. Edward L. Schapsmeier and Frederick H. Schapsmeier, "Serving under Seven Presidents: Les Arends and his Forty Years in Congress," *Illinois Historical Journal,* Summer 1992, 105.

3. Thomas B. Littlewood, *Horner of Illinois* (Evanston, IL: Northwestern University Press, 1969), 60–61. See also Edward J. Barrett, biographical questionnaire, ILBF.

4. John Stelle, interview by author, Barnes VA Hospital, St. Louis, July 3, 1962.

5. Littlewood, *Horner,* 140.

6. *Illinois Legionnaire,* October 1930, 12.

11. ECHOES OF THE PAST

1. William Pencak, *For God and Country: The American Legion, 1919–1941* (Boston: Northeastern University Press, 1989), 303.

2. State convention proceedings, September 1930, ILHF.

3. Samuel Lubell, *The Future of American Politics* (New York: Harper, 1952), 130–35.

4. State convention proceedings, September 1930.

5. Robert E. Sherwood, *Roosevelt and Hopkins: An Intimate History* (New York: Harper, 1948), 127.

6. Sherwood, *Roosevelt and Hopkins,* 127.

7. *New York Herald-Tribune,* quoted in Lubell, *Future of American Politics,* 141. Roosevelt's share of the presidential vote dropped by thirty-four points nationally between 1936 and 1940, after the outbreak of the war.

8. Pencak, *For God and Country,* 304.

9. *Chicago Daily News,* August 20, 1941, 8. The Brooks, pacifist petticoat, and *Illinois Legionnaire* quotations are from this newspaper editorial.

10. Preston W. Slosson, *The Great Crusade and After, 1914–1928* (Chicago: Quadrangle, 1958), 78, maintains that the Legion "flourished as a veterans social club and benevolent society rather than as a political power." See also Donald J. Lisio, in *The War Generation: Veterans of the First World War,* ed. Stephen R. Ward, 42 (Port Washington, NY: Kennikat, 1975).

11. Sherwood, *Roosevelt and Hopkins,* 167, suggests there were American Jews, particularly in the upper economic levels, who supported the America First Committee because of their fear of anti-Semitism, and some who were "just as ready as anyone else to 'do business' with a victorious Hitler."

EPILOGUE

1. John Gunther, *Inside USA* (New York: Curtis, 1997), 382.

2. Jennifer D. Keene, *Doughboys, the Great War, and the Remaking of America* (Baltimore: Johns Hopkins Press, 2001), 205, 212.

3. Marion County judge Frederick Merritt examined correspondence, digests of state and national executive committee Legion meetings, and other documents relating to the southern Illinois origins of the GI bill. His report was prepared with the assistance of Mariette Broughton of the *Centralia Evening Sentinel* and is taken from the Salem post files. William Pencak, *For God and Country: The American Legion, 1919–1941* (Boston: Northeastern University Press, 1989), 322, cites the Legion national archivist as the source of a version asserting that Colmery drafted the bill submitted to Congress.

4. Edward L. Schapsmeier and Frederick H. Schapsmeier, *Illinois State Historical Society Journal,* November 1977, 302–320.

5. Alan Ehrenhalt, *The Lost City* (New York: Basic, 1995), 159.

6. *Chicago Tribune,* March 4, 1973, 33.

Bibliographic Essay

The national headquarters of the American Legion urged local posts in the 1920s to designate one member as post historian. Sensitive to the criticism from some Americans that the Legion was self-serving, the organization wanted to be able to document and preserve its record of community service activities. Some of the histories from Illinois were threadbare lists of officers and dates and were of little probative value. But others were remarkably informative. On file in the Legion library in Indianapolis are several such accounts that form the base of my reconstruction of the Legion in Illinois between the world wars. They were written with literary flair by men who apparently saw no need to gild the lily as they saw it. Among the most useful of these post memoirs were Henry M. Larsen's *LaGrange Post 41: the First Twenty Years, 1919–1939,* prepared in 1940; Carl Grove's "History of Curtis G. Redden Post 210" (1939); Michael Sullivan's "History of Homewood Post No. 483" (undated); Palmer D. Edmonds's undated "History of Blackhawk Post 107"; George C. Danfield's "Did You Know That? A Story of Chicago Union Labor Post 745" (undated); Frank Hunt Garvin's "History of Marine Post 273" (undated); *A History of Lombard American Legion Post 391* (1967), for which no author is specified; and the looseleaf anonymous chronologic compilation, "History of Harold L. Taylor Post 47," that constituted the starting point for the section on that Chicago post. Most of my questions about the 1919–1922 sectional conflicts in the Illinois department were answered in Charles V. Falkenberg's excellent "The American Legion in Cook County, Illinois, 1919–1929." Two other works in the national library were indispensable: Palmer D. Edmonds's "History of the Department of Illinois, 1919–1928," and "The Illinois Legionnaire: The Official History of the American Legion Department of Illinois, 1919–1923," author and date unspecified.

More valuable even than the post histories were the verbatim typewritten transcripts of the annual meetings of the state executive committee. Most of the problems affecting the state department came before this body. Unlike the proceedings of the state conventions, which are on microfilm in the library but were obviously edited before publication, the executive committee records appear not to have been censored, at least in the early years. It is advisable to consult newspaper reports as a cross-reference. In addition, the national headquarters archivist asked prominent Legionnaires of that period to answer biographical questionnaires. Many of the leading figures in Illinois, but not all, complied with the request. Some copies of the *Illinois Legionnaire* magazine are on microfilm, but the collection is incomplete. In reading many general circulation Illinois newspapers of this period, I was astonished by the attention devoted to American Legion activities. Easily detected promotional spin can be explained by the presence of Legionnaires on the newspaper staff, but occasionally the newsworthy conflict in a situation would overcome the tendency to withhold negative news. Especially useful in my research were the *Chicago Herald and Examiner, Danville Commercial News, Warsaw Bulletin, Aledo Times-Record, Sycamore True Republican,* and *Chicago Defender.*

The Chicago Historical Society has a small American Legion collection, forty-six items, consisting of the correspondence of John S. Miller Jr., who was one of the early leaders in Chicago; some copies of the *Latrine News,* a makeshift newsletter prepared by former enlisted men in the Chicago area; the papers of Earl Dickerson; and a few scattered pamphlets and letters. It is fascinating to juxtapose Thomas R. Gowenlock's account of his Red-hunting experiences in prewar Chicago (*Soldiers of Darkness,* 1937) and Harry Haywood's *Black Bolshevik* (1978), about an African American's path to radicalism in Chicago. The papers of Scott Lucas are in the Illinois State Historical Library in Springfield. I found the Black Community Project in the Oral History Collections of the University of Illinois at Springfield to provide an insight into the importance of the Legion for blacks.

The best of the many books about the American Legion at the national level is William Pencak, *For God and Country: The American Legion, 1914–1941* (1989). Others are Thomas A. Rumer, *The American Legion: An Official History, 1919–1989* (1990); Richard S. Jones, *A History of the American Legion* (1946); George Seay Wheat, *The Story of the American Legion: The Birth of the Legion* (1919); and three consistently critical works, Marcus Duffield, *King Legion* (1931); Roscoe Baker, *The American Legion and American Foreign Policy* (1954); and William Gellerman, *The American Legion as Educator* (1938).

I consulted four other state studies for comparative purposes: Richard M. Clutter, "The Indiana American Legion, 1919–1960," an Indiana University dissertation, 1974; Terry Radtke, *The History of the Pennsylva-*

nia American Legion (1993); Jacob Armstrong Swisher, *The American Legion in Iowa, 1919–1929* (1929); and Richard J. Loosbrock, *The History of the Kansas Department of the American Legion* (1968).

Joining Willard Waller's classic *The Veteran Comes Back* (1944) are some recent first-rate studies of the return to civilian society of World War I veterans—among them Jennifer D. Keene, *Doughboys, the Great War, and the Remaking of America,* Richard Severo and Lewis Milford, *The Wages of War: When American Soldiers Came Home—From Valley Forge to Vietnam* (1989); and Weston Gladding Donehower's 1982 University of Pennsylvania dissertation, "Conflicting Interpretations of Americanism in the 1920s." Geoffrey Perret, *A Country Made by War* (1989), is a readable military history connecting the first World War and American life after the war.

There is an ever-expanding literature about the 1920s and 1930s. Frederick Lewis Allen, *Only Yesterday: An Informal History of the Nineteen Twenties* (1931) is still at the top, in my view. For the purposes of this work, I also recommend T. H. Watkins, *The Hungry Years: A Narrative History of the Great Depression* (1999); Loren Baritz, ed., *The Culture of the Twenties* (1970); Robert Wiebe, *The Search for Order* (1962); George Soule, *Prosperity Decade from War to Depression: 1917–1929* (1947); William E. Leuchtenberg, *The Perils of Prosperity, 1914–1932* (1958, 1993); Geoffrey Perret, *America in the Twenties: A History* (1982); Studs Terkel, *Hard Times: An Oral History of the Great Depression* (1970); Burl Noggle, *Into the Twenties: The United States from Armistice to Normalcy* (1974); Preston William Slosson, *The Great Crusade and After, 1914–1928* (1931); Page Smith, *Redeeming the Time* (1987); Robert Murray, *Red Scare: A Study in National Hysteria, 1919–1920* (1955); David M. Kennedy, *The First World War and American Society* (1981); and the most comprehensive yet succinct treatment of the Ku Klux Klan in the Midwest, David J. Goldberg, *Discontented America: The United States in the 1920s* (1999). Wyn Craig Wade, *The Fiery Cross: The Ku Klux Klan in America* (1987) is a good overview of the Klan.

Chicago Civil Liberties Committee, *Pursuit of Freedom: A History of Civil Liberty in Illinois, 1787–1942* (1942) catalogues the Legion's role in some of the most glaring examples of suppression of free expression. Among the many other published works that helped to establish the context of my inquiry were Marguerite Edith Jenison, *The War-time Organization of Illinois* (1923); Arthur C. Cole's chapter, "Illinois and the

Great War," in Ernest Ludlow Bogart and John Mabry Mathews, *The Modern Commonwealth, 1893–1918* (1920); Barbara Warne Newell, *Chicago and the Labor Movement: Metropolitan Unionism in the 1930s* (1961); Louis W. Liebovich, *Bylines in Despair: Herbert Hoover, the Great Depression and the U.S. News Media* (1994); and John M. Cooper Jr., *The Vanity of Power: American Isolationism and the First World War, 1914–1917* (1969). For the purposes of this study, Paul M. Green and Melvin G. Holli, eds., *The Mayors: The Chicago Political Tradition* (1987), provided a richly textured overview of Chicago political history.

INDEX

Thomas B. Littlewood is a professor emeritus of journalism at the University of Illinois at Urbana-Champaign. He worked as a newspaper reporter for almost twenty-five years in Chicago, Springfield, and Washington, D.C., before becoming head of the UIUC journalism department in 1977. His five books include biographies of two Illinois figures in the 1930s: Governor Henry Horner and *Chicago Tribune* sports editor and promoter Arch Ward.